MONEY POWER

Additional copies of this book may be purchased directly from the publisher. To order, please enclose $25.95 plus $3 postage and handling. Send to:

Book Distribution Center

Post Office Box 51488

Ontario, CA 91761-0088

Printed in the United States of America

0 9 8 7 6 5 4 3 2 1

MONEY POWER

Table Of Contents

Appendix

Free Bonus Reports

MONEY POWER

Introduction

Have you ever heard anyone say, "You can't beat the system."? Unfortunately, for many working people that statement appears to be all too true. The "system"— your employer, bank, credit card companies, the IRS, insurance companies, car dealers, etc.— is stacked against most working people. And when times are tough —as they are now—it's especially hard for the average working person to get ahead.

While the system does hold a pat hand, anyone who tells you that it can't be beaten is wrong. All you need is inside information and you can actually use the system to make more money... and to keep more money. You won't get this inside information from your banker, your insurance agent, car dealer, or other member of the system because it would cost them millions of dollars in lost profits.

The insider information provided in this book can help make the system work for you. You'll learn proven, effective money-making and money-managing strategies that can put an end to all of your money worries in just a matter of months. If used properly, the money and career strategies in this book can help you get out of debt; make more money; save more money; and achieve your financial dreams. You'll also learn how to start and operate your own profitable home-based business and where to find your dream job.

Hundreds of people have used these strategies to beat the system and ensure their own and their families' financial security. The strategies are easy to learn and easy to use by people just like you.

Besides insider tips and money-making strategies, the following pages also provide the phone numbers and addresses of important contacts and sources of information. There are chapters devoted to tax savings through legitimate deductions; sources of "free" money; high-profit, low-risk business opportunities; money-saving shopping techniques including over 60 sources for wholesale savings; and over 120 sources of products and items you can get free.

Even if your debts— mortgage, credit cards, car loans, personal loans, etc.— have you in a deep financial hole, the information and techniques in this book can help you eliminate your money problems and get you started on the road to financial and personal success. You don't have to be a college graduate or a financial wizard to use these techniques either. Thousands of people just like you have already used successfully the insider strategies described in this book to take control of their financial and professional lives.

The money-saving strategies and techniques provided in this book offer proof that the system can indeed be beaten. There are numerous ways you can go about earning and saving more money. There also are opportunities that can lead to incomes of $100,000 a year or more. If you know what you want, the following pages can provide you with insider information that may enable you to get it.

MONEY POWER

CHAPTER 1

Secrets of Success

Here's a quick "True" or "False" quiz:

1) Successful people have all been "blessed" with exceptional talents or skills.

2) Successful people are highly educated people with college degrees.

3) Successful people inherit their success.

4) Successful people get where they are by being dishonest.

If you answered "true" to all of the above, you failed the quiz. What's more, you are most likely undermining your own potential for success.

In order to unravel the "mysterious" secrets of success, it is necessary to discard several unfortunate misconceptions. First of all, success does not require superior talents or skills. It does require certain attributes or traits that are not inborn but learned. For example, successful people are typically goal-oriented, highly motivated, flexible, determined, confident, and self-disciplined.

Secondly, many of the most successful people in the world never attended college. In fact, many never even finished high school. Thomas Alva Edison— whose many inventions include the electric light bulb, the phonograph, and the motion picture camera— had only a few months of formal education. Largely self-taught, Edison learned and developed the attributes common to successful people. He once said that "genius is 1% inspiration and 99% perspiration". Insert the word "success" in place of "genius", and the statement is just as true.

A third misconception is that most successful people started out with unfair advantages. The thinking here is that successful people never get where they are by starting "from scratch". These people must have inherited financial advantages or influential contacts. The truth is, a great many success stories are "rags to riches". Many of the most successful people in America started with nothing and earned their measure of success through hard work. Finally, most successful people do not get where they are by cheating. Dishonesty is not a prerequisite to success.

Once these misconceptions have been discarded, it should begin to come clear that success is not typically a result of circumstances or aptitude. It is most often a result of "success-oriented behavior" involving certain characteristics or attributes that anyone can learn and develop. Rather than being secret, the way to success is open to anyone who has a goal and who develops the thinking, attitudes and behaviors common to all successful people.

How To Be A Winner In Everything You Do

Experts, including many leading psychologists, agree that what separates life's winners from its losers are certain patterns of thinking and behavior. Losers tend to perceive the path to success as a straight, unbroken line from beginning to end. As a result, these people are unable or unwilling to cope with setbacks along the way. If their progress is slowed or halted for any reason, they often become frustrated and give up. For these people, setbacks are failures that can not be overcome. Their motto might be, "If at first you don't succeed, give up".

Instead of a straight, unbroken line to achievement, winners view the path to success as winding and twisting upward— more often bumpy than not. These people know and accept the reality that setbacks are an inevitable part of life. They know that very few, if any, people ever achieved success without facing and overcoming adversity. Winners are not discouraged or deterred by obstacles or detours along their path. They know that, "if at first you don't succeed" you try again, and again if necessary, and that success will be your ultimate reward.

People who are successful— those people we consider winners—in their personal and professional lives share several common characteristics and attributes that allow them to deal with adversity and temporary failures. Anyone can develop these winning characteristics and attributes and actually learn how to be successful in all aspects of life. Here are seven of those winning characteristics found in common among successful people in all walks of life.

1) Goal-Oriented.

In order to be a winner, you must have a goal— some point you want to reach. That's the first and most important requirement for success. Simply put, you can't be a winner if there's nothing to win.

Both short- and long-term goals are essential elements in providing a sense of direction and purpose. Without a specific, clearly defined goal, you're like a traveler who has no destination. You have no idea of where you're going or why. You don't know how to use your time and resources to their fullest advantage. On the other hand, goal-oriented people know exactly where they are headed and why. They plan their journey carefully, keeping in mind all the detours they may face along the way, and never lose sight of their destination— their goal.

2) Motivation

Once you have set your goal(s) you must have the drive or motivation to reach it regardless of the obstacles in your way. Winners are all highly motivated people who press forward until their goals are reached. That doesn't mean that in order to achieve your goals you must exclude everything else from your life. You'll still need to socialize and to relax, but you must set priorities. Consider how much time you spend each day in unnecessary pastimes that do little more than sap your energy. If you use that time instead to focus on and work toward a specific goal, you'll increase your chances for success dramatically. The bottom line is, in order to be a winner, you must want to reach
your goal more than anything else.

3) Positive Mental Attitude

Having a positive outlook doesn't mean blissfully ignoring the many harsh realities of life. Winners understand that risks and potential setbacks are a matter of fact. Instead of dwelling on these negative aspects of life, winners are constantly looking for alternate ways to pursue and achieve positive results. After
all, how much can anyone accomplish with a defeatist attitude?

A positive approach will allow you to be your most creative and productive— both mentally and physically. Negativism will make you more vulnerable to stress and less likely to pursue your goals.

4) Flexibility

Winners are those people who accept and adapt to changing conditions. Losers tend to stick with routine and resist change regardless of potential benefits. Flexibility means being open to new ideas and new ways of doing things, and being willing to try them when old ideas and techniques no longer work. Very few people ever got to be successful by resisting change.

5) Determination

You may have a goal and possess self-motivation, a positive mental approach, and flexibility and still be a loser. That's because you lack the determination to keep going when the going gets tough. Without the necessary determination to keep pursuing your goal, regardless of the problems or adversity you may face, your chances of achieving success are slim, at best. On the other hand, if you are determined to reach your goal, even if a well-meaning friend or colleague tells you it's impossible, you probably will.

Your persistence in overcoming obstacles or a lack of faith in others is an essential characteristic for being a winner.

6) Confidence

You won't go far without a belief in yourself. Confidence in your ideas and abilities can give you the inner strength to forge ahead toward your goal even in the toughest of times. It's an essential characteristic you need to develop if you are to reach your true potential.

People who lack self-confidence are seldom positive. They're also reluctant to take risks or set goals because they believe they are bound to fail. Success requires unwavering confidence, even when others question your abilities and your judgement.

The key to developing self-confidence is knowledge. The more you know and understand about what you want, the more confident you'll become. That doesn't mean you have to be smarter. It just means that you'll need to learn all you can about the various methods available for reaching your goal. Winners are people who study what they plan to do until they understand how to do it. Armed with such knowledge and its resulting self-confidence, these people are more likely to succeed.

7) Self-Discipline

You already may possess most of the characteristics described above and still fall short of your goals. For many people, failure is due to a lack of self-discipline. No amount of confidence and determination will lead to success if you don't have the self-discipline to follow an orderly plan. That doesn't mean you can't "goof off" occasionally. It simply means that in order to achieve success you'll need to discipline yourself to do the things that need to be done, when they need to be done.

Winners are not people who go after their goals with an "I can do that tomorrow or the next day" attitude. Winners are disciplined people who know the value of getting things done on time.

One way to become a winner in everything you do is to study successful people and then follow their examples. You don't have to make yourself over in someone else's image. But you should learn and develop the winning characteristics these people have in common. It's not an impossible task. If you are willing to make the necessary changes in thinking, attitudes and behavior, you can realize your full potential and achieve whatever goals you set.

How To Get Anyone To Do What You Want

Have you ever noticed how some people seem to be able to get other people to do exactly what they want them to do? It's almost as If certain people have a special power to control the thoughts and actions of others. For example, most successful salespeople are able to convince even the most reluctant consumers to buy their products and services.

The special power these people wield is actually a form of mind-control based on techniques not unlike those used by clinical hypnotists. What's more, the techniques are not new. Some experts believe they originated in Asia over 3,400 years ago. Over the years these techniques have been refined and used by some of the most successful and influential people in the world. More important, anyone can learn these techniques and, without being domineering or intimidating, get other people to do what they want them to do.

It's not difficult to develop these ancient mind-control techniques. It requires an understanding of human behavior, and practice. The techniques work by making people feel at ease and comfortable, thereby open to suggestions and commands. Here are the basic techniques for developing this skill and making it work for you.

1) Find and build upon an area of agreement. It is essential that you establish an easy and open rapport when dealing with other people. The best way to do that is to avoid being critical or argumentative. The key to getting people to do what you want is in making them open to subtle suggestions and indirect commands. And the best way to do that is to be as agreeable as possible.

2) Emulate the other person's posture, attitude and body language. While other people won't consciously realize what you are doing, they will feel more comfortable around you.

3) Create a feeling of trust. Before you can get other people to do what you want, you must be able to gain their trust. While the first two techniques described above will help you create trust when dealing with other people, sincerity also is essential. If a person feels you are merely being polite or patronizing, he/she is not likely to trust you. If, on the other hand, you are sincere in your appreciation and approval of the other person, you are likely to gain his/her trust. Once other people trust you, they will not be nearly so resistant to your suggestions and commands.

4) Get the other person's attention and hold it. The final key in the use of subtle mind-control is to eliminate all distractions. You must be able to make the other person hear you and only you. The use of clear, slow speech and direct eye contact is an excellent way to get other people to focus on you.

Many successful businesspeople, lawyers, politicians, and other professionals have mastered this technique of capturing and then manipulating other peoples' undivided attention.

Consider the people you admire and respect and for whom you "would do anything". You might not think of these people as "spell-binding" or "mesmerizing" but they probably are. Their "persuasiveness" relies on subtle suggestions and indirect commands rather than blatant requests or orders. Most people resist direct attempts at manipulation but are vulnerable to a subtle indirect approach as described in the above techniques. If you master those techniques you may be able to get almost anyone to do what you want— and without their knowing it.

How To Get Special V.I.P. Treatment

You don't have to be rich to enjoy a rich person's lifestyle or to take advantage of a rich person's opportunities. The secret to getting treated like a millionaire, even though you're not, is image. If you can develop the image that you are successful and wealthy, that's how you're likely to be treated by other people.
As a result, opportunities which wouldn't ordinarily be open to you will now be within your grasp.

There are several proven techniques that can help you develop a "money personality" and get special V.I.P. treatment from other people. In fact, many people who are virtually broke are treated like millionaires simply because they project a money personality. These people are able to use their "money personality" image to get the things that they want and to achieve success in all aspects of life.

In order to use a "money personality" image to your advantage, you'll need to develop many of the characteristics and techniques described elsewhere in this chapter. You'll need to be self-confident, determined, and motivated in order to successfully create this image. You'll also need to invest in certain "trappings" that will help project your "money personality" image.

If you are dealing with successful professionals, you'll need to project that same image. You can do that in several ways. The most obvious way to enhance your image is through your appearance. Being well groomed, neat, and well-dressed will go a long way in projecting an image of success that is likely to impress everyone you meet. A businesslike, professional demeanor will also work to your advantage. The key to success is in convincing other people that you are an organized, highly motivated go-getter with status and permanency.

Another way to enhance your image and assure V.I.P. treatment is to acquire and use expensive business cards and high quality stationary in all of your business and social dealings. Simply put, cheap-looking business cards and stationery are not likely to enhance your image. Your chances for success in any business venture depend largely on the image you project. Impressive letterhead stationery and business cards, while superficial, can only enhance your image and increase your chances for success.

Developing a "money personality" may take a little time and practice, but it's something anyone can do. Perhaps the best way to go about it is to study the appearance, behavior, and style of successful people, and then follow their examples. Emulate their characteristics and attributes to project an image of success. If you want to be treated like a millionaire and/or get opportunities which require an appearance of affluence and competence, you need to "act" the part. If you can do that, you don't have to be a millionaire to be treated like one.

MONEY POWER

Chapter 2

Financial Matters

Done haphazardly, money-management can be a thankless task. On the other hand, focused financial planning can lead to financial security. The choice is yours. You can ignore financial planning altogether and live from paycheck to paycheck (or worse), or you can take control of your finances, stay out of debt, and save thousands of dollars every year.

This chapter of "Money Power" provides expert advice and insider techniques for managing a wide range of financial problems. You'll learn techniques for getting out of (and staying out of) debt; acquiring and using credit cards to your advantage; avoiding certain ripoffs that could cost you a lot of cash; investing; repairing damaged credit; and other financial matters.

Your financial security depends on you. You'll get very few (if any) breaks from banks, credit card companies, insurance companies, car dealers, and so on. In most cases, you'll need "inside" information on how to make the system work for you. Used properly, the information in this chapter can help you get started in the right direction in planning for your financial future.

How To Get Out Of Debt Without Filing For Bankruptcy

Debt problems can befall anyone. A sudden illness or the loss of a job can lead to a "mountain" of debt. Such indebtedness often leads to drastic measures, such as filing for personal bankruptcy. While personal bankruptcy can get you out of debt, it also can result in a black mark on your credit rating, making it difficult for you to get credit in the future. By law, a bankruptcy action can remain on your credit record for ten years.

Whatever your financial situation, there are almost always several options for getting out of debt which are less severe than filing for bankruptcy. None of the options are easy, nor will they result in a "quick fix" of your financial problems. However, with determination and a willingness to make sacrifices, there are several steps you can take yourself to resolve your financial problems without having to resort to bankruptcy.

Here are several proven "do-it-yourself" methods for getting out of debt:

— Plan a realistic budget and then follow it. This means cutting your living expenses down to the absolute necessities— housing, food, and monthly debt payments. You'll have to make some sacrifices in your lifestyle, cutting out many of the "extras", but remember, the object is to get out of debt. You don't have to forego non-essential expenses completely, but you should avoid needless spending as much as possible. For example, you can go to the movies once a month instead of once a week. You also can cut down on the number of times you dine out. The key to success is in planning a budget you can live with and then sticking to it.

— Stop using your credit cards and charge accounts. If you are like most people, credit cards and charge accounts are what caused your indebtedness to begin with. Give yourself a chance to catch up and pay off your existing debts. Switch to cash for all your purchases, using a credit card in emergencies only.

— Close out the accounts on most of your credit cards. Keep only one or two of your cheapest cards for use in emergencies only. You may be less tempted to spend if you have only one or two cards, and you also can save on interest and annual fees.

— Work out a modified payment plan with your creditors. You should take this action if you find out that you can not make your payments. Contact your creditors and explain your circumstances and try to work out a more manageable payment plan. Make sure your creditors understand that you are serious about meeting your obligations and are not trying to evade your debts. If you have made your payments on time in the past, your creditors are more likely to work with you in arranging a payment schedule that fits your budget.

— Find out about a home-equity loan. For some people, home equity loans are the best means of financing major purchases. They also can be used to pay off existing loans and credit card balances. Home equity loans appeal to some people because their interest rates are typically much lower than rates for other consumer loans, and the interest is tax-deductible. Keep in mind, this method of paying off debts involves borrowing money and may not be practical for every financial situation. For example, you would only get yourself deeper in debt if you paid off your credit card balances with the money from a home-equity loan and then ran up new debts on the cards. You'd have the credit cards to pay off again plus the home-equity loan. Consider this option carefully before applying for such a loan.

— Contact a Consumer Credit Counseling Service. If the above "do-it-yourself" methods fail to end your financial problems, a Consumer Credit Counseling Service (CCCS) can provide debt management help at little or no cost to you. The CCCS is a non-profit organization with more than 850 offices nationwide that are members of the National Foundation for Consumer Credit. CCCS counselors will contact your creditors and try to arrange for repayment plans that you can manage. The counselors also will help you prepare a budget and plan for your future expenses.

You can contact the CCCS office nearest you by checking the WhitePages of your telephone directory or by calling (800) 388-2227. You also can get information by writing or calling the National Foundation for Consumer Credit, Inc., 8611 Second Avenue, Suite 100, Silver Spring, MD 20910; (301) 589-5600.

Non-profit counseling services also are sometimes operated by credit unions, universities, military bases, county extension services, and housing authorities. They typically charge little or nothing for their services.

— Consider filing a "wage-earner" plan. Although this plan is administered under Chapter 13 of the Bankruptcy code, many experts argue that it isn't true bankruptcy at all. That's because under a wage-earner plan you are allowed to keep your property while you pay off your debts over a period of 3 to 5 years. The wage-earner plan is typically used by debtors who have regular incomes and who can make substantial repayment of their debts.

Under the wage-earner plan a trustee will be appointed to examine your financial situation and then set up a plan in which a portion of your debts is paid. The trustee will contact your creditors and get all collection actions against you, as well as all finance charges and penalties, stopped. The trustee also will administer a realistic, court-approved repayment plan. You will be required to make monthly payments to the trustee, who in turn, pays each of your creditors. Depending on your financial circumstances, you will generally have three years to repay from 10% of your debts to the entire amount.

A wage-earner plan can give you relief from bill collectors because once you file they can no longer contact you. The plan also allows you to pay off your debts—mortgage, credit cards, car loans, personal loans, etc.— under a repayment schedule that fits your budget. In essence, you pay only what you can afford to pay (as determined by a court-appointed trustee), even if it's just $20 a month.

While it will take time (at least three years), to pay off your debts under this plan, the relief from money worries can be almost immediate. Once you file, bill collectors will disappear, and you will be assured of a repayment schedule that you can live with. What's more, because you are making an honest, good faith effort to pay each of your creditors, your credit won't de damaged as severely as if you filed Chapter 7 or "straight bankruptcy".

You should consider filing a wage-earner plan only if all the do-it-yourself methods fail to get you out of debt. In that event, check with a credit counselor or an attorney who specializes in such matters and ask for information and counsel about whether or not filing a wage-earner plan is right for you and your financial situation.

How To Repair Your Credit At No Cost To You

Beware of credit repair services which promise to "cure" your ailing credit report. Their promises may be tempting but they're also expensive and virtually useless. In fact, such services can not do anything to repair your credit that you can not do yourself for free. The thing to remember is that no one can remove negative information from your credit file if that information is accurate and less than seven years old. Any credit repair service that promises otherwise can not deliver on that promise— no matter how much you pay them.

On the other hand, negative information in a credit report is often due to error and/or misinformation and under the law you can challenge such mistakes yourself for free. The credit bureau must then verify the accuracy of the disputed information and correct any errors, usually within thirty days. Once corrected of errors, resulting in the removal of negative information from your credit report, your credit will again be in "good health". What's more, you won't be out several hundred dollars to a credit repair service.

Here are the steps involved in challenging the accuracy of information in your credit report:

1) Contact the credit agency upon whose negative report your application for credit was denied and request a copy of your credit report. Under the Equal Credit Opportunity Act and Fair Credit Reporting Act, you have certain rights. If you are denied credit based on information in a consumer credit report, you have the right to contact the credit bureau involved and request a report on the "nature and substance" of all information in your file. You also are entitled to know the source(s) of the information and to know who has received a credit report on you within the past six months to one year. You are entitled to this information without charge if you contact the credit bureau within 30 days following notification of denial of credit (in practice, you can usually get the report free up to 60 days after being denied credit).

2) Photocopy the report you receive from the credit bureau. Note any errors you find on the report and then return it with an explanation as to why you dispute the information. The law requires the credit bureau to reinvestigate any disputed items. The reinvestigation must be completed within a reasonable time—generally 25 to 30 days. If the credit bureau can not prove you wrong, it must remove the disputed information from your report. (If, however, the disputed negative information in your file is accurate, it may, by law, remain in your report for 7 to 10 years).

3) Demand that a corrected report be sent to everyone who received a credit report within the past six months to a year.

4) Insert into your credit report a brief written statement explaining your side of the story regarding disputed items. You should take this step only if you disagree with the credit bureau's findings as a result of its reinvestigation.

If you assert your rights and follow the steps outlined above, you can repair your credit at no cost to you. The most important thing is to get a copy of your credit report and make sure the information is both current and accurate. If you find mistakes in the information, file a complaint with the credit bureau responsible for the report, explaining any items you dispute. If the information is indeed inaccurate or in error, you can get the report corrected and in the process repair your own credit free of charge.

NOTE: At this writing, legislation which would make it easier for people to correct mistakes in their credit records has passed both the Senate and the House of Representatives. A few minor differences remain to be resolved between the measure passed by the House in June 1994 and a similar bill passed by the Senate in May 1994. Once those differences have been ironed out, the measure can be sent to President Clinton for his signature.

Under the new legislation, credit bureaus would be required either to verify disputed information within 30 days or delete it. Lenders and other businesses that supply information to credit bureaus also would be required to investigate disputed information. Also, employers would need to obtain written consent before acquiring a person's credit report, and more restrictions would be set on who could view sensitive information contained in credit files. The legislation would serve to update the Fair Credit Reporting Act of 1970 which was designed to operate in an era when credit bureaus used handwritten card files.

Where To Get A Free Copy Of Your Credit Report

If you don't qualify for a free credit report— you haven't been denied credit or you've waited more than 30 days after denial— you must generally pay a nominal fee.

One of the three major credit bureaus (TRW), however, provides one free credit report each year upon request

You can obtain copies of your credit report by contacting any of the credit bureaus listed below.

- TRW Consumer Assistance,
  P.O Box 2350,
  Chatsworth, CA 91313.

- TRW Consumer Assistance Center
  P.O. Box 749029
  Dallas, TX.
  Phone: (800) 392-1122
  Provides one free TRW credit report on
  request annually. Otherwise, credit reports are $7.50 each or
  free after credit denial.

- Equifax
  P.O. Box 740241
  Atlanta, GA 30374
  Phone: (800) 685-1111
  Credit reports are $8.00 or free after credit denial.

- Trans Union
  25249 Country Club Boulevard, P.O. Box 7000
  North Olmsted, OH 44070
  Phone: (800) 851-2674
  Credit reports are $8.00 or free after credit denial.

Borrow $10,000 In Just 72 Hours Using Your Credit Cards.

We live in a credit card age. Practically everyone in America has credit cards, and millions of people use 20 or more cards. Many of these cards come with pre-approved cash advances ranging from $500 to $5000, depending on the card holders' creditworthiness. Such credit cards can be used as a source for unsecured loans when you need to raise a lot of cash in a hurry.

If you are like most people, you probably receive in the mail a steady stream of applications for credit cards with pre-approved cash advances. Instead of tossing those applications in the round file, apply for as many cards as you want. If you've already established good credit, you should have no trouble getting ten or more cards with pre-approved credit lines of $1000 or more. Once you have several cards, you can use your credit advances as unsecured loans to borrow the cash you need in 72 hours or less. And since credit card loans are unsecured loans, no collateral, co-signers, or credit checks are required. Once you have the credit cards, the loans are already approved.

Let's say you apply for and obtain 10 credit cards with pre-approved credit limits of $1,000 each. That means you have a total of $10,000 of unsecured credit. You can borrow the full $10,000 or just $1,000, whatever you need— no questions asked. As long as you repay your unsecured credit card loans on time, you'll always have a ready source of quick cash when you need it.

One note of caution: Credit card cash advances can be costly if you use the wrong card. Many companies get the best of card users by charging a fee of anywhere from 2% to 5% of the advance, combined with interest charges which can exceed the card's rate for purchases by almost 7%, while allowing no grace period so the interest begins to accrue immediately.

The best deal for people who use their cards for frequent cash advances is a low interest card with a "no fee for cash advances" policy. Even if the card does not have a grace period, cash advances will be less costly.

How To Borrow Up To $25,000 In Two Hours

Using your credit cards isn't the only way to raise "quick cash". Another creative financing strategy is to use overdraft protection as a line of credit. Overdraft protection is like a loan because it provides for the transfer of money into your checking account when you "bounce" checks. Many people use overdraft protection simply as a safeguard against overdrawing their checking accounts. With some smart planning and preparation on your part, you also can use overdraft protection to borrow up to $25,000 in just a couple of hours. Here's how:

The first thing you need to do is to visit five banks in your area. Open checking accounts and apply for overdraft protection with a $5,000 credit limit at each bank. As you apply for overdraft protection at each bank, don't let on to the bankers that you have such accounts at other banks. Some bankers may refuse your application if they know you have similar accounts at other banks. Don't be discouraged, even if some banks refuse your application for overdraft protection or set a cash limit lower than you requested. Maintain your checking account with the bank for several months, and then reapply. Chances are, once the bank knows you are not "overextended", it will approve your application or increase your credit limit.

Once your applications are approved, overdraft protection is automatic. You'll have a pre-approved line of credit set by each bank. You can borrow any amount, up to $25,000 simply by writing checks. For example, if you have five checking accounts with overdraft limits of $5,000 with each account, you can write five checks (one from each account) for $25,000. With only your signature, you can raise a sizable amount of cash in as little as two hours.

Of course, you'll have to pay interest on the loans (as much as 18% annual interest), so you shouldn't abuse your overdraft limits. You should use overdraft protection only when you need to borrow money in a hurry and you are certain you can handle the interest and repay the loan on time. Properly managed, overdraft protection can provide you with a "hassle-free" source of quick cash, requiring only your signature.

Five Bills You Can Pay Late Without Damaging Your Credit

If you run into a temporary shortage of money, it may be necessary to defer or finance some bills. According to financial insiders, utilities, such as gas and electric; mortgage payments; car loans; department store; and medical bills are the easiest to defer— in some cases for one to two months. You should notify the lender if you need to defer a payment or want to discuss the possibility of arranging for smaller monthly payments.

The due dates on most bills can be extended by several days by taking advantage of grace periods. Grace periods are typically eight to ten days, and even these may be extended by making arrangements with the lender(s). Even if you incur a late charge on any unpaid bill, you usually have 30 days after that to make a payment before your credit rating is affected.

Of course, if at all possible, it's always best to pay your bills before the grace period ends to avoid triggering a late charge on a lender's computer. If that isn't possible, contact the lender about deferring payment for one month or more. Failing that, you may send what you can with a note promising more payments soon. In many cases, you may be able to take up to six months to pay off a bill without having negative information reported to the credit bureau.

While some bills, such as those mentioned above, can sometimes be deferred or financed allowing you up to several months to pay, you still should make every effort to abide by the original payment schedules. If you run into financial problems, don't ignore your bills and hope they'll go away. Contact the lenders and discuss your options for deferring or rearranging your payment schedule. The key to keeping lenders from filing negative reports to the credit bureau is in your making an honest effort to pay your bills. If you do that, lenders are usually more understanding and lenient when you are short of funds.

Use This Secret Technique To Get A Visa Or Mastercard— Even If You Have A Poor Credit History

There are many financial institutions across the country which offer "secured" credit cards to people who have no credit, or who have a poor credit history. A secured card requires that you open and maintain an interest-bearing savings account as security for your line of credit (traditional, or unsecured credit cards are issued to consumers without requiring any security, but they are typically offered to people who have a good credit history).

The savings account required for a secured card may range from a few hundred to several thousand dollars, and your credit line will be a percentage of the amount you have deposited (typically from 50 to 100 percent). A secured credit card makes it possible for some people to get a line of credit of up to $15,000, even if they've had credit problems before. Secured credit cards also can help you build or re-establish your credit history.

Besides making a deposit in a savings account, you also may have to meet a few other requirements in order to get a secured MasterCard or Visa. For example, you also may have to pay application and processing fees. Such cards also typically require payment of an annual fee. There may be other eligibility requirements for obtaining a secured card, depending upon the bank to which you apply. Make sure you understand fully an institution's policies for obtaining and using such a card before you apply.

Listed below are several banks and other financial institutions which offer secured credit cards. You can call or write the numbers and addresses listed and request specific information about eligibility requirements and to request an application.

You also can get a comprehensive listing of institutions which offer secured credit cards by writing to BankCard Holders of America (BHA), a non-profit organization. BHA's "Secured Card List" is available for $4.00. Write to: BankCard Holders of America, 560 Herndon Parkway, Suite 120, Herndon, VA 22070; Phone: (800) 553-8025.

American Pacific Bank
10300 SW Greensburg Road
Portland, OR 97233
Phone: (800) 879-8757
Minimum Income Required: $1,000 per month.

California Security Bank
1694 Tully Road
San Jose, CA 95122
Phone: (408) 270-1500
Minimum Income Requirement: None.
Available for California residents only.

Community Bank of Parker
19590 East Main Street
Parker, CO 80134
Phone: (800) 779-8472
Minimum Income Requirement: $500 per month.

Consumer Fresh Start Association
217 N Church Street
Princeton, IL 61356
Phone: (800) 352-5353
Minimum Income Requirement: $1,000 per month.

Dreyfus Thrift & Commerce
P.O. Box 6003
Garden City, NY 11530
Phone: (800) 7-CREDIT [727-3348]
Minimum Income Requirement: $1,000 per month

First National Bank Of Marin
P.O. Box 3696
San Clemente, CA 92674
Minimum Income Requirement: $1,000 per month.

Service One/ Bank of Hoven
P.O. Box 9068
Van Nuys, CA 91409
Phone: (800) 777-7735
Minimum Income Requirement: $7,500 per year.

Signet Bank
11013 W Broad Street
P.O. Box C32131
Richmond, VA 23261-2131
Phone: (800) 333-7166
Minimum Income Requirement: None.

United National/First Interstate Bank of SD
4300 S Louise Avenue
Sioux Falls, SD 57106-9912
Phone: (800) 825-8472
Minimum Income Requirement: $150 per week.

U.S. Liberty, Inc./Farrington Bank
1502 Route 38
Cherry Hill, NJ O8002
Phone: (609) 488-6206
Minimum Income Requirement: $95 per week.

Where To Get The Best Deal On An Auto Loan

Nearly 80% of all car buyers arrange financing through the dealer who, more often than not, tacks two percentage points on to the annual percentage rate (APR) the bank would charge. The best advice for car buyers is to shop around for a good auto loan deal. Here are three potentially cheaper ways of financing a new car loan:

1) Credit unions. There are almost 13,000 credit unions in the United States, and most of them offer loans at lower interest rates than banks. You can contact the Credit Union National Association (800) 358-5710 for information and to find out if there's a credit union in your area that you might be eligible to join.

2) Home-equity loans. Home-equity lending is becoming more and more popular. That's because interest-rates on home equity loans are generally lower than rates on other types of consumer loans. The interest on home-equity loans (up to $100,000) also is tax deductible, unlike regular car loans. The drawback to financing an auto loan this way is the increased debt you owe against your house. If something should happen—loss of a job, or a sudden illness— and you can't make payments, you risk losing your house as well as your car. Be sure you can make the payments before financing an auto loan this way.

3) Manufacturer's low-interest financing deals. Some auto manufacturers offer low APRs as an incentive to customers. Manufacturer deals offering, in some cases, APRs as low as 3.9%, generally depend on the car model and on the state where the car was purchased.

How To Prevent ATM Ripoffs

The ready cash available from a bank's automated teller machine (ATM) is luring more and more crooks. According to banking insiders, ATM ripoffs are on the increase. Creative thieves are devising new scams in order to gain possession of ATM customers' personal identification numbers (PINs) and account numbers.

Here are several insider tips on protecting yourself from such ATM ripoffs:

— Don't write your PIN on your ATM card and don't keep it in your wallet. Only you should know your PIN. Don't tell it to anyone. As unlikely as it may seem, experts say that most ATM ripoffs are committed by someone who is acquainted with the rightful owner of the ATM card.

— Check out the area carefully before using the machine. If anyone or anything seems suspicious, walk away without using the machine.

— Take as little time as possible when using an ATM. Have your card ready when you approach the machine. If there is anyone else nearby, take your money and leave. You can count it later.

— Try to avoid using ATMs at night. If you must use a machine at night, make sure it is well-lit. If possible take a friend with you.

— Roll up passenger windows and lock all doors when using a drive-thru ATM.

— Don't leave your transaction receipts at the ATM. The receipts may have account information on them which can be used by crooks.

Turn $1,000 Into $12,400 In Two Years With This Investment

Everyone has heard about Hillary Rodham Clinton's "well-timed" trades in cattle futures. The First Lady turned an investment of $1,000 into almost $100,000 in the late 1970s and some analysts say that press coverage of her investment has spurred a new interest in the commodities market.

Evidence of a surge in activity in commodity markets can be seen in various areas: Trading in cocoa futures increased more than 50% in the first half of 1994 and cotton contracts volume jumped almost 75%. By some accounts, investment with ten of the leading agricultural commodity advisers is up by 25% from 1993 investments. Many of the investors are individuals who are venturing into the commodities game for the first time. In fact, some discount commodity brokerages report that new accounts are up from 18% to 25% over a year ago.

If you are looking for a place to invest $1,000 or so, the current market conditions may make this a favorable time to jump into the commodities market. You probably won't have the same amount of success as Hillary Clinton (few investors do), but you could turn an investment of $1,000 into $12,400 in just a couple of years as did a small investor in Connecticut. Other first time small investors all across the country also have made tidy profits of several thousands of dollars.

Obviously, any time you invest your hard-earned money there is an element of risk involved. Individual investments in commodities are no different. Contracts are highly leveraged, meaning an investor typically has to put up only from 3% to 10% of a contract's value to profit from price changes. At the same time, the amount of risk is greater. However, if you have the money, and you are willing to take the risk involved in speculating, you can earn a lucrative payback.

Before you invest, you should get as much information about commodities markets as you can. You'll need to understand how commodity futures work. Should you invest in agricultural products, metals, petroleum, foreign currencies, or stock indexes? What are the risks involved?

The more you study the commodities market the better prepared you'll be to take on the risk of investing.

There are many sources of information about commodity markets which can provide you with the basics and offer sound advice. Your public library should have a wide assortment of literature on commodity futures as well as information about other resources. The National Futures Association offers the following free pamphlets: "Understanding Opportunities and Risks in Futures Trading" and "Buying Options on Futures Contracts". You can get the pamphlets by calling (800) 621-3570. In Illinois, call (800) 572-9400. You also can write to the National Futures Association, 200 West Madison Street, Suite 1600, Chicago, IL 60606-3447.

The commodities game may not be for everyone, but for those who have a knack for picking the right investments and who enjoy the thrill of speculation, it's the most exciting and sometimes profitable game around. If that sounds like you, and you have $1,000 or so to invest, you might want to investigate investing in the commodities market.

Commodity Futures Information Resources

If you take the plunge into the commodities market you'll need to find reliable sources for commodity information, Listed below are several such resources:

— Commodity Futures Trading Commission (CFTC), 2033 K. Street, N.W., Washington, D.C. 20581; Phone: (202) 254-6387. The CFTC is a federal regulatory agency. Individuals and companies offering investments to the public— those which trade in futures contracts and options on futures contracts— are regulated by this agency.

— National Futures Association (NFA), 200 West Madison St., Suite 1600, Chicago, IL 60606-3447; Phone: (800) 621-3570. The NFA is an industry-wide self-regulatory organization authorized by Congress. This organization offers free pamphlets which provide information on futures trading for beginners. You can write or call the NFA and request the free pamphlets.

— Agricultural Commodities Market News: Deputy Administrator, Marketing Program Operations, AMS-USDA, Washington, DC 20250; Phone: (202) 720-4276. Provides reports on prices, demand, movement, volume, and quality of agricultural commodities. Anyone may subscribe to this service.

— Knight-Ridder, (800) 621-5271. This service offers charting information.

— Weather Services Corporation, Bedford, MA; Phone: (800) 634-2549. Provides global weather forecasts.

— Chicago Mercantile Exchange, (800) 331-3332. Offers a free brochure titled "Introduction to Meat and Livestock Fundamentals". Other exchanges also provide free brochures with information for beginners.

— Futures Industry's Regulatory Agencies Hotline. Call (800) 676-4632 to check out a broker and firm.

—Commodity Futures Reparations Claims; Office of the Executive Director, Office of Proceedings, Commodity Futures Trading Commission, 2000 L St. NW, Washington, DC 20581; Phone; (202) 254-3067. This office investigates customer complaints and responds to inquiries concerning commodity futures trading; hearings and reparations claims as a result of violations of the Commodity Exchange Act or regulations by persons or firms registered under the act.

MONEY POWER

CHAPTER 3

Free Money Sources

Even in the best of times, getting enough money to do the things you want can be a struggle. A college education— if not financially impossible for some families— can seriously deplete financial resources. A dream of starting a small business may have to go unrealized because of a lack of start-up capital. Whatever the need, there are sources virtually anyone can turn to for financial assistance. What's more, many of these sources offer "free money"— money that doesn't have to be paid back.

This chapter provides information about the millions of dollars of free money available for small businesses, entrepreneurs, and
college education from federal government sources. Many of the sources listed in this chapter offer grant money and direct payments and low-cost loans, designed to meet various financial needs. There are literally thousands of federal funding programs which offer this free money.

You also may have money coming to you that you aren't aware of. There are billions of dollars in unclaimed money just gathering dust in state Unclaimed Property offices. This chapter also provides information about how you can find out if any of this unclaimed money belongs to you and if so, how you can go about getting it.

How To Get Money From The Federal Government That You Never Have To Pay Back

You don't have to be friends with people in high places in order to get money from the federal government. There are hundreds of government programs offering both financial and non-financial assistance for which you may qualify. Generally, the financial assistance available comes in the form of loans, grants, loan guarantees, and contracts.

What's more, much of this money is free— it never has to be paid back to the government.

Depending on your needs and on the type of program for which you might qualify, you could get $40,000, $68,000, $100,000, or more in federal funds that never have to be paid back. There are grants (no repayment is expected), low-interest loans, and direct payments (no repayment is expected) available to small businesses, individual entrepreneurs, inventors, researchers, and other interested parties. You may apply to a program for money to use for start-up, enhancement or development of your own small business. There's also free money in the form of grants and direct payments for research in virtually every occupational field; for homeowners, renters, developers, and real estate investors; and for students.

You may not think you qualify for a government grant or loan, but it is likely that you do. That's because of the number and variety of federal programs available. Obtaining this government money first requires that you identify what assistance is available and whether or not you are eligible. The best source for that information is the "Catalog of Federal Domestic Assistance". The catalog is a government publication which provides a complete summary of all the financial and non-financial federal programs administered by the various departments and agencies of the federal government. It describes the types of assistance available as well as the requirements for eligibility for the particular assistance in which you may be interested. The catalog also provides information on how to apply for government money.

The "Catalog of Federal Domestic Assistance" can be found in the reference sections of many public libraries. State and local government agencies and officials also may have a copy of the catalog you can study. The catalog also is available by subscription (includes a basic manual and supplemental material) from:

Superintendent of Documents
U.S. Government Printing Office
Washington, DC 20402

Another source of information is the "Federal Assistance Programs Retrieval System" (FAPRS). This is a database featuring the information which is available in the "Catalog of Federal Domestic Assistance". There are certain access points in each state where you can request a computer search of the database. For more information, and a list of state access points, write to:

Federal Domestic Assistance Catalog Staff
General Services Administration
Room 101 Reporters Building
300 7th Street, SW
Washington, DC 20407
Phone: (202)708-5126.

There are literally thousands of government assistance programs described in the catalog mentioned above. Here are just a few examples of programs offering grants to eligible applicants.

—Small Business Innovation Research (SBIR)

This program offers grants (no repayment is expected) for research to small businesses and individual entrepreneurs to stimulate technological innovation. The grants range in amount from $26,000 to $220,000. The average grant is $89,000. For more information, contact SBIR Coordinator, Office of Grants and Program Systems, Cooperative State Research Service, USDA, Room 323, Aerospace Building, 14th & Independence Avenue SW, AG Box 2243, Washington, DC 20250-2243.

— Rural Development Grants

Grants are given to aid the development of small and emerging private businesses and industry in rural areas. The program is limited to private businesses with 50 or fewer new employees and a projected revenue of under $1 million. The grants range in amount from $7,000 to $500,000. The average grant is $181,000. Contact your local office of the Farmers Home Administration.

— Forestry Incentives Program

Under this program, direct payments for specified use are made to private individuals, groups, associations, or other legal entities that own non-industrial private forest land. The grants range in amount from $50 to $10,000 per year. The average grant is $1,600. Contact your local, state, and/or regional Agricultural Stabilization And Conservation Service (ASCS) office.

— Recreation And Cultural Resource Management

Project grants are available to anyone to manage and upgrade recreational and cultural resources and related facilities on public lands. The grants range in amount up to $125,000. The average grant is $10,000. Contact a Bureau of Land Management state office.

One final note: When applying for government grants, be patient. Remember, it is the government you're dealing with, so it's likely you'll encounter a certain amount of frustration and red tape. Don't give up, even if you are rejected. Try again. If you meet the qualifications and follow the application procedures to the letter, your perseverance will most likely pay off. The payoff could be a free money grant from the government.

Free Money Sources For College

Some things are unavoidable— death, taxes and now, seemingly, the ever increasing cost of a college education. Depending on the institution, today's students will need from $35,000 to $100,000 for a 4-year college degree. What's more, the American Council on Education estimates that college costs will increase by as much as 18% over the next two years. For many people, both soon-to-be high school graduates and older would-be students, these rising costs make getting a college education an almost impossible financial burden. For these people, financial assistance is essential.

There are many sources of financial aid available for anyone who wants to attend college, regardless of the cost. This assistance is typically available in three main forms: student loans (which must be paid back), student employment (work-study), and scholarships (grants, awards) which are gifts that do not have to be paid back. In essence, scholarships provide a source of free money to help defray college costs.

According to insider estimates, more than $135 million in scholarship money goes unclaimed every year. This is mostly because students and parents do not know the money is available or how to go about locating potential sources. With a little effort and investigation, virtually anyone can locate and take advantage of free money sources to help pay for a college education.

Here are the four primary sources of free money for college-bound students:

1) The colleges themselves. Colleges provide several types of financial aid including free money (scholarships and grants) from their own funds. A college may also serve as an agent for channeling certain state and/or federal awards to students. The contact for finding out about this source of free money is the financial aid administrator at each college in which you have an interest. Financial aid administrators can tell you what aid programs are available at each college and how much the total cost of education will be.

High school students also should talk to their guidance counselors who can provide information about financial aid in general and where to find other sources of information.

2) The federal government. Two of the federal government's five large financial aid programs for students involve awarding free money in the form of grants (the other 3 programs involve loans and work-study). The federal grants, which do not have to be repaid, include the following:

— Federal Pell Grant: This grant is available to undergraduates only. The amount received depends on several factors, including a student's expected family contribution, cost of education at the student's school, enrollment status, and length of enrollment. The maximum award for the 1993-94 academic year was $2,300. The deadline for application is May 1.

— Federal Supplemental Educational Opportunity Grants (FSEOG):This grant is awarded to undergraduate students only. Eligible students are those who demonstrate exceptional financial need. Priority is given to Federal Pell Grant recipients. The amount received depends on financial need, amount of other aid received, and on the funds available at a student's school. Generally, the maximum amount awarded through a FSEOG is $4,000. Each school sets its own deadline for applying for this grant.

Contact the financial aid administrator at the college you are interested in about the availability of and eligibility requirements for receiving these federal grants. You also may get information by calling the Federal Student Aid Information Center at (800) 4-FED-AID [433-3243].

3) State Programs. Virtually every state in the country has some type of financial aid for students who attend college in their own states. A few states even have awards for students who enroll in out-of-state colleges. Most state aid is in the form of scholarships. Information about financial aid in your state can be obtained from your high school guidance counselor and from your state's department of higher education.

Here are three state programs which provide free money for college-bound students:

—Robert C. Byrd Honors Scholarship Program. The Byrd program provides free money for students who demonstrate above average academic achievement and show promise of continued academic excellence. Students who meet those requirements may receive up to $1,500 a year for four years of undergraduate education. The number of Byrd Honors Scholarships available in each state is limited, but generally, at least 10 such scholarships will be made available per state. Contact the agency in your state which is responsible for public elementary and secondary schools for information about the Byrd Program.

— National Science Scholars Program (NSSP). The NSSP provides free money for undergraduate studies to graduating seniors who have demonstrated outstanding achievement and excellence in the sciences (physical, life, or computer), mathematics, or engineering. Under this program, two students from each congressional district are awarded scholarships of up $5,000 per year of postsecondary study. Contact the agency mentioned above in your state for information about the NSSP.

— Paul Douglas Teacher Scholarship Program. This scholarship provides up to $5,000 a year for outstanding high school graduates who want to become teachers after they finish college. In order to be eligible, a student must graduate in the top 10 percent of his/her high school class, and meet other selection requirements as well. Generally, recipients of this award are required to teach two years for each year of scholarship assistance received. Either the higher education agency or the agency responsible for public elementary and secondary schools in your state can provide you with information about this scholarship. Not every state participates in the Douglas Scholarship Program.

You can get the address and telephone number of the appropriate state agency from your high school guidance counselor or your financial aid administrator.

4) Private Sources. These sources of financial aid for college consist primarily of scholarships awarded by corporations, unions, fraternal organizations, foundations, civic groups, and other organizations. Your high school guidance counselor should be able to provide you with information about private sources of financial aid, especially scholarships. You also may find information in reference books in your local or school library and from your Chamber of Commerce.

Miscellaneous Sources of Free Money For College

American Council of the Blind, 1010 Vermont Avenue, N.W., Suite 1100, Washington, DC 20005. The American Council of the Blind Scholarship is available to eligible legally blind U.S. citizens. The grants range in amount from $1,000 to $1,800. Contact the Coordinator of Membership and student services at the above address.

National Federation of the Blind, 814 Fourth Avenue, Suite 200, Grinnell, IA 50112. The National Federation of the Blind offers several scholarships, including the Howard Brown Rickard Scholarship for legally blind students who are studying for professional degrees; the Hermione G. Calhoun Scholarship for legally blind female students; the Ezra Davis Memorial Scholarship for legally blind undergraduate students; the Frank Walton Horn Memorial Scholarship for legally blind students whose fields of study tend to be in architecture and engineering; and the Merit Scholarship for legally blind students. Write the above address for these and other scholarships awarded by the National Federation of the Blind.

Bureau of Indian Affairs, Office of Indian Education Programs, Code 522, Department of the Interior, 1849 C. Street N.W., Washington, DC 20240. Grants are available for some members of federally-recognized Indian tribes. Those eligible may receive grants ranging from $350 to $7,450 a year to supplement college financial aid packages. Write the above address for more information.

Daughters of the American Revolution, American History Scholarship, National Society Daughters of the American Revolution, NSDAR Administration Building,

1776 D Street N.W., Washington, D.C. 20006-5392. Based on financial need and class standing (top third), this scholarship is awarded to students who major in American history in college. Grants of $1,000 to $2,000 are awarded.

Elks, National Foundation, Most Valuable Student Award, 2750 Lake View Avenue, Chicago, IL 60614. This award is available for students who rank in the top 5 percent of their high school classes, demonstrate leadership, scholastic achievement, and have financial need. Scholarships range from $1,000 to $5,000 per year for four years of undergraduate study. Contact the Scholarship Chairperson of the State Elks Association in your state for information and requirements.

Foundation of National Student Nurses Association, Inc., 555 West57th Street, New York, NY 10019. Grants of $1,000 to $2,000 are available in several different areas of nursing studies. Write the Foundation for information.

Graphic Arts Technical Foundation, National Scholarship Trust Fund Scholarships, 4615 Forbes Avenue, Pittsburgh, PA 15213. Grants of $300 to $1,000 per year are awarded to eligible students with an interest in graphic arts careers. Write for information.

National Association of Bank Women, Inc., NABW Memorial Scholarship Awards, 500 North Michigan Ave., Chicago, Il 60611. Awards of $1,000 to $3,000 are available for eligible women who are working in business, banking, or finance and wish to further their education. Write the NABW for information.

National Association of Realtors, Herbert U. Nelson Memorial Fund, 875 North Michigan Ave, Suite 2400, Chicago, IL 60611. Grants are available to students who make a definite commitment to pursuing a degree in real estate. These grants are made directly to the college or university. Contact the financial aid administrator at the college in which you are interested for information about this award.

National Honor Society Scholarship. This scholarship is awarded to high school seniors who have been nominated by their local National Honor Society chapters. Awards of $1,000 are based on scholarship, leadership, character, and service. Contact your National Honor Society Advisor.

National FFA Foundation, P.O. Box 5117, Madison, WI 53705-0117. FFA scholarships and 4-H club scholarships are given to male high school graduates who are enrolled as freshmen in college. Eligible students must be members of 4-H or FFA and nominated by a club leader. The scholarships are awarded in the amount of $1,000 grants. Contact 4-H club or FFA advisor.

Tyson Foundation, Inc., 2210 Oaklawn, Springdale, AR 72764. Grants are awarded to eligible students who attend accredited colleges and universities and major in Agriculture, Business, Computer Science, Engineering or Nursing.

Youth Foundation, Inc., 36 West 44th Street, New York, NY 10036. Over 50 grants averaging $2,000 each are awarded to eligible undergraduate students. Contact the youth foundation at the above address for information and requirements.

Collect Up To $75,000 And More In Unclaimed Money

According to insider estimates, there may be as much as $5 billion worth of monetary items waiting to be claimed in various state "Unclaimed Property" Offices. That staggering amount of unclaimed money includes uncashed stock dividends, forgotten banking accounts (checking and passbook savings), utility deposits, safe deposit boxes, insurance payments, and many other types of income and accrued interest. These billions of dollars worth of unclaimed monetary items simply "gather dust" in state offices until the rightful owners or heirs claim what is theirs. Individual claims for this money may be as little as $20 or as much as $75,000 (or more).

Unclaimed money comes into a state's possession in several ways— people die, move away, or neglect to keep proper records of investments. In some cases, computer foul-ups can destroy files, resulting in the loss of information about the rightful owners of unclaimed assets. Whatever the cause, a holding institution, such as a bank or insurance company, will eventually declare unclaimed money "abandoned" and turn it over to a state's Unclaimed or Abandoned Property division. The state is then supposed to track down the rightful owners and return their money free of charge.

Unfortunately, in many states resources for conducting owner searches are limited. In some cases, states will list the names of owners of unclaimed money in local newspapers, but that's about the best they can do. The result is billions of dollars in unclaimed money.

If you think you may be the rightful owner or heir to unclaimed financial property currently being held by your state, contact the state's "Unclaimed or Abandoned Property" Office (see the state-by-state listing below). You can find out whether or not your name is listed as an owner or as an heir to an estate of a deceased person. If so, you will be required to fill out a claim form and furnish identification and/or proof of ownership.

State-By-State Listing of Unclaimed and Abandoned Property Offices

Alabama: Department of Revenue, Unclaimed Property Division, P.O. Box 327580, Montgomery, AL 36132-7580; Phone: (205) 242-9614.

Alaska: Alaska Department of Revenue, Income and Excise Audit Division, Unclaimed Property Section, P.O. Box 110420, Juneau, AK 99811-0420; Phone: (907) 465-4653.

Arizona: Department of Revenue, Unclaimed Property Division, 1600 West Monroe, Phoenix, AZ 85007; Phone: (602) 542-3908.

Arkansas: Auditor of the State, Unclaimed Property Division, 103 W. Capitol, Suite 805, Box 146, Little Rock, AR 72201; Phone: (501) 324-9670.

California: State Controller's Office, Unclaimed Property Division, P.O. Box 942850, Sacramento, CA 95250-5873; Phone: (916) 323-2827.

Colorado: State Treasurer, Division of Unclaimed Property, 1560 Broadway, Suite 630, Denver, CO 80202; Phone: (303) 894-2449.

Connecticut: Treasury Department, Unclaimed Property Division, 55 Elm Street, Hartford, CT 06106; Phone: (203) 566-5516.

Delaware: Delaware State Escheator, Abandoned Property Division, P.O. Box 8931, Wilmington, DE 19899; Phone: (302) 577-3349.

District of Columbia: Office of Financial Management, Unclaimed Property Division, 300 Indiana Avenue, N.W., Washington, DC 20001; Phone: (202) 727-0063.

Florida: Office of Comptroller, Division of Finance, Abandoned Property Section, Tallahassee, FL 32311-0350; Phone: (904) 487-0510.

Georgia: Department of Revenue, Unclaimed Property Section, 270 Washington Street, S.W., Room 404, Atlanta, GA 30334; Phone: (404) 656-4244.

Hawaii: Director of Finance State of Hawaii, Unclaimed Property Section, P.O. Box 150, Honolulu, HI 96810; Phone: (808) 586-1590.

Idaho: State Tax Commission, Unclaimed Property Division, 800 Park Blvd., Plaza 4, P.O. Box 36, Boise, ID 83722; Phone: (208) 334-7623.

Illinois: Department of Financial Institutions, Unclaimed Property Division, Box 19490, Springfield, IL 62794-9496; Phone: (217) 782-8463.

Indiana: Office of Attorney General, Unclaimed Property Division, 402 W. Washington Street, 5th Floor, Indianapolis, IN 46204; Phone: (317) 232-6348.

Iowa: Great Iowa Treasure Hunt, Iowa State Treasurer's Office, Hoover State Office Building, Des Moines, IA 50319; Phone: (515) 281-5540.

Kansas: State Treasurer's Office, Unclaimed Property Division, 900 Southwest Jackson, Suite 201, Topeka, KS 66612-1235; Phone: (913) 296-3171; (800) 432-0386 (Kansas only).

Kentucky: State Revenue Cabinet, Miscellaneous Excise Tax Division, Station 62, 209 St. Clair Street, Frankfort, KY 40601; Phone: (502) 564-6823.

Louisiana: Department of Revenue and Taxation, Unclaimed Property Division, P.O. Box 91010, Baton Rouge, LA 70821; Phone: (504) 925-7425.

Maine: Treasury Department, Abandoned Property Division, Station 39, Augusta, ME 04333; Phone: (207) 289-2771.

Maryland: Comptroller of the Treasury, Unclaimed Property Section, 301 West Preston Street, Baltimore, MD 21201; Phone: (410) 225-1700.

Massachusetts: Commonwealth of Massachusetts, Treasury Department, Unclaimed Property Division, One Ashburton Place, 12th Floor, Boston, MA 02108; Phone: (617) 367-3900.

Michigan: Department of the Treasury, Abandoned and Unclaimed Property Division, Lansing, MI 48922; Phone: (517) 335-4327.

Minnesota: Department of Commerce, Office of Unclaimed Property, 133 East 7th Street, St. Paul, MN 55101; Phone (612) 296-2568; (800) 925-5668.

Mississippi: Mississippi Treasurer, Unclaimed Property Division, P.O. Box 138, Jackson, MS 39205; Phone: (601) 359-3600.

Missouri: Department of the Treasury, Unclaimed Property Division, Box 1272, Jefferson City, MO 65102; Phone: (3140 751-0123.

Montana: State of Montana, Department of Revenue, Abandoned Property Section, P.O. Box 5805, Helena, MT 59620; Phone: (406) 444-2425.

Nebraska: State Treasurer's Office, Property Capitol Building, P.O. Box 94788, Lincoln, NE 68509; Phone: (402) 471-2455.

Nevada: State of Nevada Unclaimed Property Division, 2601 E. Sahara, Room 270, Las Vegas, NV 89158; Phone: (702) 486-4140; Phone: (800) 521-0019 (Nevada only).

New Hampshire: New Hampshire Treasurer's Office, Abandoned Property Division, 25 Capitol Street, Room 121, Concord, NH 03301; Phone: (603) 271-2619.

New Jersey: State of New Jersey Department of the Treasury, Unclaimed Property, 50 Barrack Street, CN-214, Trenton, NJ 08646; Phone: (609) 292-9200.

New Mexico: New Mexico Taxation and Revenue Department, P.O. Box 25123, Santa Fe, NM 87504-5123; Phone: (505) 827-0767.

New York: Administrator, Office of Unclaimed Funds, Alfred E. Smith State Office Building, 9th Floor, Albany, NY 12236; Phone: (5180 474-4038.

North Carolina: Department of the Treasurer, Escheat and Abandoned Property Section, 325 Salisbury Street, Raleigh, NC 27603-1385; Phone: (919) 733-6876.

North Dakota: Unclaimed Property Division, P.O. Box 5523, Bismarck, ND 58502-5522; Phone: (701) 224-2805.

Ohio: Division of Unclaimed Funds, Department of Commerce, 77 South High Street, Columbus, OH 43266-0845; Phone: (614) 466-4433.

Oklahoma: Oklahoma Tax Commission, Unclaimed Property Section, P.O. Box 53248, Oklahoma City, OK 73152; Phone: (405) 521-4275. Oregon: Oregon Division of State Lands, Unclaimed Property, 775 Summer Street, N.E., Salem, OR 97310; Phone: (503) 378-3805.

Pennsylvania: Abandoned & Unclaimed Property Section, Department of the Treasury, Room 218, Finance Building, Harrisburg, PA 17120; Phone: (717) 986-4641; (800) 222-2046 (PA only).

Rhode Island: State of Rhode Island, Unclaimed Property Division, P.O. Dox 1435, Providence, RI 02901; Phone: (401) 277-6505.

South Carolina: Abandoned Property Office, Department of Revenue, P.O. Box 125, Columbia, SC 29214; Phone: (803) 737-4771.

South Dakota: State Treasurer's Office, Unclaimed Property Division, 500 East Capitol, Pierre, SD 57501; Phone: (605) 773-3378.

Tennessee: Unclaimed Property Division, Andrew Jackson State Office Building, 11th Floor, Nashville, TN 37243-0242; Phone: (615) 741-6499.

Texas: Unclaimed Property Division, State Treasurer's Office, P.O. Box 12608, Austin, TX 78711; Phone: (512) 463-6060.

Utah: Utah Unclaimed Property Division, 34 South Main Street, 5th Floor, Salt Lake City, UT 84111; Phone: (801) 538-1043.

Vermont: State of Vermont, Unclaimed Property Division, 133 State Street, Montpelier, VT 05633-6200; Phone: (802) 828-2407.

Virginia: Department of the Treasury, Division of Unclaimed Property, P.O. Box 2478, Richmond, VA 23207-2478; Phone: (804) 225-2393; (800) 468-1088 (Virginia only).

Washington: State of Washington, Department of Revenue, Unclaimed Property Division, P.O. Box 448, Olympia, WA 98507; Phone: (206) 586-2736.

West Virginia: State Treasurer's Office, Unclaimed Property Division, State Capitol, E-145, Charleston, WV 25305; Phone: (304) 343-4000.

Wisconsin: Office of the State Treasurer, Unclaimed Property Division, P.O. Box 2114, Madison, WI 53701-2114; Phone: (608) 267-7977.

Wyoming: Unclaimed Property Division, Wyoming State Treasury, 122 W. 25th, 3rd Floor E., Herschler Building, Cheyenne, WY 82002; Phone: (307) 777-5590.

MONEY POWER

CHAPTER 4

Tax Savings

One of the best ways to "beat the system" and save money is by taking advantage of little-known and commonly overlooked IRS-approved tax deductions. There's a good chance that you, like many other people, are actually paying more taxes than you have to because you aren't aware of these deductions. With proper tax planning, you can find perfectly legal ways to cut your taxes and save hundreds, even thousands of dollars a year. You won't be shirking your public duty as a taxpayer or cheating the government by taking advantage of these deductions. Instead, you will be paying your fair share of taxes— the amount the law demands and nothing more.

The tax-cutting strategies provided in this chapter represent some of the least-known and most commonly overlooked IRS-approved deductions available to most taxpayers. You should consult your accountant or tax preparer for more information about these and other deductions for which you may be eligible. You also can get helpful information by sending for the free IRS publications listed later in this chapter.

Slash Your Taxes With These Commonly Overlooked Deductions

Here are several legitimate tax deductions which are commonly overlooked by taxpayers. These deductions, if applicable in your circumstances, can help you slash your taxes by $4,000 to $6,000 a year. In some cases, the deductions apply only in certain situations, such as business-related expenses. You can get more information about these and other little-known tax deductions for which you may be eligible from free IRS publications (see below) and/or your accountant or tax-preparer.

— Contributions of cash to charity are fully deductible. Keep a record of your charitable contributions, including the date, amount of contribution, and the charity(s) involved.

— Dues paid to a labor union are fully deductible.

— Depreciation of a home computer used for business purposes.

— Mortgage points which are based on a percentage of the loan.

— Fees for prepaying mortgage notes or installment contracts.

— Accounting fees paid for IRS audits and for tax preparation services.

— Moving expenses. If you are moving because you are changing jobs or you are being transferred to a new location by your employer, you may be eligible for this deduction. To qualify, your new work location must be at least 50 miles from your old home.

— Educational expenses incurred while you are employed or self-employed can be tax-deductible. You also may be able to deduct educational fees and costs if you are taking a course to improve your skills or as a requirement of your present job.

— Medical Expenses. There are many overlooked medical expense deductions for which you may be eligible, including contact lenses and solutions; birth-control pills; acupuncture; childbirth preparation classes; travel expenses incurred due to illness; orthopedic shoes; reading glasses for dyslexia; special equipment for the disabled or handicapped; and health insurance costs for the self-employed.

— Charitable mileage deduction. You can deduct for mileage (plus tolls and parking fees) incurred traveling to and from volunteer work. The deduction also applies to the mileage incurred if you are dropping off items at the Salvation Army.

— Business gifts of $25 or less per recipient.

IRS-Approved Tax-Free Income

Not all income is subject to federal taxes. For example, the rental income you derive from renting your vacation (second) home to non-family members for fewer than 15 days in a year, is tax-free. You don't even have to report the rental income on your tax return. However, you still are entitled to full deductions for property taxes and mortgage interest.

Here are several other sources of income which are free from federal taxes:

— Life and health insurance proceeds.

— A cash rebate from a manufacturer when you buy a new car.

— Worker's compensation.

— Money derived from personal injury awards.

— Money from an inheritance.

— Earnings up to $70,000 by working abroad for an American company.

— Investment income up to $600 if the investment is in your child's name. Depending on the return on your money, you can invest approximately $5,000 to $10,000 in your child's name and not be required to pay taxes on the income (up to $600).

Deduct 45% Or More Of Your Vacation Costs As Business Expenses

Combining a short vacation with a tax-deductible business trip is a smart way to travel and save money. If the primary purpose of a trip within the U.S. is business, the cost of traveling to and from the business location is fully deductible, even if you add a few days for recreation. Expenses at your destination—meals and entertainment— that are for business purposes also are deductible. In both cases, it's a good idea to be prepared to prove to the IRS that the deductions are business-related. That means being able to prove that more than half your time at the destination was spent on business.

If your spouse accompanies you on a business/pleasure trip part of your total trip expenses will not be deductible. As a rule, the nondeductible amount of such a trip is the difference between the overall expense and what it would have been if you had taken the trip alone.

If you take a business/vacation trip to a location outside the U.S., the rules change somewhat. You still can take the full business-travel deduction, explained above, unless your trip lasts for more than a week and more than 25% of your total time is spent on nonbusiness days. In that event, your transportation deduction should be adjusted accordingly.

The key to deducting 45% or more of your vacation costs is to combine pleasure with business. You must be able to justify your deductions as based on business expenses. If the primary purpose of the trip is business, you should keep good records of all your expenses and their business purpose. You also should keep receipts for expenses of $25 or more. Such records should satisfy the IRS and allow you to deduct a good portion of your vacation costs as business expenses.

Take Advantage Of These Common Property Tax Exemptions

If you are a property owner, you may be eligible for one or more of the following property tax exemptions.

—Personal property tax exemption. You may be eligible for a deduction on "necessary household items", such as a washer or dryer.

— Veterans Exemption. To be eligible you must be a veteran, or the spouse, or the child of a veteran.

— Senior citizens exemption. You must be 65 or older to be eligible for this exemption.

— Home business exemption. You may be able to deduct the portion of your home used for business.

You can get a complete list of property tax exemptions available in your area, eligibility requirements, filing deadlines, and applications from your local tax assessor's office.

How To Use Your Hobby To Save Thousands Of Dollars In Taxes

The difference in tax deductions allowed between being a hobbyist and operating a hobby as a business are considerable. Generally, as a hobbyist, your tax deductions are limited to whatever income the activity generates. If, however, you operate your hobby as a business (see chapter 5, "Turn Your Hobby Into A Profitable Full-Time Business") your expenses are deductible, even if they are greater than the business income.

In order to take advantage of business-related tax deductions, you must be able to prove to the IRS that you intended to make a profit. The key word is "intended". You can deduct losses incurred from a business as long as the IRS is satisfied that you "intended" to make a profit. If your hobby activity is not profit motivated, your deductions will be limited and the IRS will not allow any losses to offset other income.

As far as the IRS is concerned, an activity is "presumed" to be carried on for profit if it produces a profit in at least three of 5 consecutive tax years (two out of seven years if the activity involves breeding, training, showing, or racing horses). You can elect to file IRS form 5213 ("Election to Postpone Determination as to Whether the Presumption that an Activity is Engaged in for Profit Applies") and postpone any IRS determination until the first five (or seven) years have passed. If you choose to file form 5213, the IRS will not question whether or not your activity is carried on for profit, nor will it challenge your deductions claimed as a result of that activity until five years have passed.

Whether or not you choose to postpone the IRS determination, you'll want to have tangible proof that you are, in fact, engaged in an activity for profit. Here are several insider tips that can help you provide the necessary proof and reduce the risk of having the IRS challenge your deductions as hobby losses:

— Give your business a name and register it with your local county clerk. This will require filing a "doing business as" statement.

— Organize a business plan, listing your business goals and strategies.

— Establish a business bank account.

— Install a business telephone.

— Use professional-looking business cards and stationery.

— Get a business listing in the Yellow Pages.

— Advertise your business in local newspapers and on local radio/tv stations.

— Send direct mail ads to prospective clients.

— Keep detailed records of all your business transactions.

When it comes to taxes, the difference between being strictly a hobbyist or operating your hobby as a business for profit can be thousands of dollars. One former hobbyist saved over $4,200 in taxes by running her hobby as a business. If you are able to operate your hobby as a business you can take advantage of IRS-approved tax deductions and save thousands of dollars on your taxes too.

Tax-Deductible IRA Contributions

One of the best tax shelters for working Americans is an Individual Retirement Account (IRA). You can cut your taxes considerably by making a tax-deductible contribution to an IRA by the April 15th tax-filing deadline. However, the earlier in the tax year you make the contribution, the sooner the interest/dividends will begin to accrue, tax-deferred.

An IRA contribution may be tax-deductible up to $2,000 for an unmarried person; and up to $4,000 for two-income married couples; and up to $2,500 for a one-income married couple. Your IRA contribution will be fully deductible if your income Is $25,000 and you are are single— even if you are covered by a company retirement plan; or $40,000 or less for married couples who file joint returns— even if one is covered by a company plan.

How To get Extra Money In Your Paychecks

Here's some good news from the IRS: You can get extra money in each paycheck if you qualify for the Earned Income Credit (EIC). The EIC reduces the amount of income tax you pay. You may even be eligible to receive the credit "in advance" in the form of extra money in your paychecks. To qualify for EIC, you must earn less than $23,760 (in 1994) and have at least one child living at home with you.

If you meet the IRS qualifications, you can get the Advance EIC by filing form W-5, "Earned Income Credit Advance Payment Certificate", with your employer. Based on the amount you earn, your employer then adds some extra money (taken from the EIC credit) to your take home pay on each paycheck. Should your circumstances change, and you are no longer eligible to receive AEIC, you'll be required to repay the amount advanced to you when you file your federal tax return. If you need to stop the advance payments, all you do is file a new form W-5 and give it to your employer. You'll also have to file a tax return if you get AEIC in your paychecks.

You can't get the advance credit if you are self-employed. However, you may be able to claim the credit when you file your federal income tax return.

To get more information about the Earned Income Credit, contact your payroll office or call the IRS at (800) 829-3676. Ask for a free copy of "Earned Income Credit" (Publication 596), and Form W-5.

Special Deductions For The Self-Employed If you are self-employed, you pay 15.3 percent of your taxable income into Social Security (up to the limit of $57,600). There are, however, special deductions you can take when you file your tax return which are designed to offset your tax rate. You can find out about these deductions and get more information about self-employment tax rates by calling Social Security's toll-free number, (800) 772-1213. Ask for a free copy of Publication #05-10022, "If You're Self-Employed".

Free Publications From The IRS

Call (800) 829-3676 to order free copies of any or all of the following IRS publications.

— "Your Rights As A Taxpayer", Publication # 17

— "Tax Guide For Small Business", Publication 334

— "Exemptions, Standard Deductions, And Filing Information", Publication 501

— "Tax Information For Divorced or Separated Individuals", Publication 504

— "Educational Expenses", Publication 508

— "Moving Expenses", Publication 521

— "Taxable and Nontaxable Income", Publication 525

— "Charitable Contributions", Publication 526

— "Miscellaneous Deductions", Publication 529

— "Self-Employment Tax", Publication 533

— "Business Expenses", Publication 535

— "Recordkeeping For Individuals and a List of Tax Publications", Publication 552

— "Business Use of Your Home", Publication 587

— "Guide To Free Tax Services", Publication 910

MONEY POWER

CHAPTER 5

Money-Making Business Opportunities

The majority of America's self-made millionaires started with nothing— or practically nothing. Many were heavily in debt with low paying jobs that offered no prospects for advancement. Then, out of necessity, these people took advantage of various business opportunities and soon their money problems were over. Starting from scratch and in many cases, from their own homes in their spare time, these self-made millionaires discovered that entrepreneurship opens the doors to unlimited money-making possibilities.

In this chapter, we'll take a look at several of the fastest growing business opportunities of the 90s. All of the opportunities described are relatively easy to start and operate as home-based businesses on a part-time basis. While in most cases, the initial capital outlay required to start these businesses is $500 or less, the potential for growth and substantial profits is excellent.

Three Part-Time Home Businesses That can Make You $950 A Week

Starting a business in your home can be a rewarding venture— both personally and financially. The home business you choose can provide you with an opportunity to expand a hobby into a money-making business or to put into practice an "idea" you've been considering.

Whatever your reasons for starting a home business, there are several things you should consider before committing your time and resources. First of all, you should look at the possible advantages and disadvantages of making such a commitment. You might make up a list like the following:

Advantages

— Being my own boss

— Flexible work schedule
— Save on the time and expense of commuting
— Satisfaction from a sense of accomplishment
— More options for meeting child care needs
— Working at something I enjoy doing

Disadvantages

— The risk of not making a profit
— Possible distractions from family and friends
— May upset family's schedule
— Expenses required to make my business profitable

Study your list and decide whether or not the advantages outnumber the disadvantages. Keep in mind that there are many home-based businesses that you can start with minimal investment. In fact, many successful entrepreneurs started money-making home businesses with investments of less than $100.

The key to success with a home-based business is in being certain that there is a market— beyond your family and close friends- for your product or service, making it a potentially high-profit opportunity. For many people, it also is important that start-up costs are minimal ($100 or less), and that they can operate the business in their spare time. There are many businesses that have the potential of meeting all of those criteria. Here are three easy-to-start, part-time home businesses that could make you almost $1000 a week.

1) Resume Writing Service

If you have at least average typing skills and a good command of the English language, you may consider starting a resume business. The market for professionally prepared resumes is virtually unlimited. Recent college graduates looking for jobs, people who have been laid off and need to find new jobs, and people who want to change jobs or switch careers, are all potential clients for a such a service. Your income will depend on your client base and the number of hours you put into the business. One home-based resume service in Pennsylvania reports an income of $950 a week working 25 to 30 hours a week.

Not only is there a great demand for this type of service, it's also a business you can start without making a big financial investment. All you need to begin is an inexpensive personal computer, software and a printer. If you already have a computer and printer, your start-up costs can be less than $100 for various office supplies. You can make a bigger investment in equipment and facilities once your business is established and showing a profit. The important thing is to be able to produce a professional product.

To be successful, you'll need to provide your clients with professional, creative resumes. While it's true that a professionally prepared resume can not guarantee anyone employment, it can provide a decided edge with prospective employers. Such professionalism will also pay off for you in the form of referrals from satisfied clients.

Before beginning your resume service, you'll need to understand what employers look for in resumes. To do that, you'll have to invest some time in research and study. That doesn't mean you'll need to take a special college course on "resume writing". However, it does mean that you will have to become familiar with proper resume format and style. All the information you need can be found in books and manuals which are available at your local public library. You also may want to invest in a few reference books which provide up-to-date information about "job-winning" cover letters and resumes.

Obtaining clients for your resume writing business will require a small investment in advertising. One of the best, inexpensive ways of making your service known to potential clients is by placing a classified ad in your local newspaper. Your ad should appear under the heading, "SERVICES" or "SITUATIONS WANTED". It also should include such information as, "professional resume writing", "low rates", and "satisfaction guaranteed", as well as the name of your business and your phone number.

You also may reach potential clients by advertising in the Yellow pages (which requires that you have a business phone line in your home office), and by distributing leaflets and fliers around town. Your most effective form of advertising, however, is word-of-mouth referrals from satisfied customers.

Your key to success with a resume writing service is your ability to copy edit and proofread each resume you produce thoroughly. You must make sure the final product is both professional and error-free. If you can establish a reputation for producing professional, creative resumes, you'll have no problem obtaining a steady stream of clients, and earning a sizable income.

2) Collection Agency

Most businesses have neither the personnel nor the time to devote to collecting on delinquent accounts. That's where the demand for collection services comes in. Even in tough economic times the opportunities for the operator of a home-based collection agency are excellent. If you have good communications skills and you are persistent, you can earn anywhere from $15,000 to $60,000 a year operating a collection agency in your spare time or on a full-time basis.

Collecting past due accounts for various businesses doesn't require the use of intimidation and/or harassment. In fact, those approaches seldom work and may be illegal. To be successful in this business you need to be able to deal with people on a non-confrontational basis. That requires patience and understanding. You'll also need to be determined, because the higher the percentage of accounts you collect on, the more profits you'll make.

Most of your work will be done by phone or by mail. In fact, experts in the field say that after receiving one businesslike letter or one non-threatening phone call from a collection agency most people pay at least part of their past due accounts. You'll receive a commission of 30% or more for each delinquent account you collect.

Start-up costs for a home-based collection agency are minimal. Since you'll be spending a lot of time on the phone, you may want to invest in a telephone headset. You'll also need a supply of professionally printed letterheads, business cards and collection letters, and standard office supplies. Your job also will be a lot easier if you have a word processor or personal computer and printer.

To get started, you'll need to familiarize yourself with the latest state and federal regulations governing collection agencies. You can check with local and state authorities for up-to-date information and also visit your local library for information on The Fair Debt Collections Practices Act. It's essential that you are aware of and adhere to all of the regulations regarding collection agencies and the methods you may and may not use to collect overdue accounts.

The next step is building a client base. You can do that by contacting various retail stores and professionals. Doctors, hospitals, furniture stores, hardware stores, and so on are all likely candidates to need the services of a collection agency. You can contact these merchants and professionals and offer to collect their past-due accounts for a certain percentage of each bill you collect on. When getting started, you may even offer to collect delinquent accounts on a trial basis, say, for a month or two. If you collect on a high percentage of accounts during the trial period, it's likely the client will enlist your service on a regular basis.

With a low overhead, a home-based collection service can afford to collect on accounts of all sizes, including the smaller accounts big collection agencies avoid. That means a home-based
service is likely to collect on a higher percentage of a client's past due accounts. The demand is definitely there. If you have the right temperament and the necessary drive, you could earn up to $60,000 a year operating your own home-based collection agency.

3) Catering

If you have a flair for preparing creative and enticing meals, you may have what it takes to start and operate a profitable catering service. You can use your culinary skills to prepare creative dishes for wedding receptions, birthday parties, business luncheons, cocktail parties, promotional events, anniversaries, and a host of other formal and informal occasions on evenings and on weekends. Your duties would include shopping, preparing and cooking the food, serving the dishes, and cleaning up afterwards, just as you do at home, but with the added incentive of being paid for your services!

Since the emphasis is on service, you can start a catering business with little or no capital investment. In fact, many caterers have started with an investment of less than $100 by arranging to perform most of their services in facilities provided by their customers. Of course, you also can use your own kitchen to prepare your catered events if adequate facilities are not otherwise available. The important thing is that you love working with food and have a knack for whipping up culinary delights for paying customers.

Deciding what you should charge for your services may be your hardest decision. It may be helpful to check out a few catering services in markets similar to yours and use their rates as a starting point upon which to base your decision. Many experienced caterers charge a rate that is around three times the cost of the food. Others add the cost of the food and other expenses to an hourly rate that covers all of the time invested in shopping, preparing, cooking, serving, and cleaning up. The bottom line is to determine how much you want to make per hour. Keep in mind, your rates must be reasonable because most of your customers will shop around and take bids from at least one other caterer.

Besides the steady demand for this service and the low start-up costs, it's also virtually risk-free. That's because you need not invest your own money. You can require that your customers make a deposit to cover the costs of food and other expenses with the balance due at the completion of your services.

The best way to make your service known quickly and to reach a wide range of potential customers is to run an ad in your local newspapers. You also may want to invest in some thirty-second ads on a local radio or television station, once your business is established and making a profit. Your most effective advertising, however, will be word of mouth referrals from satisfied customers.

Catering is one of the easiest home-based businesses to start and operate. And like all home businesses, your income will depend on the amount of time you put in and on the type(s) of service(s) you offer. If you provide your customers with quality catering, you could make anywhere from $10,000 to $30,000 or more a year in your spare time. Not bad for something you already may have been doing every day for free!

How To Make $400 A Week From Home Clipping Newspaper Items

Are you looking for a high-profit business you can operate from home in your spare time? If so, a newspaper clipping service offers just such an opportunity. You can start and operate such a service with little or no initial investment. You'll need only the newspapers, stamps and a few office supplies. Your kitchen table can serve as a desk. No experience or college degree is necessary. All that's required is that you enjoy reading and checking newspapers for certain types of news items.

The amount of money you can make operating such a service depends on the number and length of clippings you submit. Generally, working part- or full-time, it is possible to make anywhere from $25 to $400 (or more) a week. Your profit potential will depend to some extent on the availability of newspapers in your area. You should get one or two daily newspapers, and at least one weekly paper which is published locally.

Read the newspapers carefully, looking for news items relating to one (or more) particular trade. The items can pertain to the opening of a new store, local economic trends, fire damaging a business, local business awards, promotions, etc. Be sure to pay special attention to the business, sports, obituaries, travel, society and other special sections of your local paper(s) for salable items. The idea is to find and clip any items that are likely to be of interest to other people who are involved in the same business.

Once you have several clippings, you can then locate magazines or trade journals which specialize in that particular trade. There are trade journals published for virtually every trade imaginable. Your local public library should have a directory (in the reference section) which lists every trade journal published in North America. The listings in the directory will provide you with the addresses and information about the contents of every journal published that may be a potential market for your clippings. You can also find listings of trade, technical and professional journals in other publications such as Writer's Market (Writer's Digest Books, Cincinnati, Ohio) which also may be available at your local library.

The next step involves sending the items you clip to appropriate trade journals for possible publication. Not every item you clip and submit will be published right away, but you shouldn't get discouraged. The longer you keep at it, the better you'll become in spotting and clipping salable items.

Your initial submission to a trade journal should be accompanied by a brief letter explaining your service. Without going into lengthy detail, your letter should inform the editor that you operate a newspaper clipping service and that the enclosed clipping is being submitted for approval and use. The clipping itself should be pasted neatly on a sheet of typing paper or on a letterhead sheet. Make sure each clipping you submit includes the name and address from which the clipping was obtained, the date it appeared, and your name and address. Once your service begins returning a profit, you may want to invest in a professional letterhead sheet for your clippings as well as business cards with the name of your service.

As you can see by now, it's not at all difficult to start and operate a newspaper clipping business. Anyone with some spare time and access to several daily and weekly local newspapers can take advantage of this opportunity. There are hundreds of journals and other magazines which use clippings as a source of information whenever appropriate for the subject content of their publications.

If you are willing to devote the time needed to locate and clip salable news items and send them off to the appropriate publications, you can make a decent income operating this type of business. If you persevere, and give yourself several months to get established and make the necessary contacts, you should begin to realize the profitable rewards of operating your own newspaper clipping service.

Make $2,700 A Month Turning Other People's Trash Into Cash

It may not sound too appealing at first, but there is profit to be made in trash. That's right, all those newspapers, bottles, boxes, and cans you and many other people "give away" to the garbage collector could mean money in your pocket through recycling. While most people simply put their trash in the can and forget about it, you could take the initiative and begin a profitable recycling business. Depending on the amount of time and effort you invest in the business, you could make from $200 to $2,700 a month recycling other people's trash.

The best way to begin this type of business is by recycling your own trash. Sort out all the recyclable material such as aluminum cans, glass, newspapers, bottles, cardboard boxes and cartons. When you've collected several pounds of recyclable items take them to the nearest recycling center. You can contact your local Chamber of Commerce to find out where the recycling center is in your area. You also can contact Reynolds Aluminum, (800) 222-2525 and ask about the location of the nearest recycling center.

Rates vary from location to location, but generally you can get from 5 cents a pound to 50 cents a pound depending on the types of items you have. The more you collect for recycling the more money you can make. And that's where other people come into the picture.

Once you've gained experience recycling your own trash, you can begin collecting recyclable items from your neighbors and friends. Most people will be happy to let you "haul away" their newspapers, aluminum cans and other recyclable trash. You can establish a mutually convenient day for your weekly pickups. In the event that some people are reluctant to give you their recyclable throwaways, you might offer to pay them $5 a month on the condition that they have everything ready for you to pick up on the agreed upon collection day each week.

Obviously you'll need someplace to store your "trash" until you have a sufficient amount to take to the recycling plant. Your garage, basement or a dry outbuilding will suffice until your business is established to the point of expansion. You may then want to consider adding a new, larger outbuilding or renting space in a near-by warehouse.

Once you have plenty of storage space set aside you can begin expanding your collections beyond your own neighborhood. You can place an inexpensive ad in the classified section of your local newspaper to let your community know of your service. Your ad should include the type of items you are looking for— newspapers, cardboard boxes, aluminum cans, etc., and your phone number. You also can have printed several hundred fliers outlining your service and distribute them throughout your community. You may have to offer a nominal payment for some of the items you collect, but the more people you can get involved in your recycling business the bigger your collections and your profits.

The key to success in operating a recycling business is to start out small. Don't try to collect beyond your own neighborhood and friends until you've gained the necessary experience and your business is established on a small scale. Given time and effort, your business should generate a nice profit. What's more, by recycling you will be performing an environmentally valuable service.

Turn Your Computer Into A $75,000 A Year Income

A personal computer can be one of the best investments you'll ever make. That's because a computer can provide you with the means to start and operate your own profitable part- or full-time home-based business. You can use your computer to provide hundreds of money-making services, many of which you can start with little or no initial investment and in your spare time. Depending on the type of service(s) you provide and the number of hours you put in, you could generate an income of $75,000 or more a year!

Here are five of the fastest-growing computer related businesses you can start with little or no money.

1) Mailing List Service

This is one of the best computer-related home-based businesses to get into. Your biggest initial investment will be a computer. If you already have a computer, your start-up costs will be minimal, at most. What's more, the growth potential for this type of business is excellent— even in a weak economic climate. And the income potential from a mailing list service ranges from $10,000 to $75,000 a year!

With your computer, you can provide several mailing-list services including creating and maintaining mailing lists. There are several ways to go about building mailing lists. One of the best ways is to run a short classified ad in various mail-order publications offering a free report on some type of money-making opportunity. To get a copy of the report, each person responding must send you a self-addressed, stamped envelope. While each person who responds gets a free copy of your money-making report, you get names and addresses for your list.

You also can create specialized mailing lists for your local community and/or specialized markets. For example, read all your local newspapers and compile the names and addresses of all new parents and all newlyweds. These lists can be sold to such clients as furniture stores, appliance dealers, photographers, department stores, cleaners and so on. You also can build a good mailing list by using your clients' existing records, including invoices and client files.

With your computer and an inexpensive database program, you can build a marketable database of names which you can sell as sets of ready-to-use mailing labels. The lists also can be sold as reports featuring names, addresses and phone numbers. To add value to your service, you can conduct regular phone interviews to verify or update your information or to gather additional information which you can use to create specialized lists.

2) Word Processing

This is another home-business that you can start with a minimal investment. All you need is a computer, a good word-processing program and basic typing skills. You may land jobs typing book manuscripts, letters, documents, legal briefs, screenplays, or business reports. You can charge anywhere from $2 to $20 a page, depending on how complex the material is. Some home-based word-processors gross over $50,000 a year handling overflow work from businesses, law firms, publishers, and other sources.

Getting clients for your word-processing business will require an initial investment in advertising. You can run ads offering your service in area newspapers and local newsletters. You also can advertise your service on community and college campus bulletin boards for free. Ads in writer's magazines, such as "Writer's Digest" (1507 Dana Avenue, Cincinnati, OH 45207) also can reach potential clients. Once you've built a solid reputation, much of your business will come from current client referrals.

3) Indexing

Indexing is one of the most popular and least-expensive-to-operate computer-related businesses of the 1990s. It's a service that provides back-of-the-book indexing and computer-database indexing for book publishers and database companies. Some home-based indexers charge $30 and more an hour, depending on the complexity of the material. The potential income from such a business ranges from $10,000 to $40,000 or more a year.

Generally, start-up costs for this type of business include the purchase of a computer with lots of memory, letter-quality printer, and word-processing and indexing software. Once your business is established and making a profit, you also may want to invest in a modem and a fax machine.

You don't need any formal training to be a successful indexer, however, basic training (by correspondence or from a university) can give you a decided edge in landing the highest-paying jobs. The U.S. Department of Agriculture's graduate school offers correspondence courses for fledgling indexers. You also may begin by reviewing indexes in a variety of books and by researching and learning how to use indexing software.

Most successful home-based indexers say that the best way to get clients is to contact publishers and database companies directly. Your contact should be in writing and include a brief cover letter, resume and sample indexes. "The Writer's Market" and "The Literary Marketplace" are two good sources for locating publishers. Both books are updated every year and are available for review in most public libraries.

For more information about indexing, write to the American Society of Indexers (ASI), P.O. Box 386, Port Aransas, TX 78373. ASI publishes a book entitled "Freelancers on Starting & Maintaining an Indexing Business". The book is available to ASI members for $15— nonmembers may purchase the book for $20.

To get information about correspondence courses offered by the USDA, write to: Correspondence Study Program, Graduate School, USDA, South Agriculture Building, Room 1114. 14th & Independence, S.W., Washington, DC 20250.

4) Medical Transcription

Medical Transcription is one of the fastest-growing computer-related business of the 1990s. It's a business that requires good typing skills and a knowledge of medical diagnostic procedures and terminology. You'll also need a computer and a transcribing machine.

Transcriptionists listen to cassette tapes which describe such things as patient care, operations, lab reports and autopsies and then enter the information into a computer. The income you can generate from providing such a service depends on whether you work full- or part-time, and your client base. However, many home-based medical transcriptionists report yearly incomes ranging from $25,000 to $40,000.

To get clients for your medical transcription business, you'll need to contact doctors, hospitals, and/or lawyers who handle medical disability cases. You also can advertise your service in medical publications and respond to "Medical Transcriptionist Needed" ads in the same publications. Another method for obtaining clients is to take on overflow and/or referral work from other transcriptionists.

As to the training you'll need, you may be able to take some courses at your local community-college or university. You also can enroll in a home-study course (see Chapter 7) or get on-the-job training in a doctor's office or a medical laboratory.

For more information about starting a home-based medical transcription business, contact the American Association for Medical Transcription, 3460 Oakdale Road, Suite M , Modesto, CA 95355; (800) 982-2182.

5) Small Business Billing Service

The demand is high among small businesses for billing services. That's because most small businesses can't afford to hire a full-time staff to take care of the administrative work involved in billing and invoicing. These businesses find it more cost (and time) effective to pay an outside billing service to do the job for them. The result is a potentially profitable, low-overhead, home-based business opportunity for anyone who can take on the job of billing quickly and accurately.

You can operate a general business billing service from a home-based office in your spare time or on a full-time basis. You won't need any specialized training—just an ability to use a computer and to get the work done accurately and on time. If you already own a computer and printer, start-up costs will be $500 or less for software and assorted office supplies. A successful home-based billing service can generate a yearly income ranging from $25,000 to $100,000 and more a year.

Potential clients for this type of service include small, service oriented businesses. You can contact such businesses and offer them your services free for one month. Most businesses will jump at such an offer, and if you are prompt and accurate in handling their accounts, will sign on as clients after the free trial period. You also can reach potential clients by running ads in local newspapers and other business-oriented publications. Once your business is established, many of your accounts will be referrals from your original clients.

For additional information about starting a billing service, contact the American Association of Billing Professionals (813) 365-3357.

How To Make Big Profits In Mail Order

What does it take to get rich in mail order? The most obvious requirement is a marketable idea, product or service. Combine that with persistence and a desire to succeed, and the opportunities for mail order riches are virtually unlimited. In fact, almost anyone, regardless of previous experience, educational background or training, is qualified to start and operate a successful mail order business.

The first thing you should understand about mail order is that while it is a potentially very profitable business, no one gets rich overnight. The second thing to understand is that like any other job, mail order requires time, effort, and a willingness to learn. The more you understand about the business of mail order, the better prepared you'll be to take advantage of its vast moneymaking potential.

Besides the potential for huge profits, mail order also attracts many fledgling entrepreneurs because start-up costs can be relatively low. Many successful mail order businesses began as spare time, "kitchen table" operations which required very little start-up capital. Once these operations were turning a profit, they expanded into more "businesslike" home-based and outside offices. Most of your initial investment in such a kitchen-table operation will be for advertising and/or making mailings.

To get started in mail order, you'll need to choose a product that has the potential to bring you substantial profits. While just about anything can be sold by mail, specialized information is one of the most sought after and profitable products in mail order today. People are always looking for information and/or specific knowledge on a seemingly endless list of subjects— everything from astrology to yodeling. You can actually become rich by providing basic but valuable information in the form of reports, manuals, books, tapes, etc. to thousands, even millions of mail order buyers.

Selling information in reports of 4 to 20 pages is one of the easiest and most profitable ways to begin a kitchen-table mail order business. That's because you can use your own area of expertise and special knowledge as subject matter or through basic research choose from a bottomless well of topics. For example, "how-to" reports are good sellers because they offer specific information and advice on how people can cope with or correct certain problems or achieve certain goals.

Your aim then is to write an informational report drawn from your own experience or research. If you have no special talent for writing, you can enlist the services of someone who has. This could be a friend, relative or colleague or someone they know who can write your knowledge down. Such a collaboration can be on a royalty basis, and you won't have to pay any up-front or advance money. You also may contact a freelance writer and offer him/her the assignment on a royalty basis.

Whether or not you write your own report, you will be responsible for marketing it. If the report provides useful information on a subject of interest, you should be able to sell as many as you can produce. The good thing about reports is that they can be duplicated again and again for just pennies per copy and sold for several dollars per copy. Conceivably, you can duplicate your report as many times as needed, meaning the potential for profits exists as long as the report is available.

In order to sell your report, you'll need to write a winning sales letter to send to potential customers. Your sales letter should be professional in appearance and focus in clear concise language on how each customer will benefit from purchasing a copy of your report. The key to your initial success will be in your ability to write an effective sales letter.

After your sales letter is written you'll need to take advantage of "targeted" market lists and classified advertising to get your offer to the people who are most likely to buy your report. One of the most effective ways to do that is to get a targeted mailing list from a reputable mailing list broker. Explain your product to the broker you contact and ask for help in choosing a mailing list that will target the most potential customers. Send each person on the list a copy of your sales letter and order form. You also can invest in classified advertising in appropriate publications, offering "Free Information" about your report. Each person who responds should in turn receive a copy of your sales letter and order form.

How much money can you make from a single 4 to 20 page "how-to" report? That depends on a number of factors, including the number of potential buyers on your mailing list, the percentage of people who respond, and how much you charge per report. For example, a 15 percent response from a 5000 name mailing list (750 buyers) for a $10 report would mean an income of $7,500. A 20% response would bring in $10,000, and so on.

Considering the low initial investment, the profits from this type of mail order business can be phenomenal. Using your kitchen table as an office, and with an initial investment of $500 or so, you can make thousands of dollars in just a few months. Of course, you'll need a marketable product and the know-how to make it available to your most likely buyers. While you may not get rich overnight, you can, with enough time and effort, reap substantial financial rewards in mail order.

Turn Your Hobby Into A Profitable Full-Time Business

Your hobby can be more than a rewarding pastime— it also can be a money-making business. If your hobby involves producing anything—crafts, artwork, photography, and so on—there's a good chance you can turn it into a profitable part- or full-time business by marketing your creations. Here are seven ways you could turn your hobby into a profitable enterprise.

1) Sell your home-made products (quilts, stuffed animals, dolls, woodwork, ceramics, artwork, etc.) to friends and co-workers. You also can hold your own garage sale and have some of your work on display. At this stage, you are "testing the waters" to see if there is a market for your special talents.

2) Expand your base of customers. Once you find out that there is a market for your products and you begin to make a small profit, you can then offer your creations to other potential buyers. Word-of-mouth will bring in some customers, but to reach a wider customer base, you'll need to advertise. If you're artistic, you can create inexpensive fliers on brightly colored paper and distribute them door-to-door, or on cars in parking lots. You also can have fliers printed for relatively little cost. Running a classified ad in your local newspaper also is an inexpensive method of reaching more potential customers.

3) Sell your crafts at craft fairs. Check with shopping centers and malls for dates during the year when they rent space to craftspersons who wish to sell their products. You can rent a temporary booth set up in a high traffic area and make a good profit selling your craftwork. Craft fairs are typically well-advertised and usually attract large crowds. They offer a great opportunity for profit.

4) Sell your products at flea markets. Many hobbyists have turned their creativity into money-making propositions by selling at flea markets. These events offer a variety of unusual items and attract collectors, tourists and bargain hunters who are looking for handmade items.

5) Sell your items on consignment. This type of selling means that you leave your work with a store and receive your money only after it sells. The price you set is the amount you want to make from your work. The store owner will then mark up your work for a retail price so that he/she makes a profit also.

6) Prepare and distribute a monthly newsletter. You can make good profits from your hobby by providing a newsletter for people with similar interests.

7) Give lessons. Many hobbyists make extra income by giving lessons and teaching their special skills. A community college extension program might afford you such an opportunity. Lessons also can be given in your home.

Your hobby may provide the money-making opportunity you've been looking for. The only way to find out is to offer your creations to potential buyers. You could end up with a highly profitable full-time business.

How To Buy A Profitable Business In Your Area For No Money Down

The owner of a profitable business has given you the option to buy the company. You want to buy the company but you don't have the cash. What can you do?

One method of financing which is becoming more and more popular in such circumstances involves securing an investment from a certain type of investment fund. This investment fund, also known as a blind pool, is established by a group of individuals who want to invest in promising businesses. These investment funds are set up so that the pool of investors assume an equity position in the businesses they buy but are not involved in the management of those businesses.

Here's an example of such a financial arrangement: You have the option to buy a profitable business in your community. You approach a group of investors who have established an investment fund or blind pool. The pool has a certain amount of cash to invest and its stock is traded on the over-the-counter market. You provide the pool management with comprehensive information about the company and its potential for profit. You also provide evidence that you are both qualified and capable of running the business successfully.

If the investors decide to buy the company, you will assign your option to buy to the blind pool. In exchange, you will receive a majority of stock in the blind pool. The money for the down payment on the company will come from the pool. Your majority of stock in the pool serves as security for the remaining payments to the seller which will come from the company's continued cash flow. In effect, you will become a majority owner of a company without using any of your own money.

Under this type of financial arrangement, you not only get the majority of stock in the business, you also get to run it with little or no interference from the investors. Of course, the success of this type of arrangement depends on the continued growth and prosperity of the company. Remember, your stock in the pool is security for the payments.

You can get more information about blind pools—how they work, how to locate them in your area, and what to avoid—by contacting your accountant or attorney. They should be able to refer you to a professional who specializes in venture capital financing.

How To Make Money During Tough Economic Times

You've heard the old saying, "When the going gets tough, the tough get going". The implication is, that rather than giving in to setbacks, some people attack their problems head-on and find new ways to succeed. Those people who do, realize that in order to survive and prosper they must work harder, and develop new and better ways of doing things.

For the average small business owner that means taking a more aggressive approach to marketing his/her product or services during tough economic times. That may sound impractical, but experts say that cutting back on marketing activities or taking a "wait and see" attitude during an economic recession may be a costly mistake. On the other hand, the key to financial success when times are tough, is in using smart, aggressive strategies not only to maintain but to increase sales and profits.

Here are several expert strategies for surviving a weak economy and ensuring your personal and family's financial security:

— Develop a new and aggressive marketing plan. Instead of wringing your hands and bemoaning slow times in business, put your time to good use devising a marketing plan that will bring in new customers and produce more sales from existing customers as well. The marketing plan you implement should recognize the needs of your customers and offer them more value and service for their money.

— Keep advertising. You don't necessarily have to spend more money on advertising — just take a slightly different approach. For example, you may try a direct mail advertising campaign to attract potential customers. Your mailing could consist of a brief description of your product or service and a special "introductory offer" for those who reply right away. Inexpensive newspaper and radio ads also can be effective in letting potential customers know about your service. Remember, during tough economic times, people are looking for special values and for ways to save money. Your advertising should address those concerns. It isn't enough simply to sell products or a service, a successful business also provides value when customers need it most.

— Don't skimp on promotional activities. Whatever you do during slow times in business, don't cut back on your promotional activities. Promoting your business is more important than ever during tough times because you'll need to communicate with existing and potential customers about the benefits of your product or service. If that means passing out fliers and/or business cards to potential customers, do it.

— Offer "money-saving" coupons. Most shoppers love coupons which they can redeem for reduced prices on products or services. Regardless of the type(s) of product or services you offer, a coupon which can be redeemed for a reduced price on what you have to sell is a great way to attract new customers. It also can produce more sales from existing customers.

— Improve and expand customer service. During slow economic times, customer needs are likely to change. If you are alert to these changes and respond in kind by adjusting and expanding your services you are likely to have an edge over a competing business which simply sells a product. You should provide as many "free" services as possible—home delivery, consulting, etc. The key is to provide your existing and potential customers with a way to get more for their money. If you can do that, you'll not only get a lot of repeat business, you'll get more new business through referrals from appreciative customers.

— Join business and professional organizations. Membership in such organizations (and your local chamber of commerce) will bring you into contact with colleagues and other businesspeople. You can share and exchange ideas about marketing, promotion, advertising, customer service, and other business concerns. This type of networking is a good way to gain new insights into more effective ways to operate your business and to attract potential customers (You can find a listing of professional and trade associations in various publications, such as "National Trade and Professional Associations of the United States", available at your local public library).

— Take advantage of free consulting services. The Service Corps of Retired Executives (SCORE) in cooperation with local SBA offices can provide small business owners with free advice on all sorts of business-related topics, including strategies for surviving a weak economy. To take advantage of this service, contact your local SBA Hotline, (800) 827-5722; or the main office of SCORE, (202) 205-6762.

Your ability to make even bigger profits during tough economic times depends largely on whether or not you both recognize and accommodate the needs of your customers. To do that, you will need to be aggressive and creative in your marketing strategies. By making plans and taking action during tough times, you can give yourself a decided edge over a competitor who decides to just "sit back" and hope the economy improves. And that edge can mean the difference between failure and financial prosperity for you and your family during tough economic times.

MONEY POWER

CHAPTER 6

Money-Saving Shopping Techniques

The money-saving techniques provided in this chapter can help you "beat the system" with smart shopping. These are proven, effective techniques you can use to save thousands of dollars every year on all of your purchases— food, clothing, furniture, medicines, and so on. By using these insider shopping techniques, you'll be able to avoid marketing campaigns and other tricks many stores employ to get your money. You'll also learn where to shop for savings of 70% and more on everything from baby clothes to wallpaper, and how to take advantage of special money-saving coupon and refund offers.

How To Avoid A Dirty Trick That Stores Use To Rob You Of Money

The average American consumer spends hundreds, even thousands of dollars a year buying on impulse. Such purchases are typically for items the consumer doesn't need, and sometimes cannot really afford. Most stores employ an assortment of "tricks" to get consumers to spend more than they intended or to pay the highest prices. One of the most successful tactics used by stores is placing the most appealing and expensive items at eye level where they are most likely to be selected on impulse.

Supermarkets are especially adept at using that and other tactics to entice shoppers to spend more money than they planned to on impulse and convenience items they don't really need. In fact, most supermarkets are designed and laid out in such a manner that shoppers are unwittingly "encouraged" to buy as many impulse items as possible. For example, staples that many consumers buy on every trip to the supermarket, such as milk, usually are strategically placed at the rear of the store forcing consumers to pass several impulse temptations before they get there. Other staples are placed in various locations throughout the store to ensure that shoppers will have to walk through as many aisles and pass as many impulse items as possible before they get to the items they actually need.

These tricks and others are employed for the sole purpose of getting you to spend more than you have to. You can, however, use some "tricks" of your own to avoid impulse shopping and save hundreds, even thousands of dollars a year. Here are several effective money-saving strategies:

— Shop from a list of items you need. Stick to your list and avoid the store's carefully placed impulse distractions along the aisles.

— Clip and use coupons only for products you would normally buy. You're not really getting a bargain if a manufacturer's coupon for a high-profit impulse item leads you to buy a product you wouldn't purchase ordinarily.

— Avoid buying "convenience foods". Food companies and supermarkets make their biggest profits on so-called convenience items. While convenience foods may provide you with some convenience at meal-time, they generally cost much more. You can save a good deal of money by making foods such as soups, cakes, etc. from scratch, whenever you have the time.

— Limit your shopping trips to once every week or less. The more often you go shopping, the more likely you are to make impulse purchases.

— Shop alone whenever possible. Children can be a distraction, whining for impulse items such as candy, cereals, ice cream and so on, causing you to give in and spend more money than you intended on items you don't need.

— Buy sale items whenever possible. Check for weekly ad inserts in local newspapers and stock up on high-priced sale items that you use frequently.

— Buy some items in bulk. It may be more expensive initially, but ultimately, buying staples and dry goods (toilet paper, paper towels, canned goods, pasta, soap and detergent, and toothpaste) in bulk quantities can save you hundreds of dollars a year. You can stock up on non-perishable items whenever they are on sale at the supermarket, store them on basement shelves, and use them as needed. Warehouse stores and membership clubs also can be excellent sources of savings when buying in bulk.

— Buy store brands. Many store brand items are just as good (some are even better) than their more expensive, heavily marketed, brand-name counterparts. That includes items you may shop for every week such as vegetables, lunch meats, soft drinks, snacks, and other products you may buy only once or twice a month. You can save $1,000 or more a year if you buy lower-priced store brands whenever you have no strong preference for a name brand product.

— Check unit prices and comparison shop. Buy some products in larger sizes or in quantity whenever it means a lower price per unit.

— Finally, never shop when you're hungry. You are less likely to buy items on impulse when you aren't hungry.

Save Up To $2,400 With These No-Pain Shopping Secrets

Here are 12 ways you can save up to $2,400 (and more) a year on everything from clothing to utilities:

1) Shop only when there are specific items you need to buy. Browsing in stores and malls often leads to impulse purchases. You'll save money if you shop only when necessary.

2) Buy from wholesale sources. You can save 70% and more on virtually everything you need by taking advantage of the bargains offered by wholesale suppliers (see "Wholesale Sources" elsewhere in this chapter).

3) Shop for clothing at thrift shops and factory outlets. This is a great way to save from 30% to 75% off typical retail prices on virtually all of your clothing needs without sacrificing quality. Why pay full price when you can get perfectly good clothing for everyone in the family for much less?

4) Find clothing bargains for women in the boy's department. Women can find some real money-saving bargains on shirts, sweaters, pants, jackets, robes and belts for themselves by shopping in the boys' department. Many items, including designer boys' clothes are priced at 20% to 50% less than similar items in the women's department.

5) Shop at garage sales and flea markets. Such events offer everything from baby clothes to tools at great prices. You also can find bargains on such items as furniture, collectibles and antiques. This is a good way to get many of the things you need without paying department store prices.

6) Use fluorescent light bulbs. True, they're more expensive than incandescent bulbs, but they last from 10 to 14 times longer and use up to 75% less electricity. That could mean a savings of $20 to $40 per month on your electric bill.

7) Dry your clothes on an old-fashioned clothes line. You'll be surprised at how much you can save by hanging your clothes to dry rather than using your dryer. Depending on the amount and the frequency with which you do laundry, you could cut your electric bill by $20 to $40 per month.

8) Use direct deposit. You can get an extra days' worth of interest by having your pay check, Social Security, or any other check you receive on a regular basis, deposited directly into your bank account.

9) Buy your checks by mail instead of from your bank. Many banks mark up checks they sell to customers by 100% and more. You don't have to pay such a high price for your checks. You can save 50% and more when you order direct from an established mail order vendor (see "Wholesale Sources" later in this chapter).

10) Buy name-brand and generic medications from mail-order pharmacies. You can save 10% to 90% on prescription and over-the-counter medications when you order by mail (see "Wholesale Sources" later in this chapter).

11) Don't buy extended warranties on appliances. Such warranties are typically overpriced. Save your money instead.

12) Pay your bills monthly or annually to save on the interest and handling fees. For example, pay credit card balances in full each month and pay insurance premiums annually.

Slash Your Grocery Bills With Coupons And Refund Offers

More and more consumers are using coupons to save money on groceries. In fact, a recent study by the Food Marketing Institute reveals that couponing ranks second, behind "cutting back on gourmet items", among the most commonly practiced money-saving techniques. And a recent survey, conducted by a major coupon-processing firm, shows that in 1993 smart shoppers redeemed almost 7 billion coupons worth around $4 billion. While that's a lot of coupons and a lot of savings, less than 3% of all coupons issued are ever redeemed. That means that there still are plenty of consumers who are not taking advantage of a great money-saving technique.

If you're one of those people who consider finding and clipping coupons too much bother, consider this: Experienced coupon shoppers say they save, on average, $5 to $20 for every $100 they spend on groceries by redeeming coupons and cashing in on rebate offers. Depending on the amount of time and effort you invest in finding and clipping coupons, you could save $500 or more a year on your grocery bill.

The first order of business is locating money-saving coupons and refund offers for products you normally buy. You can find such coupons in many different sources, including the following:

— Free-Standing Inserts (FSI's).

FSI's are distributed in Sundaynewspapers and account for over 1/3 of all manufacturers' coupons issued. Instead of throwing FSI's in the trash, clip and redeem
the coupons for products you normally use. Besides using the coupons in your
own Sunday paper, you also can cash in on coupons from papers you collect from
friends and neighbors.

— Daily Newspapers.

Many stores distribute their advertising circulars in local newspapers on
Wednesdays or Thursdays. These circulars often include "in-ad" coupons to be
used only at specific stores. The redemption period on these coupons is usually
about seven days. You'll also find "one-on-a-page" coupons in most daily newspapers.

— Magazines.

Women's magazines, such as "Ladies Home Journal"; "McCalls"; and "Woman's
Day", and some general interest magazines such as "Reader's Digest", provide
avariety of money-saving coupons within their pages.

— Home Mailers.

Most people receive coupons in the mail. These coupons are sent by large marketing firms and manufacturers and their representatives. Not all of these
coupons will be of value to you, but many of them could be for products you normally use.

— In-Store Coupons.

You'll find these coupons and rebate offers printed on product packages or inside
the packages. These coupons can be redeemed only if you make another purchase of the same product. For example, inside your favorite box of cereal may
be a coupon worth 50 cents off your next purchase of that cereal.

— Direct From The Manufacturer.

In some cases you may be able to get coupons just by asking for them. You can
call the numbers listed on product packages or write to different companies and
ask them to send you product coupons if any are available. Not all companies provide free coupons upon request, but some do.

— Instant Coupon Machines.

Thousands of stores nationwide now have these machines positioned at "end-of-aisle" displays. All you have to do is press a button on one of these machines and you'll get a coupon for the particular product being promoted. Some stores also have instant coupon machines located in the middle of aisles within easy reach of the products being promoted.

— Checkout Line Coupons.

This is a relatively new marketing technique in which coupons are issued for products which are either complementary to or in competition with current purchases. These coupons are issued at the check-out line as purchases are being made and are redeemable on future purchases.

Once you find several sources for coupons, you can begin using the following "couponing" techniques for even more savings:

— Increase the value of your coupons by using them during sales and double-coupon promotions. Many stores redeem "double-coupons" at least one day a week providing you with extra savings on those days. Coupons also may be used in combination with items that have already been reduced in price because they are on sale. You can save even more if you buy sale items in quantity when you have coupons.

— Look for refund offers on fresh foods. You'll often find "money-back" offers on meat, fruit and other fresh foods. You may get $2 or more off your next purchase by mailing in such a refund offer.

— Buy whatever brand is on sale and for which you have a coupon. Unless you have a definite preference for a specific brand name product, your best value will be the brand that is on sale and "couponed".

— Use coupons to buy the smallest-sized packages of products you're not familiar with. For example, let's say you have a 50-cent coupon for a new breakfast cereal. Instead of using the coupon for the largest-size package which is priced at $3.50, use it for the smallest-size package, priced at $1.50. If you buy at a store that offers double coupons, you can buy and try the cereal for just 50 cents. This is an inexpensive way to try new products.

The key to saving money with coupons and refund offers is to clip and redeem as many as you can on products that you normally use. If you are willing to invest the time and effort it takes to find and clip coupons and refund offers, you can save hundreds of dollars a year on your grocery bill.

Ten Commonly Overlooked Every-Day Bargains

1) Public Library Card

It would be hard to find a better bargain than the services provided by public libraries. Besides circulating books, magazines, videocassettes, and other materials, your public library offers a number of other services including story hours for children, reading clubs, after-school programs for students, local art exhibits, and seminars.

2) Museum Membership Card

While it's true that a museum membership won't get you into a rock concert or to see the latest movies, it can provide you and your family with other types of quality low-cost entertainment. Such a family membership costs about $25 and entitles you and your family to reduced admission exhibits, various discounts, lectures, films, tours, and in some cases, monthly newsletters.

3) Baking Soda

There's no fancy packaging or inane advertising involved with this product. It costs about 50 cents-a-pound and in addition to its use in baking, it can be used effectively for many household cleaning chores, as a deodorizer, toothpaste, and to ease acid indigestion.

4) Renting College Dorm Rooms

This is an inexpensive way for budget-minded travelers to save on accommodations. Many colleges and universities offer dormitory rooms for rent as low as $10 per person. The best time to find such low-cost accommodations is during the summer. Dorm rooms also are available to rent during school holidays, such as Christmas and Spring break.

5) Plain Brown Paper Bag

There are many uses for these multi-purpose paper bags. In addition to use as a handy carrier for an assortment of items, brown paper bags can be used as lunch bags, packing material, gift wrap, and to cover and protect school textbooks.

6) Crayons

An inexpensive box of crayons (priced at less than $1.00) and a coloring book can keep a child busy for hours. Crayons also provide a great way to unleash and nurture a child's creativity.

7) Old-fashioned Sneakers

In this day of expensive, "high-tech" footwear, it's nice to know that old-fashioned sneakers still are available and still in fashion. Such sneakers are washable and available in a number of colors at prices which start at under $30.

8) Cotton T- Shirts

Even the best 100% cotton T-shirts can cost less than $10. Considering the fashion versatility, that can be quite a bargain.

9) Canned Tuna

For a little over a dollar a can (6 1/8 ounces), tuna provides a healthful and tasty food. It's low in fat and high in protein and can be used in a number of delicious recipes.

10) Medical Consultations

You may not know it but there's a good chance that your family doctor offers a free consultation service. Many physicians allocate one hour per day to talk with their patients (over the phone) about nonemergency medical problems.

Watch Out For Supermarket Scanner Errors

Don't take for granted that the supermarket scanner is error-free— it isn't. A recent study suggests that scanner errors do indeed occur. What's more, such errors are more likely to result in overcharges than in undercharges.

Here are several insider tips for protecting yourself from being overcharged by supermarket scanner errors:

— Shop from a list and write down prices as you place individual items in your cart.

— Keep sale items together at the check-out so you can watch the cash register and see that the items are rung up properly.

— Compare the register tape with your list when you get home.

— If you find a mistake, take your records to the store for reimbursement or credit.

Tax-Free Shopping

You can save from 3% to 9% on all your purchases by shopping, whenever possible, in states that don't have a sales tax. Those states include New Hampshire, Delaware, Montana and Oregon. If you are planning a vacation, it might pay you to visit one of those "tax-free" states and do some shopping too.

Save Up To 70% On Clothing By Shopping At Factory Outlets

According to industry insiders, there are now close to 300 factory outlet shopping centers nationwide. The growing popularity of factory outlets is due to the great bargains available on all sorts of merchandise including brand name and designer clothing for men, women and children.

Savings at factory outlets typically range from 30 to 70% on clothing for every season and for every member of the family. Outlet retailers are able to offer such discounts because they sell directly to customers, avoiding the middleman and the high mark-ups common at most clothing and department stores.

The Merchandise at factory outlets typically consists of manufacturers' overruns and closeouts. You'll also find some seconds and irregulars among the merchandise offered. That means you should examine each potential purchase carefully before buying.

Overall, the merchandise at factory outlets is of high quality and the prices are unbeatable. Smart shoppers are finding that they can save thousands of dollars by shopping at outlets for most of their clothing needs.

Most factory outlets are located outside of metropolitan areas where operating costs are lower. Many of these outlets are located off main highways in large shopping malls. Depending on where you live, you may have to travel 30 to 50 miles or more to find an outlet, but the resulting savings can more than make up for any inconvenience.

If you are interested in designer clothing at discount prices, check the following list for an outlet in your shopping area.

Anne Klein

Boaz, AL; Casa Grande and Sedona, AZ; Barstow, Cabazon, and Gilroy, CA; Naples and Orlando, FL; Calhoun, GA; Michigan City, IN; Freeport and Kittery, ME; Perryville and Queenstown, MD; Birch Run, MI; Osage Beach, MO; North Conway, NH; Flemington, Secaucus and Shrewsbury, NJ; Central Valley and Lake George, NY; Blowing Rock, NC; Stroud, OK; Lancaster and Tannersville, PA; Hilton and Myrtle Beach, SC; Pigeon Forge, TN; San Marcos, TX; Manchester Center, VT; Williamsburg, VA; Martinsburg, WV; and Kenosha, WI.

Calvin Klein

Foley, AL; Orlando, FL; Freeport and Kittery, ME; New Bedford, MA; West Branch, MI; North Conway, NH; Flemington and Secaucus, NJ; Central Valley and Niagara Falls, NY; Reading, PA; Manchester Center, VT; Williamsburg and Woodbridge, VA; and Kenosha, WI.

Liz Clairborne

Boaz and Foley, AL; Casa Grande, AZ; Gilroy and Lake Elsinore, CA; Silverthorne, CO; Calhoun and Commerce, GA; Williamsburg, IA; Gonzales, LA; Kittery, ME; Perryville and Queenstown, MD; Buzzards Bay and Medford, MA; Birch Run, MI; North Branch, MN; North Conway, NH; Secaucus, NJ; Central Valley, NY; Burlington, NC; Stroud, OK; Mt. Pocono and Reading, PA; Pigeon Forge, TN; Conroe and Hillsboro, TX; Manchester, VT; Waynesboro and Williamsburg, VA; Burlington, WA; Martinsburg, WV; and Kenosha, WI.

Ralph Lauren

Boaz and Foley, AL; Page, AZ; Anderson, Barstow, Eureka, Mammoth Lakes, and Redding, CA; Durango, CO; Valdosta, GA; Michigan City, IN; Williamsburg, IA; Colby, KN; Eddyville, KY; Freeport and Kittery, ME; Lawrence, MA; West Branch; MI; Osage Beach, MO; Billings, MT; North Conway, NH; Cohoes, Lake George, Niagara Falls, Plattsburgh, and Watertown, NY; Blowing Rock, NC; Reading and

Somerset, PA; Rapid City, SD; Chattanooga and Pigeon Forge, TN; St. George, UT; Manchester, VT; Williamsburg, VA; Martinsburg, WV; Appleton, WI; and Jackson, WY.

Here are several other popular factory outlets located throughtout the country. To find out whether or not there is a factory outlet from the following list in your shopping area, call (800) 33-Outlet.

— Men's, Women's and Children's Apparel

Brooks Brothers Factory Store

Hang Ten

Kids Express

Today's Child

Fruit of The Loom

The Gap Outlet

Gitano Factory Stores

Guess? Factory Store

Jockey

Jordache

L.L. Bean Factory Outlet Store

Levi's Outlet By Design

Levi's Outlet By Most

London Fog Factory Stores

OshKosh B'Gosh Factory Stores

Arrow Factory Stores

Banana Republic Outlet

Bugle Boy Outlet

Eddie Bauer Outlet Store

Geoffrey Beane Company

J. Crew Factory Store

Laura Ashley

Oxford Sportswear Outlet

Hosiery/Lingerie

Barbizon Lingerie Co., Inc.

Carole Hochman Lingerie

E.J. Plum Socks

Formfit

LaLingerie

Footwear

Acme Boot Company Factory Outlet

The Branded Shoe

Buster Brown

Converse Factory Outlet Stores

Endicott Johnson

Florsheim Factory

Nike Factory Store

Perry Ellis Shoes

Timberland Factory Outlet

Jewelry/Accessories

Charles Jourdan Factory Outlet

Coro Fashion Jewelry

Time World

Tower Jewelry Outlet

Save Over 70% On Everything You Buy With These Little-Known Wholesale Sources

Smart shoppers can save on virtually everything they need when they take advantage of the thousands of bargains offered by wholesale suppliers. Discount prices are available on all types of quality name-brand merchandise for home use or for resale at huge profits.

Wholesale savings of up to 70% and more are available on everything from automotive supplies to contact lenses and you don't have to buy in large quantities. Most of the wholesale sources listed below have no minimum order requirements so you can order individual items for personal use. Dealers also can order in quantity for resale.

Most of the wholesale suppliers and manufacturers listed below have catalogs, brochures and/or price lists available which you can get free upon request. Others may charge a nominal fee ($1 to $10) which is often refunded with the first order.

Many of the listings provide toll-free phone numbers which you can call for information, price quotes and to request merchandise catalogs. Allow six to eight weeks for delivery of each catalog you order.

Before you order from any company, make sure you are familiar with its required methods of payment, return policy, minimum order requirements (if any), customer service, and so on.

This information should be available in the company's product catalog. Contact the company with any questions you may have about its policies before you place an order.

Appliances/Electronics/Audio/Video

E.B.A. Wholesale Corporation
2361 Nostrand Ave.,
Brooklyn, NY 11210.
Phone: (718) 252-3400.
E.B.A. offers a large selection or refrigerators, washers, dryers, dishwashers, and ranges at savings of up to 40%. Quality brand names available include Frigidaire, Amana, G.E., Hotpoint, Whirlpool, Kitchen Aid, Magic Chef, and oth-

ers.TVs and video equipment also are available at wholesale prices.

Call or write (include a SASE) for a price quote.

Electrosonic,
8400 Alameda,
El Paso, TX 79907.
This company features wholesale and below prices on quality car stereos, equalizers, speakers, amplifiers, woofers, tweeters, speaker box supplies, alarms, and more. Send $2.00 for a catalog.

Crutchfield,
Phone: (800) 336-5566.
Crutchfield sells a wide selection of home and car audio equipment at discount prices. Call for price quotes and to request a catalog.

Foto Electrical Supply Company,
31 Essex Street,
New York, NY 10002.
Send a SASE for price quotes by return mail on large appliances, TVs, and audio/video equipment.

Irv Wolfson Company,
3321 W. Irving Park Road,
Chicago, IL 60618;
Phone: (312) 267-7828.
In business since the early 1950s, Irv Wolfson offers a selection of large appliances at savings of up to 40% below typical retail. Both large and small appliances are available. Call or write (include a SASE) for a price quote.

Wisconsin Discount Stereo,
Phone: (800) 356-9514;
in WI (608) 271-6889.
Offers a good selection of audio and video equipment.
Call for a price quote.

Carpeting

Carpet Wholesale Outlet,
Dalton, GA 30720;
Phone: (800) 628-4412.
Carpet Wholesale has been selling quality carpeting whole-
sale to the public for many years. The company also offers
wholesale prices on a good selection of handmade and
machine-crafted rugs.
Call the toll-free number for information.

Johnson's Carpets,
Inc., 3239 S. Dixie Highway,
Dalton, GA;
Phone: (800) 235-1079.
This company offers direct-from-the-mill carpeting at
savings of up to 80%. Carpet padding, vinyl flooring and
custom area rugs also are available. Free samples are
available.
Call or write for information.

Checks By Mail

American Check Printers,
2197 East Bayshore Road,
Palo Alto, CA 94303-0818;
Phone: (800) 262-4325.

Offers computer checks at a savings of 39%.
American's checks are 100% compatible with the leading
financial packages such as Quicken and MS Money.
Call the toll-free number for information.

Artistic Checks,
One Artistic Plaza,
P.O. Box 1501,
Elmira, NY 14902-1501;
Phone: (800) 224-7621.
Artistic Checks offers a variety of check styles, from simple
design to fine art, at prices up to 53% less than banks
charge.
Call the toll-free number for complete details.

Checks In The Mail,
P.O. Box 7802,
Irwindale, CA 91706;
Phone: (800) 733-4443.
Buy direct and save on all your checks, consecutively num-
bered and printed to conform to all of your bank's require-
ments. Business and computer checks also are available.
Call or write for more information and/or to request a free
brochure.

The Check Store,
790 Quail Street,
P.O. Box 5145,
Denver, CO 80217-5145;
Phone: (800) 4CHECKS.
The Check Store has over 70 years of check printing expe-
rience and offers savings of 50% and more off traditional
check-printing prices. Buy direct and save on all your
checks.
Call for a free business and computer check brochure.

Current Checks,
Product Division,
P.O. Box 18500,
Colorado Springs, CO 80935-8500;
Phone: (800) 533-3973. In business for over 40 years,
Current offers direct-to-you checks at discount prices.
Call the toll-free number for information.

Designer Checks,
P.O. Box 12966,
Birmingham, AL 35202;
Phone: (800) 239-9222.
This company has over 20 years of experience in the pro-
duction of checks and encoded documents for the financial
industry. Prices range from $4.95 for 200 single Designer
checks to $20.80 for 600 duplicate checks.
Call the toll-free number for more information.

Clothing & Accessories

Baby Clothes Wholesale,
60 Ethel Road,
West Piscataway, NJ 08854;
Phone: (800) 568-1930.
Choose from a large selection of clothing for children rang-
ing from newborn to boys and girls' sizes. Savings of 50%
off typical retail prices.
Send $3.00 for a catalog.

D & A Merchandise Company,
22 Orchard Street,
New York, NY 10002;
Phone: (212) 925-4766.
This company offers savings of 25% to 35% on most brand

name lingerie and men's and women's underwear. A price
quote is available by phone or by mail with a SASE.
A product catalog is available for $2.00.

Lands' End, Inc.,
1 Lands' End Lane,
Dodgeville, WI 53595-0001;
Phone: (800) 356-4444.
Lands' End offers savings of up to 40% on many items of
casual apparel for men, women and children.
Call or write for a free catalog.

New Concept,
P.O. Box 6756,
Laguna Niguel, CA 92607.
Offers lingerie at wholesale prices.
Write the company for catalog information.

No Nonsense Direct,
Box 26095,
Greensboro, NC 27420-6095.
Get No Nonsense panty hose and other hosiery with slight
imperfections at savings of up to 60% off usual retail prices.
A free catalog is available upon request.

Olsen Mills Direct,
(800) 829-4979.
Offers the Osh-Kosh line of children's clothing at factory-
outlet prices. Send $2.00 (refundable with first order) for a
catalog.

Eyeglasses/Contact Lenses/Sunglasses

House of Eyes II,
Greensboro, NC 27420;
Phone: (800) 331-4701.
Savings of up to 70% on brand name eyewear and frames are available from House of Eyes II. Fashion and sport styles are available. Call the toll-free number to request a free catalog and/or for a price quote.

Sunglasses USA;
(800) 872-7297.
Offers discount prices on Bausch & Lomb, Ray-Ban, and other brand-name sunglasses. A catalog is available free upon request.
Contact Lens Discount Center,
Phone: (800) 780-LENS [5367].
The Contact Lens Center offers the same contact lenses your doctor prescribes at a savings of up to 75%. Brand names include Bausch & Lomb, Cooper Vision, Barnes Hind, and others.
Call the toll-free number and request a free brochure.

The Ultimate Contact,
721 North Beers St.,
Holmdel, NJ 07733;
Phone: (800) 432-LENS.
The Ultimate Contact offers all brand-name lenses at savings of up to 70%. Choose from disposable, soft, hard, gas permeable and toric.
Call the toll-free number for information.

Furniture

Highpoint Furniture,
Jamestown, NC;
Phone: (800) 359-6320.
In business for over 15 years, Highpoint Furniture offers savings of over 50% on most major lines of bedroom, dining room and living room furniture.
Call the toll-free number for more information.

Homeway Furniture Company,
P.O. Box 1548
Mt. Airy, NC 27030;
Phone: (800) 334-9094;
or (910) 786-6151.
Homeway offers factory direct savings on quality furniture from over 400 manufacturers.
Call or write for information and/or a free brochure.

James Roy Furniture Company,
15 E 32nd St.,
New York, NY 10016;
Phone: (212) 679-2565.
Offers a selection of furniture and bedding from various famous manufacturers. Discounts of one-third (and more) off suggested retail prices. Call or write the company for price quotes.

Loftin-Black,
111 Sedgehill Drive,
Thomasville, NC 27360;
Phone: (800) 334-7398;
FAX: (919) 472-2052.
Loftin-Black has been in business since 1948. The company offers most major brands of furniture, bedding and accessories at prices of 35% to 50% below manufacturers

suggested retail prices.
Call or write for a free brochure.

North Carolina Showrooms,
Hickory, NC;
Phone: (800) 227-6060.
This company offers savings of 30% to 50% on hundreds of
brand name furniture items. Call the toll-free number with
the brand-name and style number you want.

Quality Furniture Market of Lenoir,
2034 Hickory Blvd. SW,
Lenoir, NC 28645;
Phone: (704) 728-2946.
Offers discounts on furniture and bedding from hundreds of
quality manufacturers. Price quotes are available by phone
or by mail.

Health

AARP Pharmacy Service,
144 Freeman's Bridge Road,
P.O. Box 2211,
Schenectady, NY 12301-2211;
Phone: (800) 456-2226.
The AARP Pharmacy Service offers savings of up to 90%
on generic equivalents of brand-name drugs. Men and
women who are 50 years of age or older can pay a $5 mem-
bership fee and get mail-order savings on both brand-name
and generic medications.
Call or write for a free catalog and price quote.

Action Mail-Order,
P.O. Box 787
Waterville, ME 04903-0787;
Phone: (800) 452-1976.
Offers brand-name and generic prescription and OTC
medications at discount prices.
Call or write to request a free catalog.

Healthhouse USA,
Box 9034,
Jericho, NY 11753;
Phone: (516) 334-9754;
FAX (516) 334-6920.
Offers low prices on a wide assortment of health and fitness
related products. A recent catalog lists cardio-walker
machine for under $90, "Walk-N-Jog" fitness shoes, heavy-
duty back braces, magnifying reading glasses, wheelchairs,
safety bath tub and shower seats, massagers, home health
test-kits, and many other items.
Write for a free catalog.

Medi-Mail,
P.O. Box 98520,
Las Vegas, NV 89193-8520;
Phone: (800) 331-1458.
This mail-order pharmacy offers prescription medications—
both brand-name and generic— and OTC remedies at
savings of 50% and more. A catalog is available free upon
request.

Pharmail,
Phone: (800) 237-8927.
Offers mail-order discount prices on generic and brand-
name prescription medications.
Call the toll-free number for a price quote and/or to request
a free catalog.

Pet Care/ Supplies

Echo Discount Aquarium & Pet Supply,
Box 145,
Westland, MI 48185;
Phone: (313) 453-3131.
This company offers mail-order fish and pet supplies for
dogs, cats, hamsters, gerbils, and birds at savings of up to
70%. Complete aquarium outfits and supplies also are
available.
Send $1 for a product catalog and/or call or write
(include a SASE) for a price quote.

The Kennel Vet Company,
Box 835,
Bellmore, NY 11710.
Kennel Vet offers a selection of nutritional foods, health
products, leashes, kennels and other supplies for dogs and
cats at savings of 35% to 75% off typical retail prices.
Write the company and request a free catalog.

Northern Wholesale Veterinary Supply Company, Inc.,
P.O. Box 7526,
Omaha, NE 68107;
Phone: (800) 356-5852.
Call or write the company to request a free catalog featur-
ing a wide assortment of pet supplies and equipment. The
catalog lists savings of up to 50% on some items.

Sporting Goods/Equipment

The Austad Company,
P.O.Box 1428,
Sioux Falls, SD 57196-1428;
Phone: (605) 336-3135.
Although Austad sells a variety of sporting goods and equipment, the company is best known for golfing equipment and supplies.
You can save from 15% to 40% and more on some items, including overstocked and closeout goods.
Call or write the company to request a free catalog.

Cabela's, Inc.,
812 13th Avenue,
Sidney, NE 69160;
Phone: (308) 254-5505.
This company offers a good selection of brand name hunting and fishing gear at savings of up to 40%.
Send $2 for Cabela's big catalog.

Las Vegas Discount & Tennis,
5325 South Valley Blvd.,
Las Vegas, NV 89118;
Phone: (702) 798-6847.
Offers discount prices on a wide selection of name brand sports equipment including golf clubs and other golfing equipment, tennis racquets, and other racquet equipment.
Price quotes are available by phone or by mail (with SASE).
A catalog is available free upon request.

Wallcoverings

Headquarters Windows & Walls.
8 Clinton Place,
Morristown, NJ 07960;
Phone: (800) 338-4882.
Offers first-quality blinds and wallcoverings. All brands available at up to 81% off retail prices.
Call with book, name and pattern number.

#1 Wallpaper,
2914 Long Beach Road,
Oceanside, NY 11572;
Phone: (800) 423-0084;
in New York state call (515) 678-4445.
Has over 100,000 rolls of wallpaper in stock at savings of up to 80% off typical retail prices. Wholesale discounts also are available.
Free delivery.

Nationwide Wholesaler,
P.O. Box 40,
Hackensack, NJ O7602;
Phone (800) 488-9255.
Nationwide offers a selection of wallcoverings, fabrics, and blinds at savings of 50% to 75%.
Call for a price quote.

Peerless Wallpaper & Blind Depot,
39500 14 mile road,
Walled Lake, MI 48390;
Phone: (800) 999-0898;
FAX: (313) 553-8605.
Peerless offers savings of up to 80% off typical retail prices on 1st quality wallpaper and blinds.

Silver's Wholesale Club,
30001-15 Kensington Ave.,
Philadelphia, PA 19134;
Phone: (800) 426-6600.
Silver's features wallcoverings and blinds at savings of 80%
and more. Brand names available include Levolor, Riviera,
Mark I, and Ovation.

Smart Wallcoverings,
P.O. Box 2206,
Southfield, MI 48307;
Phone: (800) 677-0200.
This company offers savings of up to 80% on every wall-
covering pattern in every book.
Also available are custom blinds at savings of up to 78%.

Southern Discount Wallcoverings,
1583 N. Military Trail,
West Palm Beach, FL 33409;
Phone: (800) 699- WALL (9255).
Southern offers discount prices of up to 80% off list on 1st
quality name brand wallcoverings.
Call with book and pattern number and number of rolls
needed.

Worldwide Wallcoverings & Blinds, Inc.,
333 Skokie Blvd.,
Northbrook, IL 60062;
Phone: (800) 322-5400;
FAX: (708) 559-9000.
Worldwide offers savings of up to 80% off typical retail
prices on blinds including Verticals, Duettes, Pleated
Shades, and Horizontals.
Also available are name brand wallcoverings at savings of
up to 78% off retail prices.
Call with book and pattern number.

Miscellaneous

Artcraft,
P.O. Box 90616,
Columbia, SC 29209.
Artcraft offers a huge selection of quality brass products at
wholesale prices.
Send $5.00 for a catalog and sample pack.

Beautiful Visions,
810 Broadway,
Hicksville, NY 11801;
Phone: (516) 576-9000.
You can call or write Beautiful Visions and request a free
catalog which lists brand name cosmetics and toiletries at
discount prices.

Bailey's Wholesale Floral Supply,
P.O. Box 591,
Arcadia, IN 46030.
This company offers silk flowers, supplies and accessories
for crafters at wholesale prices. A catalog is available for
$3.00 (refundable).

Christy's Wholesale,
Bloomington, IN 47401;
Phone: (800) 332-4713.
Christy's offers a selection of vintage, collectible and
rare watches and jewelry.
Over 700 pieces—priced from $5 to $50,000 are in stock.
Brand names available include Timex and Rolex.
Christy's also features watch and clock repair and
restoration.
Call the toll-free number for complete information.

Commercial Culinary,
P.O. Box 7258,
Dept NC-330,
Arlington, VA 22207;
Phone: (800) 999-4949.
Offers savings of up to 40% on quality cookware, cutlery, and appliances. A catalog is available free upon request.

Cook Brothers, Inc.,
240 N. Ashland Ave.,
Chicago, IL 60607;
Phone: (800) 345-8442.
Cook Brothers is a wholesale distributor for a large variety of products. The selection of brand-name merchandise includes everything from watches and jewelry to toys.
Send $1.00 for a wholesale catalog.

Durham Wholesale,
Box 132,
Plainview, TX 79073;
Phone: (806) 293-8909.
Offers wholesale bargains on thousands of products including games, gift items, carpeting, household items, software, office supplies, computers, stereos, and more. Name brand items available at wholesale and below wholesale prices.
Call or write the company for catalog information.

Good 'N' Lucky Promotions,
P.O. Box 1185,
Chino Valley, AZ 86323;
Phone: (602) 636-1649.
In the closeout business since 1971, Good 'N' Lucky is a Dun & Bradstreet rated firm which offers bargains on jewelry, toys and novelties.

Samples are available on many items listed in the company's catalog.
Minimum order is $30.
A wholesale merchandise catalog is available for $3.00.
Call or write the company for information.

Flash Print,
35 Bath Street,
Ballston Spa, NY 12020;
Phone: (800) 374-6114.
Flash Print promises quality work on all your business print-ing needs including stationery and envelopes, business forms, brochures, and booklets at the lowest possible prices. Call or write for a free catalog. Instant price quotes also are available by calling the toll-free number.

House Sale Co.,
2379 Hwy 157,
Department 248,
Judsonia, AR 72081;
Phone: (501) 729-4746.
Offers wholesale and below wholesale prices on a selection of custom printed caps, T-shirts and transfers, sweat shirts, socks, work gloves, towels, wash cloths, jewelry, leather wallets, key rings, panties, panty hose and many other items.
Send $1.00 (refundable) for a price list.

Hyman's,
P.O. Box 71171,
N. Charleston, SC 29415;
Phone: (803) 747-5433;
FAX: (803) 566-0470.
Phone or write Hyman's for a color catalog featuring a selection of uniforms including work shirts and pants, lab-coats, scrubs, and coveralls at wholesale prices.

Also available are Oxford shirts and jackets.
No minimum order is required.

Interstate Label Company,
P.O. Box, 1239,
1715 E. Main Street,
Freeland, Washington 98249;
Phone: (800) 426-3261.
Factory direct savings of up to 35% on labels of every size,
shape and type, including custom labels, mailing labels,
computer labels, primary product labels, custom and stock
tags, and more.
Interstate has been in business for over 23 years and will
provide a catalog of products free upon request.

J.C. Whitney,
1917-19 Archer Ave.,
P.O. Box 8410,
Chicago, IL 60680;
Phone: (312) 431-6102.
J.C. Whitney offers savings of 40% and more on a complete
line of automotive parts and accessories for all makes and
models of cars, trucks, vans, motorcycles, and RVs.
The company has been in business since 1915.
Call or write the company for information and to request a
catalog.

Netherland Bulb Company,
13 McFadden Road,
Easton, PA 18042;
Phone: (610) 253-8879.
This company offers the finest bulbs imported from Holland.
The selection includes tulips, lilies, hyacinths, narcissu
crocus, iris, daffodil, and many others.
A bulb catalog is available upon request.

Oriental Trading Company, Inc.,
4206 S. 108th Street,
Omaha, NE 68137-1215;
Phone: (800) 327-9678.
The Oriental Trading Company features a selection of toys, gifts, party supplies, stationery, candy, and more at direct-to-you prices. There are over 10,000 inexpensive items to choose from.
Send $1.00 for a catalog.

Reasonable Solutions Software,
1221 Disk Drive,
Medford, OR 97501-6639;
Phone: (503) 776-5777.
Reasonable Solutions is an approved vendor of the Association of Shareware Professionals.
The company offers savings of up to 40% on some software for IBM PCs and compatibles. All types of shareware are available including, Windows applications, utilities, games, business and financial, religious, educational, clip art, and more.Call or write the company and request a catalog.

Rings & Things,
114 Fifth Avenue,
New York, NY 10011;
Phone: (800) 445-0057. Classic and high fashion jewelry at savings of up to 75% are available from Rings & Things.
Call or write the company to request a free catalog.

Roussels,
107 Dow,
 Arlington, MA 02174-7199;
Phone: (508) 443-8888.
Offers a selection of wholesale craft supplies and jewelry. Close-out jewelry also available.
Send $1.00 for a catalog of products and prices.

Sentry Table Pad Company,
Phone: (800) 328-7237 Ext. 240.
Sentry Table Pad offers custom table pads from America's oldest and largest manufacturer at factory direct prices.
The company has been in business for over 20 years.
Call the toll-free number for information.

Surplus Traders,
P.O. Box 276,
Alburg, VT 05440;
Phone: (514) 739-9328.
In business since 1975, Surplus Traders offers electronics and computer surplus at discount prices.
Call or write the company for catalog information.

Topnotch,
Box 608,
Mount Sinai, NY 11766.
Offers wholesale prices on a selection of work gloves and raingear.
Send $1.00 for a wholesale catalog.

Ultra Computer Supplies,
P.O. Box 616,
Howell, NJ 07731;
Phone: (800) 423-1239.
Offers computer supplies and furniture at discount prices.
A catalog is available free upon request.

MONEY POWER

CHAPTER 7

Insider Money-Saving Secrets

Imagine being able to travel almost anywhere in the world free. How about cutting all of your insurance costs by 50% without lowering your coverage? Do you believe it's possible to find a dream job, with high-pay and great benefits— or to live rent-free in a new home? All of this, and much more, is indeed possible if you know how to make the system work for you. By using the insider money-saving techniques described in this chapter, you can get many of the things you want out of life at little or no cost. These techniques have worked for others and if used properly, they also can work for you.

Secret Techniques For Winning Huge Sweepstakes Cash And Prizes

Forget about luck. Being chosen as a sweepstakes winner has more to do with down-to-earth organization and strategy than with being lucky. In fact, experienced sweepstakes winners agree that "beating the odds" is mostly a matter of entering as many sweepstakes as you can as often as you can. Simply put, the more entries you submit to a particular sweepstakes, the more you increase your chances of winning. Some sweepstakes winners have submitted hundreds of entries to individual sweepstakes.

Of course, making multiple entries to every sweepstakes you find can be quite expensive. Few people can afford to submit hundreds of entries to every available sweepstakes. The winning secret here is to be selective and pick the right sweepstakes to enter.

The first thing to consider in picking which sweepstakes to enter is what prizes are being offered. You can narrow your choices by selecting and entering only those which offer prizes that you want and can use. Obviously, any sweepstakes offering a large cash prize is worth entering. Once you find a sweepstakes which offers prizes that are of special interest to you, submit as many entries as you can.

Besides the prizes being offered, it also is a good idea to consider the type of sweepstakes you want to enter. Some people prefer Random Drawing Sweepstakes wherein winners are determined by a random drawing from all the entries received. Entries in this type of sweepstakes are in sealed envelopes and the winners are drawn by an unbiased official. Random Drawing Sweepstakes are appealing because they are easy to enter, generally requiring that entrants submit their names and addresses only. On the other hand, Card Game Sweepstakes often require more time and effort. In this type of sweepstakes, entrants may be required to collect and match many different pieces, collect a series of cards, or simply scratch a card with a coin to reveal some important information.

Sweepstakes may also be local, regional, or national. Your chances of winning will be better when you enter local or regional sweepstakes because they won't have as many entries as national sweepstakes. However, national sweepstakes usually offer the most valuable prizes.

Whichever type sweepstakes you enter, keep in mind that state and federal laws ensure that "no purchase is necessary" in order to enter and win. It makes no difference whether your entry is submitted on an official entry form or a specified size card or piece of paper. Your chances of winning are the same. The majority of sweepstakes employ outside judging agencies to guarantee their drawings are handled in a completely unbiased manner.

While there is no specific technique which will guarantee that you'll win a sweepstakes, you can do several things to improve your chances. Picking the right sweepstakes and submitting as many entries as you can are the two most important winning techniques, however, the following tips also can give you a better chance of winning:

— Make sure you follow all sweepstakes rules and regulations exactly. For example, in lieu of an official entry form, some sweepstakes require entries be submitted on a 3" x 5" piece of paper or card. Always read the fine print to be sure of entry requirements, and then follow them to the letter.

— Mail your entries from different zip codes whenever possible. You can have relatives and/or friends who live in different zip codes mail entries for you.

— Don't mail all of your entries at one time. Mail them a few days apart in the weeks preceding the closing date specified for the sweepstakes. Make sure your last entry is mailed several days before the close.

— Send your entries in envelopes of various colors. Use colored pens or magic markers to print your name and address in block print (all capital letters). Also make sure the envelopes are the proper size as specified in the sweepstakes entry rules.

— Don't mail more than one entry per envelope.

— Mail your first entries as early as possible. Many sweepstakes offer additional "early bird" drawings for the earliest entries.

How To Boost Your Odds Of Winning A Million Dollar Lottery

There are several ways you can give lady luck a helping hand and increase your chances of winning a million dollar lottery. Here are a few insider suggestions for boosting your odds of winning a random number jackpot.

1) Be a part of a lottery pool. Overall, this may be the best way to improve your chances of winning a lottery. If you form a lotto pool with trusted colleagues, friends, and relatives, you can improve your chances of winning dramatically. Depending on the number of members in your pool, you could increase your chances of winning by anywhere from 10% to 400%. For example, if there are 20 members in your lotto pool who each buy two tickets per lottery, you'll have 40 chances instead of only 2. Of course, you'll have to split any lottery winnings equally with all the members of the pool, but your chances of winning will increase.

When forming a lottery pool, make sure every member understands and agrees to abide by the group objective. It's best to have such an agreement in writing. The written records for your pool should include a statement of purpose indicating that all members have an equal share and interest in all tickets purchased and any subsequent winnings. Your records also should include the number of tickets purchased and the dates of every drawing in which the pool participates. You also should list the dollar amount contributed by each pool member for every drawing. Every pool member should sign the record for each drawing.

2) Pick a number higher than 31. This strategy might not increase your odds of winning a lottery, but it will diminish the likelihood that you'll have to share the loot if you win. That's because many lottery players choose numbers based on special dates, such as birthdays, anniversaries and so on. Obviously those players choose numbers of 31 or lower (since months never have more than 31 days). As a result, a winning combination with one or more numbers higher than 31 will most likely be shared by fewer people.

3) Try wheeling. This strategy involves "playing a field" of more than six lotto numbers, combined in such a way that if some of them are drawn the player has a bet-

ter chance of winning. You can choose to play a "full wheel" in which all possible combinations of the numbers chosen are covered. A less expensive option would be a "partial wheel" which allows players to use up to 20 numbers but does not require betting on all possible combinations.

Save 50% Or More On All Of Your Insurance

Here are several insider strategies which can help reduce your auto, homeowners, and health and life insurance by 50% or more without lowering your coverage:

Auto Insurance

— Request higher deductibles. By raising your deductibles on collision and comprehensive (fire and theft) coverage you can reduce your costs 15% to 30% without diminishing your coverage. Ask for a deductible that you can afford to pay with money from your savings if you should have to make a claim.

— Cancel collision and/or comprehensive coverages on older cars. You can save 35% to 40% by canceling this coverage on a car that is more than 5 years old and whose market value has dropped below $1,000 dollars. In such a case, the annual costs and deductible amounts are likely to be nearly as much as any claim you might turn in. A trusted auto dealer or mechanic should be able to tell you the worth of your car. You also can check the National Automobile Association's "N.A.D.A. Official Used Car Guide" for an estimate of your car's worth.

— Take advantage of discounts. Some insurers offer discounts for more than one car, no accidents or moving violations in 3 years, drivers over 50 years of age, automatic seat belts and/or air bags, anti-theft devices, good grades for students, college students away from home without a car, and driver training courses. Ask about those and other driver discounts for which you might be eligible.

Homeowners Insurance

— Take stock of your possessions. Make a personal inventory of your household possessions (both written and on video)—furniture, clothing, silverware, jewelry... everything of value. Since premiums are based on the types of possessions you have and their value, you can save money by not guessing and overstating their worth. You'll also have proof that you owned certain items if you make a claim.

— Inquire about homeowner discounts. You may qualify for a discount if you have smoke detectors, vehicle insurance with the same company, a burglar alarm wired to the police department or the alarm company, a sprinkler system, and deadbolt locks on all exterior doors.

— Buy your coverage direct from the insurance company. If you buy direct, you'll be able to eliminate the use of an agent, and therefore an agent's commission. You'll also lower your premiums.

Health and Life Insurance

— Avoid credit life insurance. This type of insurance may bring you peace of mind knowing that your payments will be made if you become disabled or die. It is also generally overpriced. You can save money and still get protection by increasing your basic life and disability coverage.

— Don't buy life insurance for your child. Unless you depend on your child's earnings for your own financial stability, this type of insurance is totally unnecessary. The primary reason for buying life insurance is to protect the dependents of the person being insured from an immediate loss of income.

— Avoid special policies for cancer and other diseases. Comprehensive major medical coverage can provide protection against virtually any medical eventuality.

How To Drive A New Car Absolutely Free, With No Down Payment Or Credit Check

It may sound impossible or illegal, but it's neither. In fact, hundreds of people are already taking advantage of this little-known strategy to own a new car every year. The strategy involves the use of IRS-approved tax shelters. It also requires initiative, and a certain amount of business acumen. Managed properly, this business strategy could enable you to own the car of your choice — Cadillac, Mercedes, BMW, Jaguar, Lincoln, whatever— absolutely free in just a matter of months.

In order for this strategy to work you will first need to form a small, car-leasing corporation. Incorporating will allow you to keep your car-leasing business separate from other businesses and to raise the money you need by selling corporate stock. Once your corporation has been organized, visit a dealer who sells the type of car you want. Make an offer to purchase 10 cars per year for the next five years in return for a new car for yourself each year of the agreement. Most car dealers are likely to agree to such an offer because they rarely have the opportunity to sell so many cars to one customer. In effect, you are offering to buy in volume (10 new cars per year) in return for a discount (one new car for yourself every year).

As soon as a car dealer accepts your offer, you can begin contacting prospective stockholders. Use the Yellow Pages to make a list of around 300 high-tax-bracket professionals from your area. Your list should include the names of attorneys, doctors, dentists, top business executives, and so on. Another way to get a list of top professionals is to contact a reputable mailing list broker.

You should be able to get a good list of 1000 professional people for around $75. Once you have a sizable list to work from, you should send an introductory letter to as many professionals as possible. Your letter should be brief— three or four paragraphs— and explain the following:

— That you represent a car leasing company which has a plan designed for top professionals who are in a 50% tax bracket.

— That the plan will enable professionals who take advantage of the opportunity to own and drive a brand new car without cost for a full year and then take delivery on another new car the following year.

— That the arrangement may be extended for as long as he/she chooses.

— That you would be happy to arrange for a personal meeting to discuss the plan in detail (include your phone number).

Your letters should be individually addressed and on quality stationery with your company letterhead. You also should include an impressive business card with every letter. If you present yourself and your opportunity in a professional manner, you are more likely to receive favorable responses, increasing your chances of success.

During your personal meetings with each professional who responds to your letter explain that the plan works by taking advantage of legitimate tax shelters, the professional's 50% tax bracket, and by maintaining a high resale value (2/3 of original cost) of each car. Also provide each professional with a complete financial statement detailing exactly how the plan works. The statement should include a complete breakdown of the financial arrangements, including the amount of the loan being financed for the ten cars; each stockholder's equity in the corporation; each stockholder's monthly tax deductible payments to the corporation; and each stockholder's total tax deduction (taking into consideration the 50% tax bracket of the stockholders); and each car's expected resale value at the end of one year. The end result will be a net cost of -0- for each stockholder.

Leave a copy of the financial statement with each professional you talk with. Encourage them to have their accountants or tax advisors study the plan and confirm that it is legitimate, and that if the cars retain their resale value at about 2/3 of their original costs, it really works. Once your prospects understand the plan and are satisfied that it can work for them, you should have no problem getting your ten stockholders. Once you do, you'll be driving the new car of your choice absolutely free.

Become A Travel Writer And Travel Almost Anywhere In The World Absolutely Free

If you have a talent for writing and a yen for travel, you may want to consider a career as a travel writer. There's a good market for travel writers who can both entertain and provide current, reliable and useful information to travel-minded readers. In fact, travel writing is one of the easiest types of writing to sell because of the vast number of publications which use travel information.

Travel and special interest magazines, and newspapers all carry travel-related articles on a regular basis. Markets include magazines for women, men, families, outdoorsmen, sports enthusiasts, and organization members. In some cases, freelance writers sell travel articles to such publications and make enough money to cover all of their travel expenses. Freelancers also may be able to deduct much or all of their travel expenses from their taxes. Many magazines and newspapers also have staff writers who are assigned to write travel-related articles from exotic locations all over the world. These writers always travel first class with all of their expenses paid by their employers.

One way to gain experience as a travel writer is to visit and write about tourist attractions in your immediate area. Your travel articles should be written to entertain and inform readers. The key is to create a sense of excitement and "travellust" with your written words, transporting your readers vicariously to the wonderful place you've described. You should make readers feel as if they simply must travel to the destination you are describing. You also can take your own photographs to add to the effect of your written description. Such a complete package (text and photographs) is more likely to impress an editor and give you an edge in making a sale.

There are several ways to find potential travel stories in your immediate surroundings. Local historical societies, chambers of commerce, convention bureaus, and departments of tourism all can provide you with valuable information. You should collect as much information as you can about historical sites of interest, recreational attractions, campsites and off-road hiking trails, industries, restaurant and hotel accommodations, and other items of interest to tourists. This information will provide useful background text for your travel article.

For authenticity and credibility, always visit the area about which you are writing. This will enable you to convey personal insights into what the area has to offer tourists. Describe, in your own words, your experiences while visiting the area.

Finding a market for your travel-related article(s) will require some research. "Writer's Market" (Writer's Digest Books, Cincinnati, OH) lists several travel, camping and trade magazines as well as trade publications which publish travel features. You can check at your local library for the latest "Writer's Market" and other sources of information.

For general information about travel writing, you can contact the Society of American Travel Writers, 1100 17th Street, N.W., Suite 1000, Washington, DC 20036.

The key to success as a travel writer lies in your ability to share with the reader the appeal of unique destinations. It isn't enough to provide factual information. You'll also have to be able to generate in the reader a genuine interest in visiting the spot your article describes. If you can do that, you can establish a steady income that more than covers all of your travel expenses, making it possible for you to travel almost anywhere absolutely free.

How To Live Rent-Free In A Beautiful New Home

Are you responsible, trustworthy and of good standing in the community? If the answer is yes, you meet three of the most important qualifications for becoming a professional "house sitter", and getting to live in a beautiful new home, rent-free.

The demand for professional house sitters is growing at a rapid rate. More and more people have to be away from their homes for long periods of time. Families, couples and single homeowners leave town year-round on business, extended vacations, sabbaticals, traveling, and so on. Many of these people are turning to professional house sitters to care for their homes while they are away, either on a short- or long-term arrangement.

The duties and responsibilities of a house sitter vary from home owner to home owner but generally, you will move into a house as soon as the owner is ready to leave it. You'll live in the house, rent-free, until the owner returns. Typical house sitting duties include taking care of a pet(s), watering plants, answering telephone calls, taking care of the mail, light housekeeping (dusting and vacuuming), making sure all windows and doors are secure, and giving the home a lived-in appearance just as though it were your own home. Some assignments, depending on the region and season, also may include tending the lawn or supervising lawn care by a contractor.

There are several ways you can go about starting a house sitting service. First of all, you should find out whether or not such a service is already being offered in your community. If it is, contact the operator(s) of the service and ask about local house sitting rates. If no such service is available locally, contact a service in a nearby community and inquire about rates. This information can serve as a guideline for the rates you set for your service. Generally, house sitting fees are based on a per-day, per-week, or per monthly rate with additional charges for any special individualized services you might offer.

The best way to market a house sitting service and attract potential clients is to advertise in local and area newspapers. Inexpensive classified ads can make your service known throughout the community, and should result in inquiries from local homeowners who have to be away from their homes for extended periods of time. You also can advertise your service in shopper's newsletters and on public bulletin boards (supermarkets, libraries, city buildings, etc.).

Another method of reaching prospective clients is to print up professional-looking fliers for distribution in appropriate locations. Your fliers can be distributed in likely residential and suburban areas, at country clubs, condominium developments, and at various civic organizations. You also should contact your local Chamber of Commerce and provide it with information about your service.

Both your classified ads and fliers should stress the service(s) you offer, reasonable rates, and that references are available upon request.

House sitting is not for everyone. Obviously, if you don't enjoy taking care of pets and houseplants, doing light housework, yard-work, etc., for yourself, you probably wouldn't like doing it for someone else either. However, if you don't mind such household duties, and you would like to make some extra money while living rent-free in a beautiful home, house sitting may be the opportunity you've been looking for.

How To Get A Full College Degree Without Going To A Single Class

In this day and age, having a college degree is a virtual necessity in order to get and keep a good-paying job. Unfortunately, many people who are already working don't have the time or money necessary to attend a college or university for four or more years to earn a degree. Without a college degree, these people are often the last to be considered for promotions to high-paying jobs. In other cases, people without college degrees are turned away when responding to various job opportunities which require specific skills and training.

Home study (or correspondence study) can be a viable alternative for people who can not (for whatever reason) attend classes on a regular college campus. Home study enables you to increase your earning power and enhance your career opportunities by earning a college degree (bachelors, masters, doctorate) at home without ever going to a single class on campus. You don't have to leave home, give up your job, lose income, or find childcare. You can work at your own pace, setting your own study-hours because, in essence, your own home will become a classroom.

Generally, home study involves enrolling in an educational institution which provides a "self-directed" course of study. There are home study schools which offer academic degree programs in accounting, business, medical transcription, health, engineering, environmental studies, and many other fields of study.

Individuals who enroll in educational institutions which offer home study courses receive their lessons one-at-a-time by mail. Each lesson is completed and then returned by mail to the institution. Qualified instructors correct and grade each lesson and then return them to their students. The instructors also make comments on the student's work, and provide personalized guidance. Instead of the student going to the college, the college comes to the student.

The time it takes to earn a degree through home study varies, depending on the school and the course of study. Generally, it will require three or four years of conscientious study.

If you desire a college degree, but you can not attend college or university classes, you may want to consider enrolling in an accredited home study school. Accreditation requires that an institution meet several high educational standards, including maintaining a competent faculty, and offering educationally sound and "up-to-date" courses.

Listed below are several such schools which can provide you with information about specific academic degree programs, including requirements and costs. All the schools listed below are fully accredited by the National Home Study Council (NHSC) which is listed by the U.S. Department of Education as the "nationally recognized accrediting agency" for home study institutions.

(The NHSC publishes a "Directory of Accredited Home Study Schools" which is available free upon request. Write to National Home Study Council, 1601 18th Street, N.W., Washington, D.C. 20009.)

NHSC Accredited Home Study (Correspondence Study) Schools

> BEREAN COLLEGE, 1445 Boonville Avenue, Springfield, MO 65802; Phone: (417) 862-2781. Berean College is a division of the Assemblies of God and offers an Associate Degree in Bible-Theology, and a Bachelor of Arts in Bible-Theology.

> CALIFORNIA COLLEGE FOR HEALTH SCIENCES, 222 West 24th Street, National City, CA 91959; Phone: (619) 477-4800.
> Degrees offered include Associate of Science in Medical Transcription, Allied Health, and Early Childhood Education; Associate in Applied Science in Respiratory Care; Bachelor of Science in Health

Services Management; and Master of Science in Community Health
Administration and Wellness Promotion.

CLEVELAND INSTITUTE OF ELECTRONICS, INC., 1776 East 17th
Street, Cleveland, OH 44114; Phone: (800) 243-6446. Offers Associate
degree courses in electronics engineering and electronics technology.

GRANTHAM COLLEGE of ENGINEERING, 34641 Grantham College
Road, P.O. Box 5700, Slidell, LA 70469-5700; Phone: (504) 649-4191.
Offers Associate and Bachelor degrees in electronics engineering
and computer engineering technology.

GRIGGS UNIVERSITY, P.O. Box 4437, 12501 Old Columbia Pike, Silver
Spring, MD 20914-4437; Phone: (301) 680-6570. Griggs University
is a division of Home Study International and offers Associate of Arts
Degrees in Personal Ministries, Bachelor of Arts in Religion, and Bachelor
of Arts in Theological Studies.

ICI UNIVERSITY, 6300 North Bell Line Road, Irving, TX 75063;
Phone: (800) 444-0424. Offers Associate Degree in Bible-Theology,
Bachelor of Arts in Bible-Theology, and Master of Arts in Biblical Studies
and Ministerial Studies.

INSTITUTE OF PHYSICAL THERAPY, 201 Health Park Boulevard,
Suite 215, St. Augustine, FL 32086; Phone: (904) 826-0084. Offers a
combination home study-resident course leading to a Master of
Science in Physical Therapy.

ICS CENTER FOR DEGREE STUDIES, 925 Oak Street, Scranton, PA
18515; Phone: (717) 342-7701. The ICS CENTER is a division of
International Correspondence School—National Education Corporation
and offers Specialized Associate degree programs in business, engineering, technology, and electronics technology.

IMC-INTERNATIONAL MANAGEMENT CENTRES, Castle Street,
Buckingham, England MK 18 1BP; Phone: (44-280-817222). Offers
Bachelor and Master level programs in all major fields of professional
management.

INTERNATIONAL SCHOOL OF INFORMATION MANAGEMENT (ISIM),
University Business Center, 130 Cremona Drive, Santa Barbara, CA
93117-2360; Phone: (800) 441-4746. Offers Master of Science in
Information Resources Management and Master of Business
Administration.

PARALEGAL INSTITUTE, INC., 3602 W. Thomas Road, Suite 9, Drawer 11408, Phoenix, AZ 85061-1408; Phone: (800) 354-1254.
Offers courses leading to an Associate Degree in Paralegal Studies.

PEOPLEs COLLEGE OF INDEPENDENT STUDIES, 233 Academy Drive, P.O. Box 421768, Kissimmee, FL 34742-1768; Phone: (407) 847-4444. Offers Specialized Associate Degrees in Travel and Tourism Management, Computer Programming and Electronics Technology.

SOUTHERN CAREER INSTITUTE, 164 West Royal Palm Road, Boca Raton, FL 33432; Phone: (407) 368-2522. Offers a Specialized Associate Degree in Paralegal Studies.

WORLD COLLEGE, Lake Shores Plaza, 5193 Shore Drive, Suite 113, Virginia Beach, VA 23455-2500; Phone: (804) 464-4600.
World College is an affiliate of Cleveland Institute of Electronics and offers a Bachelor of Electronics Engineering Technology.

Where To Find A High-Paying Job With Great Benefits

Some people seem to be naturally lucky. They find ideal employment situations right away after graduating from high school or college. Many others, however, expend a great deal of time and effort trying to find good-paying jobs they enjoy. In the meantime, they're stuck in unsatisfying, low-paying jobs. These people spend a lot of time reading the "help-wanted" ads in newspapers hoping to find a better job— both in pay and personal enjoyment.

More often than not, relying solely on job leads from newspaper ads can lead to a dead end and discouragement. While hundreds of jobs are listed in newspapers, many of the best job openings are not. The key to finding the job you want is in locating sources of information about available jobs in your field of interest and expertise. Here are several insider sources for locating such job openings that may never be advertised in newspapers:

— State employment service offices. Sometimes called the Job Service, these offices work in cooperation with the Labor Department's U.S. Employment Service. Through approximately 1,700 local offices (also known as employment service centers), these services help jobseekers find the jobs they want. The offices also help employers find qualified workers at no cost to themselves. To locate the office nearest you, look in your telephonedirectory under "Employment" or "Job Service".

— "America's Job Bank". This is a computerized job network system run by the U.S. Department of Labor. The Job Bank lists 50,000 to 75,000 job openings every week. You can access "America's Job Bank" through personal computers located in local public service offices. Some state employment agencies also have set up access to the Job Bank in other locations, including libraries and shopping malls. The listings in "America's Job Bank" include a wide range of job openings in all fields.

— Federal Job Information Center. Employment with the U.S. Government can mean higher-than-average wages and excellent benefits. For information about the availability of government jobs, call the Federal Job Information Center, operated by the Office of Personnel Management at (202) 606-2700; or write to Federal Job Information Center, 1900 E. St. NW, Room 1416, Washington, DC 20415.

— Professional and trade associations and labor unions. These sources can provide a variety of free or inexpensive job information, including specific job training, requirements, and potential opportunities in the field of your interest. Most of these groups and organizations publish professional journals and trade magazines which feature listings of job openings within specific trades and professions. Publications such as the "National Trade and Professional Associations of The United States", and "The Encyclopedia of Associations" provide comprehensive listings of trade associations, professional societies, labor unions, and other organizations which can provide you with valuable job leads. Both publications can be found in most public libraries.

— The "Occupational Outlook Handbook". Based on extensive research by the U.S. Department of Labor (updated every two years), the "Handbook" describes approximately 250 occupations, covering over one million jobs. While it doesn't list job openings, the "Handbook" does provide an excellent reference for job seekers and career changers. It features a job outlook section which provides projections on job opportunities covering a 10- to 15- year period. It also provides information on the necessary skills and training required to land the fastest-growing, and highest-paying jobs, and average salaries for each occupation listed.

In a manner of speaking, the "Handbook" is a "what jobs are hot, and what jobs are not" book. The information it provides can help you get an edge in knowing where the best job opportunities are and how to take advantage of them. For example, the 1994-1995 edition of the "Occupational Outlook Handbook" projects that opportunities for the following jobs will increase much faster than average through the year 2005:

● Professional specialty occupations: Computer scientists and systems analysts; operations research analysts; psychologists; human service workers; school teachers; occupational therapists; registered nurses; respiratory therapists; speech language pathologists and audiologists.

- Executive, administrative occupations: Construction contractors and managers; general managers and top executives; health service managers; management analysts and consultants; and restaurant and food service managers.

- Technicians and related support occupations: Dental hygienists; EEG technicians; nuclear medicine technologists; radiologic technologists; and paralegals.

- Marketing and sales occupations: Cashiers; retail sales and travel agents.

- Administrative support occupations: Adjusters; investigators and collectors; general office clerks; secretaries; and teachers' aides.

- Service occupations: Corrections officers; guards; chefs and cooks; food and beverage service workers; medical assistants; nursing aides and psychiatric aides; flight attendants; gardeners and groundskeepers; in-home health aides; janitors and cleaners; and preschool workers.

- Mechanics, installers and repairers:General maintenance mechanics.

- Transportation: Truck drivers.

Knowing where the best opportunities are is the first step in landing a high-paying job. The U.S. Department of Labor's "Occupational Outlook Handbook" can help you find those opportunities. The "Handbook" is available in most local public libraries.

— State employment security agencies. Through extensive research and analysis, these agencies develop detailed information about local job market and career information. You can contact these agencies for information about job opportunities in your area. A state-by-state listing of addresses and phone numbers for these agencies can be found in the "Appendix", following chapter 8.

No one can guarantee you a high-paying job with great benefits. It will take time and effort on your part to find the best opportunities that are suited to your own interests and expertise. Many people have taken advantage of the free or inexpensive sources described above and found their "dream jobs"— some at double their current salaries, and all with excellent benefits. If you have the desire and the motivation, you too can use these sources to help you find your dream job.

How To Quit Your Job Now And Get The Same Salary For The Rest Of Your Life

Your love of crafts, cars, sports, reading, collecting or anything you might now consider a hobby, can actually turn into a money-making business. In fact, thousands of people have quit their nine-to-five jobs and earned the same or a higher salary from their hobbies!

What kinds of hobbies or interests can you turn into a steady income? Here are some examples of hobbies and special interests other people have already turned into money-making businesses:

— Children's Bedtime Stories On Tape.

Recording traditional children's bedtime stories on cassette tape is perfect for people who enjoy reading. Tapes can be mass-produced easily and marketed by mail order and/or in retail outlets.

— Baby Shoe Bronzing

There's a big demand for preserving a baby's first pair of shoes in bronze (or silver, or gold). Many people have gone from hobbyists to operating their own successful home-based bronzing businesses. Start-up costs are minimal.

— Custom Made Quilts

If needlework is your hobby, you might consider making quilts to order as a money-making business. Other people who are skilled in needlework have found a steady demand for custom-made quilts. If you're good at what you do and invest in some initial advertising, you could make a good living with this type of business.

— Home Sewing/Mending

If you like to sew in your spare time, you'll probably enjoy doing it as a full-time occupation as well. There are many ways you can use your sewing skills and equipment to earn a good income.

— Auto-Painting

One Ohio man combined a talent for painting with a love of automobiles and started his own auto-painting shop. He started working out of his garage, offering custom painting for automobiles. The demand for his services soon led to an expansion of his business and his income sky-rocketed . If you have an "artistic flair" and a love of automobiles, you may want to give this business a try.

— Bookfinding

Many avid readers enjoy trying to help other readers locate rare or out-of-print books. Some successful bookfinders operate from home-based offices. Start-up costs for this type of service are minimal. As a bookfinder you can earn a living while indulging your love of reading by pouring over library volumes and various library journals.

— Photography

If your hobby is photography, you have excellent money-making potential. Many hobbyists began successful careers in photography by taking baby pictures. By watching birth notices in local newspapers, these entrepreneurs were able to line up lots of new parents as paying customers. There's a steady market for good photography making this a good business to get into. And if you know what you are doing, this can be one of the most profitable hobby-turned-business opportunities.

— Pet Sitting Service

Animal lovers can make a lot of money with this type of service. Many successful pet sitting services started out on a small scale. The operators took care of pets for friends, colleagues, and relatives who did not want to leave their animals in kennels. Once word gets around, there's no limit to the amount of business a pet-sitting service can generate. Income with such a service depends on how many pets you can handle at one time. To be successful with this business, you'll need to have a love of animals and adequate facilities for taking care of several pets at one time.

The eight examples described above represent just a small fraction of the money-making possibilities inherent in peoples' hobbies and special interests. Generally, if you produce anything from crafts or you have an area of expertise in which you can instruct others, you have the potential to quit your regular job and earn a comfortable salary. You already have the knowledge and the skills required.

With initiative on your part and a minimal investment you can begin by marketing the products of your hobby on a part-time basis. Once you've established a market for your products, you can decide whether or not to expand to a full-time operation.

There are a few things you should consider before you quit your job and devote full-time to your hobby as a business. First of all, you should consider whether or not there is a long-term market for your products. The market will need to be steady and generate an income that is at least equal to that of your present job. Another consideration is whether or not you have money set aside to live on until your business is generating a profit. Most experts agree that anyone considering such a move should have at least six months income saved up to live on. If you're sure of your market, and you have saved enough money to live on for six months to a year, you then may consider quitting your regular job.

Don't expect riches overnight. It will take time and effort to get your business established and earning the kind of salary you want. Many people are satisfied with generating the same income they've been receiving from the regular jobs. Others have gone on to double their salaries by profiting from their hobbies. How much you can earn from such an endeavor depends on your product, your market, the time and effort you devote to your business and, in large part, how much you want to get paid.

Being your own boss and earning at least as much money as you now make in your regular job is certainly enticement enough to consider your hobby as a potential money-making opportunity. Just imagine doing something you enjoy and getting paid for it! If you have a hobby or special expertise, you may be able to quit your regular job and do just that! The steps for turning your hobby into a money-making, full-time business are given in chapter 5, "Money-making Business Opportunities".

How To Collect Social Security At Any Age

Most people think of Social Security as a retirement program. While it's true that most Social Security beneficiaries (almost 60%) receive retirement benefits, many others get benefits because they are disabled; or are dependents of someone who gets Social Security; or are widows, widowers, or children of someone who has died. In fact, depending on your circumstances, you and your family members may be eligible to receive over $800 (the amount of your Social Security benefit depends on several factors including your age, the type of benefit you are applying for, and your earnings) in Social Security benefits at any age from one of the following programs :

Disability Benefits: You qualify for disability from Social Security if you have a "physical or mental impairment" that will keep you from doing any "substantial" work for at least one year, or if your condition is expected to be terminal. Members of your family also might be eligible for payments. For example, disability benefits can be paid to the following family members:

— Your wife or husband (at any age) if she/he is caring for your child who is under 16 or disabled and receiving Social Security benefits).

— Your unmarried children who are under 18; or under 19 but in school (elementary or secondary) as full-time students; or 18 or older and severely disabled (if the disability starts before age 22).

For more information about the disability program, call Social Security at (800) 772-1213 and ask for a free copy of the booklet "Disability" (Publication # 05-10029).

Survivor Benefits: Family members who may collect benefits when a family bread-winner dies include the following:

— A widow/widower who is 60 or older; or who is 50 or older and disabled; or who at any age is caring for a child under 16 or a disabled child who is receiving social security benefits.

— Unmarried children under 19 who are in school (elementary or secondary) as full-time students; or 18 or older with a severe disability that started before age 22.

The amount payable to survivors is generally 75% to 100% of the deceased's Social Security benefit. You can get more information about survivors benefits by contacting Social Security and requesting a free copy of "Survivors" (Publication # 05-10084).

Supplemental Security Income (SSI): People of any age (including children) are eligible for monthly SSI payments if they are blind or disabled and their income and assets are below certain limits. Generally, the basic monthly SSI check is $434 ($652 for a couple). You could get more or less than that amount depending on what state you live in (some states add money to the basic rate) and on your other income (you get less than the basic rate if you have other income).

For more information about the Supplemental Security Income program, contact Social Security and ask for a free copy of the booklet, "SSI" (Publication # 05-11000).

How To Sue And Win A Large Settlement

The key to winning a large settlement in a law suit is in having a good lawyer present your case in court. In fact, with the right lawyer, you can win a settlement of $25,000 to $1 million or more if you have been injured financially, physically, emotionally, or verbally.

Of course, no one can guarantee those results. Obviously, your claim must be based on provable injury, supported by solid evidence. A good lawyer can, first of all, tell you whether or not you have legitimate grounds for suing someone. If you do, the lawyer can organize and present the facts and evidence of your claim in a winning manner in court. Without the right legal help, your chances of winning a large settlement— even if your claim is valid—are not nearly as good.

There are several techniques you can use to find a lawyer who specializes in personal injury matters. Many people find the right lawyer by responding to advertisements on radio and television, in newspapers, and in the Yellow Pages. Most people, however, find their lawyers through personal referrals from friends, relatives, and colleagues. The best referral comes from a satisfied client who gives a glowing recommendation of his/her attorney. But even with such a recommendation, you still should "shop around", considering cost and compatibility as well as expertise. Besides personal referrals and advertisements, you also can find the names of lawyers by consulting the following sources:

— The "Martindale-Hubbell Law Directory", available at many public libraries. This directory provides information such as a lawyer's age and educational background, area of specialization (if any), and titles of published articles. The directory also features ratings on many of the lawyers listed based on recommendations from fellow lawyers and judges. The ratings take into consideration several factors, including a lawyer's legal ability, and professional ethics and reliability.

— Local, county, state, and national bar associations. Your local or state bar association can provide you with names of lawyers through their referral services. A national association, such as The Association of Trial Lawyers of America also may be helpful.

— Your banker, accountant or other business professional whose judgement you trust and respect.

— The alumni offices of law schools.

— Your employer's attorney or law firm.

Once you have the names of several lawyers who specialize in personal injury matters, make appointments to see each one. Even if each lawyer comes highly recommended, you should base your decision whether or not to hire him/her on your own opinion. To do that, you'll need to ask several key questions, including the following:

— How long have you been a member of the bar? You should go with experience. Choose a lawyer who has been practicing for three years or longer (specializing in your kind of case).

— How strong (or weak) is my case? A good lawyer will tell you honestly, whether or not your case has any merit and generally what your chances are of winning a settlement.

— How soon can you begin working on my case? "Immediately", would be a good answer to this question.

— What kind of strategy do you propose to employ on my case? A good lawyer will explain to you all possible options, as well as the strategy he/she feels offers the best chance of winning a large settlement.

— How often will you keep me informed on the progress of my case? You should expect to receive a status report on your case at least once a month, and in some cases as often as every week.

— What are your hourly rates and how many hours do you expect my case will require? Depending on the lawyer, you can expect to pay $100 per hour (or less) to $250 (and up) per hour.

— How much of the work required will you do yourself, and how much will you delegate to an associate or paralegal? A competent associate who is qualified to handle most of the legal work on your case can save you a lot money.

— Will you provide a written estimate of all costs of my case before you begin work? When deciding on which lawyer to hire, legal costs are obviously an important consideration. You should get an agreement in writing that includes the lawyer's fees, estimate of additional costs and expenses, as well as a statement that he/she will get your permission before exceeding a specific dollar amount.

You can cut down on your legal costs by doing as much of the "leg work" as possible yourself. That means organizing all the relevant papers and information, providing necessary documents such as police or medical reports, delivering documents to the courthouse, helping locate witnesses, and being on time for appointments and court appearances. In short, do everything you can to help your attorney save time. After all, when dealing with an attorney, time is indeed money.

No one should consider filing a lawsuit without having a legitimate reason. Litigation should not be used in a frivolous manner as a means of attempting to make some "easy money". In other words, be certain you have been injured before you consider suing another person you believe is responsible. If you believe you have a valid unresolved legal claim against someone, you should enlist the services of a good lawyer. By using the techniques described above, you should be able to find and hire a lawyer who is right for your case. If you do, you'll have a very good chance of collecting big money in a winning settlement.

Little-Known Government Programs Can Save You 50% On Your Rent Or Mortgage Payments

The federal government sponsors many little-known programs designed to help people find suitable places to live. Many of these programs are offered by the Department of Housing and Urban Development (HUD). Through rent subsidies and/or mortgage insurance, eligible renters and homebuyers can find affordable housing with the government paying as much as 50% of rent or mortgage payments.

Depending on your income and other circumstances, you may qualify for one of the following government programs:

— **Rural Rental Assistance Payments**

This program offers assistance in the form of direct payments to be used to subsidize rents paid by low-income families and senior citizens. To be eligible to receive this assistance, beneficiaries must be low-or very-low-income families, handicapped, or senior citizens who live in rural rental housing. For more information about this program and eligibility requirements, write to your local Farmers Home Administration office, or write Multifamily Housing Services and Property Management Division, FmHA, U.S. Department of Agriculture, Washington, DC 20250.

— **Section 8 Rental Voucher Program and Section 8 Rental Certificate Program**

These two section 8 programs provide direct payments to subsidize rents paid by very-low-income families. For information and eligibility requirements write to your local HUD office, or write Rental Assistance Division, Office of Assisted Housing, HUD, Washington, DC 20410.

— **Lower Income Housing Assistance Program ("Section 8")**

This section 8 program is designed to make up the difference between approved contract rent and the family's contribution which is based on income. Eligible beneficiaries must be very-low-income families. For information write to your local HUD office, or to Office of Multifamily Housing Management—HUD, Washington, DC 20410.

— **Interest Reduction Payments— Rental And Cooperative Housing For Lower Income Families ("Section 236").**

This program provides direct payments to subsidize mortgages (both insured and non-insured) on rental or cooperative housing developed for the low and moderate income. Eligible beneficiaries include individuals and families, including the elderly or handicapped with locally determined income limits. Contact your local HUD office for details, or write Director, Office of Multifamily Housing Management—HUD, Washington, DC 20410.

Use This Insider Secret To Get Free Home Repairs 22. The federal government has over 950 programs through which hundreds of billions of dollars in grants and direct payments (money that never has to be paid back) are awarded to help people buy and/or repair housing (See chapter 3, "Free Money Sources"). Grants awarded for repair or rehabilitation of existing homes may be used for a number of home improvements including room additions, remodeling bathrooms and kitchens, and weatherization.

If you own and occupy a home in a rural area or certain urban areas you may qualify for one (or more) of the following government programs:

— Rural Housing Preservation Grants

This program is designed to assist low-income rural homeowners (and rental property owners) repair or rehabilitate their housing. The average grant awarded is $7,500. For more information about this program and eligibility requirements, write to your local Farmers Home Administration (FmHA) office, or write Multiple Family Housing Loan Division, FmHA, U.S. Department of Agriculture, Washington, DC 20250.

— Very-Low-Income Housing Repair Loans And Grants ("Section 504")

This section 504 program provides grants of up to $5,000 to eligible rural homeowner-occupants for repair or modernization of their existing homes. Grants awarded range from $200 to $5,000 with the average being $3,500. In order to qualify, you must be at least 62 years of age and own and occupy a home in a rural area. For more information, write your local county FHA office.

—John Heinz Neighborhood Development Program

Low-to-moderate-income persons who live in neighborhoods served by community-based organizations may be eligible beneficiaries of this program designed to, among other things, help rehabilitate existing housing. For information on this program and eligibility requirements, write to your local Department of Housing and Urban Development (HUD), or write Office of Technical Assistance, Community and Neighborhood Management Division, HUD, 471 7th Street SW-Room 7218, Washington, DC 20410.

— Weatherization Assistance For Low-Income Persons

Low-income households (especially the elderly and the low-income handicapped) may be eligible for Department of Energy (DOE) grants ranging up to $1,700. The grant money may be used to cover the costs of attic insulation, storm windows, furnace and cooling system modifications, and replacement furnaces and boilers. For information and eligibility requirements, write to the nearest DOE office.

— HUD Homes

There are several advantages to buying a HUD Home— especially if you buy a home that needs fixing up. HUD may lower the price on the home in consideration of the fact that the buyer will have to invest money to make improvements. In some cases, HUD might offer a special program that includes money for improvements as part of an FHA-insured financing program. Contact a real estate broker in your area who participates in the HUD Homes program for more information.

How To Buy Homes, Office Buildings And Apartment Buildings With Little Or No Money Down

Whether you're interested in buying a home for your family or investing in real estate as a money-making venture, there are smart, low-cost ways of achieving your goals. In fact, many real estate millionaires have started from scratch buying property for next to nothing and then selling it for huge profits. In many cases, their secret technique for success involves locating and buying distressed (foreclosures) properties, including homes and apartment and office buildings, at large discounts.

Foreclosed government homes and properties can provide home-buyers and investors with some especially good bargains. Qualified buyers can take advantage of low-cost government financing through various favorable loan programs. For example, many Farmers Home Administration (FHA) and Veterans Administration (VA) loan programs feature little or no down payment, lower interest rates, and assumable mortgages.

Fortunes have been made buying foreclosed properties which are in need of major repairs for as little as $1 down, making the necessary repairs and then renting or reselling the properties for astronomical profits. The key to success with this technique is in knowing where to find foreclosures. According to real estate industry insiders, here are five of the best sources for locating such properties:

— The Resolution Trust Company (RTC)

The RTC was created by the federal government and charged with disposing of the foreclosed properties of failed Savings and Loans (S & L's). The RTC listings include thousands of residential properties including single- and multi-family homes, permanent mobile homes with land, townhouses, condominiums, and land zoned for residential use. The RTC also has commercial properties for sale, including office complexes and apartment buildings. This foreclosed property is disposed of in four different ways: individual sales, sealed bids, auctions, and portfolio sales at various national, regional, and local RTC Sales Centers. (See the Appendix following chapter 8 for a listing of RTC sales center offices.)

NOTE: The RTC can not make any guarantees as to the condition of any of its listings. The property is sold in "as is" condition. That means that home buyers and investors should make every effort to have the properties inspected by a professional before making a bid.

For general information and to request a free copy of the RTC booklet "How to Buy Real Estate", call (800) 842-2970; or write to National Sales Center, 1133 21st Street, NW, Washington, DC 20036.

For a listing of foreclosures in your area, call the RTC at (800) 782-3006 (there's a $5 fee).

—The U.S. Department of Housing and Urban Development (HUD)

HUD foreclosed properties are put up for sale when a mortgage lender forecloses on a mortgage insured by the Federal Housing Administration— a HUD agency. At the lender's request, HUD pays the balance due on the mortgage and then takes title to the foreclosed property. The property, which may include single-family homes, townhouses, and condominiums, is then offered for sale to the general public.

Instead of the usual 10%-20% required as a down payment, you can buy many HUD foreclosed properties for just 3% down. You can buy some HUD foreclosed homes which are in need of fixing up for as little as $100 down! In fact, most HUD foreclosures are sold on an "as-is" basis, meaning the buyer is responsible for making any repairs or renovations. HUD may even reduce the sale price on the property to offset the investment the buyer will need to make on improvements. This property can provide super bargains for investors who make the necessary improvements and then resell it for huge profits.

You can get a list of HUD foreclosed properties for sale by contacting your local HUD office and asking for one.

—The Veterans Administration (VA)

You may find some great buys and investments among the properties repossessed ("repos") by the VA. These are houses that have been foreclosed on after the veterans who bought them defaulted on their payments. What you may not know is that many of these repos are available to anyone— service veteran or not. You may be able to buy a VA repo even if you're not a veteran and even if you're not buying the home to live in yourself. What's more, you also may be eligible for a VA low-interest loan, and you may be able to buy the home with little or no down payment required.

To find VA repos in your area, contact area real estate offices and ask if any of their brokers handle the sales of these properties. You also can contact your state Veterans Administration Office and request a list of foreclosures in your area.

— Bank Real Estate Owned (REOs)

REO's are foreclosed properties owned by banks. The banks may dispose of this property any way they see fit. The best way to find out information about REOs in your area is to contact your area banks. Write the banks' foreclosure or REO department, explaining the type of property you are looking for and ask them to call you if such a property comes onto the list.

To locate other banks that are likely to have a good deal of foreclosed property for sale, call the RTC at (202) 416-6940 and order a list of thrifts in conservatorship. These are banks which have been taken over by the RTC, but are selling their own property. Most banks in conservatorship are eager to sell their REOs and can make deals without all the red tape normally encountered when dealing with the RTC. If you know what you're looking for, you may find some really great bargains among the foreclosed property sold by these institutions in conservatorship.

— Delinquent Property Tax Sales

These sales are held in all local communities in order to recover unpaid taxes on properties. When property tax bills go unpaid, local tax collectors seize and sell the property at publication. Some investors have purchased parcels of undeveloped land at tax sales for less than $50 each, developed the property, sold it and made a substantial profit.

You can contact your local tax assessor's office and ask for a list of sale properties as well as sale dates and locations. In most areas, property is auctioned off three or four times a year.

While the above sources for locating foreclosed property bargains are some of the best, they are by no means the only sources. The Federal National Mortgage Association (Fannie Mae) distributes a leaflet titled, "How To Buy A Foreclosed Home", and provides you with a list of foreclosed properties it offers for sale. To get the leaflet and to request the foreclosed property list, write to :

Fannie Mae, Public Affairs
3900 Wisconsin Ave. NW
Washington, DC 20016 ; Phone:(800) 553-4636.

You can get some really great bargains on foreclosed property, but you must do your homework and be prepared to battle a certain amount of rod tape. Most foreclosures are sold "as is", so buyers and investors should beware. It wouldn't be a good investment to buy a property that was beyond fixing up. The best advice is to inspect thoroughly each property you are interested in before making a bid. If you take the time to do it right, you can buy a home, or an apartment or office building with little or no money down, and at a large discount.

How To Get Free Car Repairs— Even After The Warranty Expires

Repeated auto repair attempts can be frustrating as well as costly. You may even feel that you are virtually powerless and at the mercy of auto repair shop mechanics. The good news is that a little-known law— one your auto repair shop mechanic isn't likely to tell you about— can protect your rights to own a safe, operable, relatively trouble-free automobile.

If your new car is constantly in the shop for repairs, it may be a "lemon" and as such subject to action under federal and state laws. Lemon laws vary from state to state but they all have in common certain provisions enabling consumers to demand and receive refunds or replacement vehicles if successful repairs can not be made.

Generally, lemon laws cover new cars which experience chronic problems resulting in substantial reduction in the vehicles' use, value or safety. Coverage also may extend after the manufacturer's warranty has expired if the owner can prove the car failed to operate properly due to a defect that was not repaired successfully during the warranty.

Before exercising your lemon-law rights you should give the dealer a chance to fix your car. You'll need to keep accurate records of all repair orders, including the number of repairs attempted and the number of days your car is out of service. If the problem has not been corrected after two repair attempts or if your car has been out of service for 15 days, you should contact the manufacturer's regional office and request assistance in getting your car repaired. If the problem persists after three repair attempts— or your car has been out of service for 20 days— contact the manufacturer's headquarters and explain that unless successful repairs are made you will exercise your lemon-law right to a refund or a replacement vehicle. You can find contact information for the manufacturer in the owner's manual provided with your vehicle or from the dealship where the car was purchased.

After four unsuccessful repair attempts for the same problem—or after the car has been inoperable for 30 days—you should invoke your lemon-law right and demand a refund or replacement. If the manufacturer refuses to reimburse you or to replace your vehicle, you can take the matter to court or arbitration. Under both federal and state lemon laws your attorney fees can be redeemed if you take such action. You can get a referral for a lawyer who specializes in lemon-law cases by sending a SASE to:

> The Center for Auto Safety
> 2001 S. St. NW,
> Washington, DC 20009

Your success in getting a refund or a replacement vehicle depends on your ability to prove that your car is indeed a lemon. In order to do that you'll need to keep accurate records of unsuccessful repair attempts as well as the number of days your car is inoperable. If you can supply such records as proof that your new car cannot be repaired successfully, you can get your money back or get a replacement by exercising your rights under federal and state lemon laws.

How To Save 50% Or More On Airfare, Hotels, And Rental Cars

Shopping for travel bargains can be as much of an adventure as the trip itself. That's especially true now that the travel industry is more competitive than ever in battling for your travel dollars.

Money-saving bargains are available in almost every area of travel— if you know where to look. In fact, travel industry insiders say you can save 50% or more on airfare, hotel accommodations, rental cars, and other travel business every time you take a trip. However, without some prompting, most travel agents aren't likely to tell you where you can get such travel bargains.

To make sure you get the most for your travel dollars, follow these insider strategies:

Air Fare Savings

— Book your reservations at least two weeks in advance, whenever possible.

— Shop around for the lowest fares. You can have your travel agent do a computer "fare search". Such a search will reveal which airlines offer the lowest fares to your destination.

— Take advantage of lower rates during airfare wars. You also may be able to take advantage of fare war prices even if you purchased your ticket before prices dropped. Although airlines don't advertise this policy, you may be able to exchange a ticket you've already bought for a lower-priced fare. You have to pay a ₵25 to ₵00 fee to make such an exchange, but you still can end up saving $100 or more.

— Travel on Tuesday, Wednesday and Saturday. Fewer people fly on those days, so most airlines lower their ticket prices in order to fill seats. There are fewer discounted tickets on Friday afternoon and Monday morning flights when there are more business travelers.

— Book your flight on a low-fare airline. While most low-fare airlines offer fewer frills (no meals, movies, or advanced-seat assignments) and fly limited routes, they can save you as much as 70% off regular airfare. If you're concerned about safety, keep in mind that all low-fare airlines must meet the same federal safety standards as major carriers. (For a listing of several leading discount airlines, see "Low-Fare Airlines" elsewhere in this chapter.)

— Book a flight through a consolidator. These firms buy blocks of tickets from airlines at wholesale prices and then resell them to consumers at a 10% to 25% discount. On overseas flights, consolidator tickets can save you as much as 50% off the regular fare. You can have your travel agent book tickets through a consolidator or you can locate consolidator fares in the travel section of your Sunday newspaper.

Be aware that there are usually restrictions that apply to a consolidator ticket. For example, you may not be able to change your itinerary after you've purchased your consolidator ticket. Also, during a fare war, consolidator tickets may be no cheaper than those bought directly from an airline.

— Check out domestic charter flights. Some charter flights can be as much as $100-$200 below advertised fares of the major airlines. Ask your travel agent to check on charter flights before you buy a higher-priced ticket from a major airlines.

Rental Car Savings

— Rent by the week or on weekends, whenever possible. Week long rental rates offer the best value, and weekend rates are lower than one-day rentals.

— Take advantage of club discounts. You may qualify for a travel club rental car discount if you are a member of AAA, AARP, frequent flyer clubs, or other unions and professional groups.

— Negotiate for a better rental rate. Car-rental rates depend on the demand and may vary from day to day. Shop around, asking several rental agencies to beat the rental rate you've been quoted. The bottom line is that car-rental companies want and need your business and will often lower their prices or give you a better car for the quoted price.

— Choose rentals that come with unlimited mileage. Some rental car firms offer rental cars with unlimited mileage. That means you can drive the car as many miles as you want during its rental period without incurring any additional mileage charges. Other companies impose limited mileage on rental cars and charge an additional 20 cents or more for every mile you drive over the limit.

— Don't use the empty-tank option. This option "allows" you to pay in advance for a full tank of gas so you won't have to be bothered with having the tank filled before returning the car. The problem is, you may not use that full tank of gas. For example, if you pay in advance for a full tank of gas and then return the car with three-quarters of a tank, you'll lose $10 to $15 on the deal.

— Ask your travel agent if he/she can get you a car-rental rate discount. Some travel agents who deal with large-volume rental companies can get discount coupons good for up to 10% off the typical rental rate.

Low-Fare Airlines

Travelers can save from 20% to 70% off regular airfare by flying on any of the following low-fare airlines:

CARNIVAL AIRLINES, (800) 824-7386. Based in Ft. Lauderdale, Florida, this airline has 30 to 40 flights a day between New York area airports and several cities in Florida and San Juan, Puerto Rico. Also flies from Miami to LA.

KIWI INTERNATIONAL AIRLINES, (800) 538-5494. Based in Newark, New Jersey, Kiwi International connects New York with Chicago, Atlanta, Orlando, Tampa, and San Juan, Puerto Rico. Also flies between some of those cities.

LEISURE AIRLINES, (800) 538-7688. Flies several times a week Boston-Orlando, and Hartford, Conn.-Orlando. Also has a Boston-LA flight several times a week, as well as Boston-Atlanta.

MARKAIR, (800) 627-5247. Based in Anchorage Alaska, this airline offers several low-fare flights between Denver and Seattle, LA, Kansas City, Chicago, New York, Atlanta, and other cities in the U.S.

MIDWAY AIRLINES, (800) 446-4392. Midway is based at Chicago's Midway Airport and offers flights between Chicago and New York, Philadelphia, Washington, D.C., Denver, and Dallas/Ft. Worth.

MORRIS AIR, (800) 466-7747. Most of this airline's flights are in the Western United States.

RENO AIR, (800) 736-6247. Flies between Reno and all major cities in California and the Northwest.

TOWER AIR, (800) 221-2500. Flies daily between New York and LA and Miami. Also flies between New York and San Francisco, Orlando, and San Juan.

ULTRAIR, (800) 858-7247. Flies between New York and Ft. Lauderdale, Orlando, Miami, West Palm Beach, Florida, and other cities.

VALUJET, (800) 348-6937. Offers flights between Atlanta and several major cities in the South, Mid West and East.

These Cruise-Only Travel Agencies Can Save You Up To 60%

You can save 25% to 60% off regular cruise rates by booking with a cruise-only travel agency. Industry insiders suggest that you contact at least three agencies to compare prices before booking your cruise. Some of the leading cruise-only travel agencies include:

> Cruise Headquarters, (800) 424-6111
> Cruise Line of Miami, (800) 777-0707
> Cruise Value, (800) 551-1000
> Cruises of Distinction, (800) 634-3445
> Family Cruise Club, a division of CruiseMasters in Los Angeles (800) 242-9000
> Landry & King in Coral Gables, Fla. (800) 448-9002
> Spur of the Moment, (800) 343-1991
> World Wide Cruises, (800) 882-9000

The National Association of Cruise-Only Agencies, 3191 Coral Way, Suite 630, Miami, Fl 33145, can provide you with a list of cruise-only travel agencies located near you.

Avoid Travel Scams With These Insider Tips

According to travel experts, consumers will be bilked of an estimated $12 billion dollars this year by crooks peddling bogus "dream vacations" and "free" getaways. The best way to avoid travel scams is to buy travel from reputable companies you or trusted friends or colleagues have used with satisfactory results.

Here are several other insider tips for avoiding travel scams.

— Throw away mail that informs you that "you have won" or that "you have been selected to receive" a "free" or discount vacation (or any other unnamed prize). Unsolicited phone salesmen proclaiming similar good news are not to be trusted either. Remember this rule: If it sounds too good to be true, it probably is.

— Don't give your credit card or bank account numbers to anyone you don't know and trust.

— Forget about any "free" offer that requires you to pay a processing fee or to pay for lodging and/or airfare in advance and doesn't add in taxes.

— Be suspicious of any deal that requires you to book immediately. Ignore such a deal altogether if you are not provided with a contract and time to look it over.

— If you do book a trip and make a deposit with a phone salesman, check with all hotels, tours, air lines, etc. to make sure they received your deposit. You also should reconfirm the dates and services you ordered.

There are several things you can do if you believe you are the victim of a travel scam. First of all, you should file a complaint with the attorney general's office in the state where the company offering the deal is based. You also can report the scam to your local postmaster and by calling the National Fraud Information Center Hotline at (800) 876- 7060.

Charity Scam Alert

Before you contribute to a charity you're not sure of, check it out with the Council of Better Business Bureau's Philanthropic Advisory Service (PAS). Send a business-size SASE— along with the names of up to three charities— to:

Philanthropic Advisory Service
CBBB, Dept. 024
Washington, D.C. 20042-0024
You'll receive a report on each charity. The report will tell you whether or not the charity meets PAS standards.

MONEY POWER

CHAPTER 8

126 Products You Can Get Absolutely Free

Who says there's nothing free anymore? Listed below are 126 things you can get absolutely free, including catalogs, toys, magazines, booklets, educational and instructional brochures, posters, recipes, sample products, and other items you can get free, simply by writing to the appropriate addresses or by calling toll-free phone numbers.

When sending away for any of the free items listed below, be sure to follow all directions and instructions as each listing may specify. In some cases you will be required to include a SASE (self-addressed, stamped envelope) with your request. You may also be required to send a specified amount to cover postage and handling.

You also should should keep in mind that these offers do not last indefinitely. Giveaways are available in limited quantities and may be no longer available when you send for them.

Freebies For Kids

"Astronaut Fact Book": This book features biographical sketches of America's astronauts. Pictures of planets, posters, and other material is also available by writing to the NATIONAL AERONAUTICS AND SPACE ADMINISTRATION EDUCATIONAL PUBLICATIONS, CODE FEO-2, WASHINGTON, DC 20546.

Coloring Book: Get a 48-page coloring/activity book by sending .75 for postage and handling to SAV-ON GIFTS, 5341 E. GREENWAY STREET, MESA, AZ 85205. Ask for the 48-page coloring/activity book.

Dinosaur Tattoos: Relive the days of the dinosaurs with two, 2" removable dinosaur tattoos. The tattoos are easy to apply and remove. The tattoos are free (one request per address) and are available upon written request to the ALVIN PETERS COMPANY, P.O. BOX 2400, EMPIRE STATE PLAZA, ALBANY, NY

12220. Ask for two dinosaur removable tattoos, and include a long SASE.

Learn About Money: Liberty Financial offers a free 50-page booklet of easy-to-read basic financial information for kids. For a copy of the booklet, call Liberty at (800) 403-KIDS [5437]. Ask for "Young Investors: Parents' Guide".

Educational Coloring Books: Get two free educational coloring books for children from the maker of Triaminic cough and cold medicines. The coloring books are designed to help children understand the effects of illness and disease on loved ones, and show them how they can help. The books deal with such illnesses as diabetes, epilepsy, and Alzheimer's disease. To get the free educational coloring books, write to JEFF'S COMPANION ANIMAL SHELTER, C/0 SANDOZ PHARMACEUTICALS, 59 ROUTE 10, E. HANOVER, NJ 07936-1951.

Children's Dental Care Guide: The makers of Crest toothpaste offer a free booklet, "Care of Children's Teeth: A Guide From Crest". The booklet explains when and how to begin caring for your children's teeth and gums. The information includes easy instructions for proper brushing. Get the booklet by writing to CREST, 303 E. WACKER DRIVE, STE. 440, CHICAGO, IL 60601.

Coloring Book: To get a coloring book with a safety theme, send a business-sized SASE to AETNA LIFE & CASUALTY CO., CONSUMER INFORMATION DEPARTMENT, 151 FARMINGTON AVENUE, HARTFORD, CT 06156. Request the "Play It Safe Coloring Book".

Animal Bookmark: This bookmark is ideal for kids who have pets and who love to read. The bookmark features information about the care of many different animals. To get a free bookmark, send a business-sized SASE to ANIMAL PROTECTION, P.O. BOX 22505, SACRAMENTO, CA 95822. Request the Animal Bookmark and include what pet is your favorite.

Socks The Cat: You can request a free picture of the "first cat" Socks and/or President Clinton. Send a letter along with your request to the OFFICE OF PRESIDENTIAL CORRESPONDENCE, WHITE HOUSE, WASHINGTON,DC 20500.

Fossil Imprinter: Create the skeletal outline of three different creatures with a free, 2" embossing device. Use the embossing device with clay, foil or paper to make your own fossils. To get a free fossil imprinter, send a long SASE (send $.75 for 3 imprinters) to THE GIFT BOX, P.O. BOX 1237, GWINN, MI 49841.

Toy Manufacturer's Guide To Safe Toys & Play: This booklet from the Toy Manufacturers of America provides information on choosing safe, age-appropriate toys for children. There's also several tips on how children can get the most out of playtime. Request a free copy of this booklet by writing to TOY BOOKLET, P.O. BOX 866, MADISON SQUARE STATION, NEW YORK, NY 10159-0866.

Shoelaces: McVehil's Mercantile offers a free pair of shoe laces for children's shoes. The laces are covered with colorful trolls, guaranteed to brighten up any pair of shoes. The troll laces can also be used as hair ribbons. To get a pair of Troll shoelaces, send $.50 for postage and handling to MCVEHIL'S MERCAN-TILE, DEPT. T, R.D. #8 BOX 112, WASHINGTON, PA 15301.

Children's Guide To Investing: The free guide, "Young Investor" provides information to help children become familiar with money and successful investing. Send for a free copy by writing to LIBERTY FINANCIAL COS., 600 ATLANTIC AVE., BOSTON, MA 02210.

Forest Fire Prevention: Posters, bookmarks, rulers, and other materials featuring Smokey Bear teach children how to prevent forest fires. The material is available free upon request by writing to SMOKEY BEAR HEADQUARTERS, U.S. FOREST SERVICE, 14TH AND INDEPENDENCE AVENUES N.W., WASHINGTON, DC 20205.

Puzzle Kit: Get a free "Solar System Puzzle Kit" that includes patterns and other materials for building a solar system. This is a good learning experience for children and adults available free from the NATIONAL AERONAUTICS AND SPACE ADMINISTRATION,EDUCATIONAL PUBLICATIONS, CODE FE0-2, WASHINGTON, DC 20546.

Mini Glow-In-The-Dark Stickers: Get two free "mini-kits" with a total of 54 stickers. These stickers come in the shapes of stars, moons, and planets. If you include a long SASE with your request, you will receive two more free mini-kits, making a total of 108 free stickers. To get the stickers, send $1.00 for postage and handling to M. WORMSER, P.O. BOX 50904, PHOENIX, AZ 85076-0904.

Catalogs

Arts Catalog: Get the National Gallery of Art's catalog of free-loan films, videos, slides and laser discs, by writing to: DEPARTMENT OF EDUCATION DIVISION, NATIONAL GALLERY OF ART, FOURTH STREET AND CONSTITUTION AVE. NW, WASHINGTON, DC 20565.

Business Catalog: Get a free catalog of business books for sale by the U.S. Government. Write to, FREE BUSINESS CATALOG, U.S. GOVERNMENT PRINTING OFFICE, OFFICE OF MARKETING, STOP SM, WASHINGTON, DC 20401.

Consumer Information Catalog: This is a free resource catalog, listing both free and low-cost government publications. The catalog features a listing of booklets on a wide assortment of topics. For a free copy of the catalog, write to CONSUMER INFORMATION CENTER, DEPARTMENT KO, PUEBLO, CO 81009.
Educational Toys Catalog: Educational toys and games for children are featured

in this free catalog. Get a free copy of the catalog by writing to CHILDCRAFT, INC., 20 KILMER ROAD, EDISON, NJ 08818.

Gift Catalog: This free catalog features an assortment of inexpensive dinosaur and fossil gifts. Get a free catalog by writing to TRILOBITE TREASURES, P.O. BOX 232, THOMPSON, CT 06277.

Consumer Guide: McCool Communications offers a free booklet, "Consumer's Guide to Renting a Car", which provides information about insurance, discounts and other related car-renting matters. Send a business-sized SASE (52 cents postage) to McCOOL COMMUNICATIONS, BOX 13005, ATLANTA, GA 30324.

Philatelic Products Catalog: Stamp collectors can get a free mail order catalog of philatelic products by writing to: PHILATELIC FULFILLMENT SERVICE CENTER, US POSTAL SERVICE, PO BOX 449997,KANSAS CITY, MO 64144-9997.

Insurance Information Booklets

"A Consumer's Guide to Annuities": This booklet provides information on the various types of annuities, how they work, and the costs involved, etc. To get a free copy, write to AMERICAN COUNCIL OF LIFE INSURANCE, 1001 PENNSYLVANIA AVE. NW, WASHINGTON, DC 20004.

"Insurance For Your Home and Personal Possessions": Get answers to questions about your coverage and how to improve it in this free booklet. Write to: INSURANCE INFORMATION INSTITUTE, 110 WILLIAM STREET, NEW YORK, NY 10038.

"Life Insurance in Your Personal Financial Plan": This booklet provides information on ways to decide how much coverage you need, what kind to buy, and more. The booklet is available free upon request by writing to MASSACHUSETTS MUTUAL LIFE INSURANCE COMPANY, SPRINGFIELD, MA 01101.

"A Shopper's Guide to Long-Term Care Insurance": This guide provides information on the different types of polices available and how they work. Includes a checklist for policy comparison. For a free copy, write to NATIONAL ASSOCIATION OF INSURANCE COMMISSIONERS, 120 W. 12 ST., SUITE 1100, KANSAS CITY, MO 64105.

Freebies For Your Pet

"Introduce Your Dog To Your New Baby": Send for this free booklet which explains how to establish a loving relationship between your dog and your newborn. You'll also receive a 50-cents off coupon for Gaines Cycle Dog food. Write to QUAKER PROFESSIONAL SERVICES, "INTRODUCING YOUR DOG TO YOUR NEW BABY", ITEM # 1180, 585 HAWTHORNE COURT, GALESBURG, IL 61401.

Dog Snacks: Get a free sample of Purina Beggin' Strips—bacon-flavored snacks for your dog. Write to: BEGGIN' STRIPS FREE SAMPLE, DS 223A, P.O. BOX 15510, MASCOUTAH, IL 62224.

Canine Cookie Treat: Gourmet Canine Cookies are nutritious snacks made especially for dogs. You can get your dog a free cookie sample by writing to BARKEY'S CANINE BAKERY, BOX 519, STONY BROOK, NY 11790. Ask for a Gourmet Canine Cookie sample. Include $.52 in loose postage stamps.

Dog Training Manual: Have fun teaching your dog "new tricks" with the information provided in the Friskies Training Manual. The Free 18-page manual features information on both casual and competitive play. To get the manual, send a long SASE to FRISKIES TRAINING MANUAL, P.O. BOX 2092, YOUNG AMERICA, MN 55553-2092. Request the manual by name.

Gourmet Bird Food: Get a free trial size sample of Lafeber's Avi-Cakes Gourmet Bird Food for your pet bird. Avi-Cakes are a nutritional bird treat especially for Parrots, Parakeets, Cockatiels, Conures, and Love Birds. Request your Avi-Cake sample by writing to, LAFEBER COMPANY, RR #2, ODELL, IL 60460.

Allergy Information: "Can My Pet Really Be Allergic?", is a free booklet which features information on pet allergies and what you can do to keep your pet "allergy-free". To get the booklet, write to "CAN MY PET REALLY BE ALLERGIC?", 460 PARK AVE., SOUTH SUITE 1100, NEW YORK, NY 10016.

Alpo "Lite" Dog Food: Does your dog have a weight problem? If so, send away for this free 12-page booklet, "Q & A on Overweight Dogs" and a coupon for a free can of Alpo "Lite" Dog Food. To get the free booklet and coupon, send a business-sized SASE to the ALPO PET CENTER, P.O. BOX 25200, LEHIGH VALLEY, PA 18002-5200.

Financial & Investment Booklets

"Directory of Small Business Investment Companies": This free directory features lists of names, addresses, telephone numbers, and investment policies of the companies listed. To get the directory, write to : INVESTMENT DIVISION, ADMINISTRATION, 409 3RD STREET S.W., WASHINGTON, DC 20416.

Money Matters: Newlyweds can benefit from the information provided in a free booklet titled, "Money Matters for Newlyweds". The booklet provides information on how to establish a strong financial foundation, savings and investments, insurance, and more. Write to : CITIBANK PROCESSING CENTER, BOX 17029, BALTIMORE, MD 21208.

Treasury Securities: "Treasury Investors...Make The Smart Exchange" provides information about which safety measures to take if you still hold Treasury securities in paper form. The information is available free by writing to CONSUMER INFORMATION CENTER, DEPARTMENT 571A, PUEBLO, CO 81009.

Fixed Income Investing: Get sound investment information such as how to select investments and buy bonds in "The Guide to Successful Fixed Income Investing". For a free copy, write to US CENTRAL SECURITIES, 19800 MACARTHUR BLVD., SUITE 700, IRVINE, CA 92715.

"How To Get Safety Information From Your Financial Institution": This free booklet provides a list of questions you should ask your bank, insurance company, or brokerage firm to find out whether or not your money is safe and in good hands. Write to WEISS RESEARCH, 2200 N. FLA. MANGO ROAD, WEST PALM BEACH, FL 22409.

Investment-Oriented Coins: "American Eagle Gold and Silver Bullion Coins", provides answers to the most commonly asked questions about investment-oriented coins issued by the United States Mint. Send for a free copy by writing to CONSUMER INFORMATION CENTER, DEPARTMENT 570Z, PUEBLO, CO 81009.

Financial Planners: Get a free copy of "The Value of Investment Management Counseling". This guide provides information about the qualifications of financial planners who have CIMC certification. The guide is available free upon written request from THE INSTITUTE FOR INVESTMENT MANAGEMENT CONSULTANTS, 3101 N. CENTRAL AVE., # 560, PHOENIX, AZ 85012.

Newsletters

"The Bankers Secret Bulletin": To get a free sample copy of this newsletter, send a long SASE to THE BANKERS SECRET BULLETIN, P.O. BOX 78, ELIZAVILLE, NY 12523.

"Cheapskate Monthly": Get a sample copy of this newsletter which features money-saving tips by sending a long SASE to CHEAPSKATE MONTHLY, P.O BOX 2135, PARAMOUNT, CA 90723.

HUD USER: You can learn about housing conditions in your area, low-income housing, community development programs, environmental hazards, land development regulations, housing for the elderly and the disabled, and other housing information in a free newsletter and other materials offered by HUD USER, a service of the U.S. Department of Housing and Urban Development. To get a copy of the newsletter, write to HUD USER, P.O. BOX 6091, ROCKVILLE, MD 20850.

"The Penny Pincher": Request a free sample copy of this newsletter by writing to THE PENNY PINCHER, P.O. BOX 809, KINGS PARK, NY 11754. Include a long SASE.

"The Tightwad Gazette": A sample copy of this newsletter is available upon request in writing from THE TIGHTWAD GAZETTE, R.R. 1, BOX 3570L, LEEDS, ME 04263. Include a long SASE.

Magazines

"Consumers' Research": This magazine provides consumer information and advice on a number of consumer topics. Send $1.00 to cover postage and handling to CONSUMERS' RESEARCH, SAMPLE ISSUE OFFER, 800 MARYLAND AVENUE, NE, WASHINGTON, DC 20002 and request a sample issue.

"Science Weekly": This magazine provides information that helps kids learn science and math. It also helps youngsters improve their language skills. The magazine is issued weekly for 7 different grade levels (K to 8). Get a free copy by writing to SUBSCRIPTION DEPARTMENT, SCIENCE WEEKLY, P.O. BOX 70154, WASHINGTON, DC 20088-0514.

"National Geographic" for Kids: The National Geographic Society offers a free copy of "National Geographic World", a special magazine for kids. The magazine features articles on science, nature, world events and many other interesting and educational topics. To get a free sample copy of this magazine, write to NATIONAL GEOGRAPHIC WORLD, 17TH AND "M" STREETS, SUITE 687, WASHINGTON, DC 20036. Ask for "National Geographic World" magazine.

Recipes

"Quick & Easy Charcoal Grilling": The Kingsford Company offers a free leaflet, which provides 10 recipes as well as tips for marinades and flavor enhancers. For a free copy, send a SASE to KINGSFORD GRILLING IDEAS, P.O. BOX 24304, DEPARTMENT 384N, OAKLAND, CA 94623-1305.

"America's Best Dressed Salads": This free leaflet contains entree salad recipes from several well-known chefs. To get a copy, send a SASE to AMERICA'S BEST DRESSED SALADS, THE ASSOCIATION FOR DRESSING AND SAUCES, SUITE 500-G, 5575 PEACHTREE-DUNWOODY ROAD, ATLANTA, GA 30342.

"Recipes for Sensational Desserts": The National Dairy Board offers a collection of butter-rich sweet goodies in this free booklet. The recipes in the booklet were contributed by several pastry chefs across the United States. For a free copy, write to NATIONAL DAIRY BOARD, 928 BROADWAY, BOX FR4, NEW YORK, NY 10010.

"WATERMELON": The National Watermelon Promotion Board provides several recipes, as well as nutrition information in this free leaflet. To request a free copy, write to THE NATIONAL WATERMELON PROMOTION BOARD, P.O. BOX 140065, ORLANDO, FL 32814-0065; or call (800) 55-MELON [556-3566].

"The B & B Experience": The makers of B & B Liqueur offer a free brochure which feature award-winning recipes from country inns throughout the U.S. For a copy of this brochure, call (800) 532-6336. Ask for the brochure by name.

Wish-bone Marinade Recipes: Get a free cookbook featuring easy-to-prepare recipes using Wish-bone Italian Dressing. Write to FREE COOKBOOK OFFER, P.O. BOX 1148, GRAND RAPIDS, MN 55745-1148.

"Marvelous Marinades": This publication, from the makers of ZIPLOC storage bags, features tips and recipes for marinating. For a free copy, write to MAR-VELOUS MARINADES, ZIPLOC STORAGE BAGS, DEPARTMENT 8200-PK, P.O. BOX 78980, NEW AUGUSTA, IN 46278.

"The Great Taste of Spam": This 48-page booklet features several contest-winning recipes from major state and county fair competitions. The booklet also contains several selected recipes from the kitchens of Hormel Foods. To get the booklet, write to "THE GREAT TASTE OF SPAM" RECIPE BOOK OFFER, P.O. BOX 5000, DEPARTMENT P, AUSTIN, MN 55912. Include $1 for postage and handling.

"Easy Entertaining—Award-Winning Deli Meat Recipes": This free brochure, produced by the National Live Stock % Meat Board, features recipes and tips for party hosts. There are 12 recipes as well as color photographs, preparation times, and calorie counts in the recipe brochure. For your free copy, send a long SASE to the NATIONAL LIVE STOCK MEAT BOARD, 444 N. MICHIGAN AVE., DEPT. EE, CHICAGO, IL 60611. Ask for the Easy Entertaining Brochure.

"Egg Classics: Often Requested Recipes": This is an 8-page leaflet featuring an assortment of favorite egg recipes. Also available is another 8-page leaflet, "Egg Favorites...With Less Fat", which provides low-fat egg recipes. To get the leaflets, send a long SASE to THE INCREDIBLE EDIBLE EGG #62, P.O. BOX 858, PARK RIDGE, IL 60068-0858.

"Backyard Barbecue Basics": Recipes, tips and a grilling guide are featured in this leaflet from Weber. The leaflet is available free upon request by calling the WEBER GRILL-LINE, (800)- GRILL-OUT.

"Low Sodium Information You Can Bank On": This booklet can help you reduce your daily salt intake by providing over 20 low-salt recipes as well as health and cooking tips. To get a free copy of the booklet, send a long SASE to :
ANGOSTURA, 20 COMMERCE DRIVE, BOX JD, CRANFORD, NJ 07016.

"Winning Ways With Grilled Veal": This leaflet features winning recipes from the Favorite Veal Recipe Contest. Tips on grilling are also included in the leaflet. For a free copy, send a business-sized SASE to MEAT BOARD TEST KITCHEN, DEPARTMENT WWGV, 444 N. MICHIGAN AVE., CHICAGO, IL 60611.

"Hearty Home Cooking": Pepperidge Farms provides a 12-panel brochure which features 10 recipes for preparing old-fashioned meals, such as meat loaf, Pot Roast and chicken and dumplings. To get a copy of this brochure, send a long SASE to PEPPERIDGE FARM GRAVY, P.O. BOX 964, BENSALEM, PA 19020.

"The American Collection": The Catfish Institute provides a free brochure which features farm-raised catfish recipes from several chefs. To get a copy of the brochure, send a SASE to THE AMERICAN COLLECTION, P.O. BOX 536, GIBB-STOWN, NY 08027.

"Fit For Life With Fresh Citrus": This booklet, produced by Sunkist Growers, features recipes and nutrition information. Get the booklet by sending a SASE to SUNKIST GROWERS INC., MS 236-FIT, BOX 7888, VAN NUYS, CA 91409-7888.

"Smucker's Summer Recipes": Get a brochure featuring quick tips and Smucker's recipe cards with easy-to-prepare recipes. The recipes include English Berry Pudding and Lemon Apricot Marinade. Send for your free quick tips brochure and recipe cards by writing to "SMUCKER'S SUMMER RECIPES", STRAWBERRY LANE, ORRVILLE, OH 44667.

"Delectable Gifts for all Occasions": This leaflet features several recipes, including Buttered Almond Biscotti and Nippy Nuts. Also included in the leaflet are creative tips for wrapping and gift wrapping. For a free copy, send a business-size envelope to DELECTABLE GIFTS, NATIONAL DAIRY BOARD, 928 BROADWAY, SUITE 600, BOX DG-2, NEW YORK, NY 10010.

"Idaho Inspirations": Award-winning potato recipes are featured in this free booklet. Send a SASE to IDAHO INSPIRATIONS, 27TH FLOOR, 1633 BROADWAY, NEW YORK, NY 10019.

"Cheese Makes It Better Recipes": This leaflet, featuring "old recipes" made new by adding cheese, is available by sending a SASE to CHEESE RECIPES, NATIONAL DAIRY BOARD, 928 BROADWAY, SUITE 600, BOX 2111, NEW YORK, NY 10010.

Recipes for Drinks: The makers of Angostura aromatic bitters offer a free brochure, featuring recipes for drinks. Learn to mix both classic and new drinks—with or without alcohol. The booklet also includes tips for mixing drinks.
To get a copy of the brochure, send a business-sized SASE to ANGOSTURA, 20 COMMERCE DRIVE, SUITE 100, CRANFORD, NJ 07016.

Product Samples

Coffee: Get a free sample of 100% Colombian coffee by writing to: 100% COLOMBIAN COFFEE SAMPLE OFFER, P.O. BOX 8545, NEW YORK, NY 10150. Ask for "free coffee samples", and include a business-sized SASE.

Lip Conditioner: Keep your lips moist with a free sample of Stay Moist Moisturizing Lip Conditioner. Get the sample by sending .75 for postage and handling to: STANBACK COMPANY, P.O. BOX 1699, SALISBURY, NC 28145.

Sea-Bond Denture Adhesive: Denture wearers can get a sample of Sea-Bond denture adhesive by writing to SEA-BOND SAMPLE, DEPARTMENT 4, P.O. BOX 8046, MARSHFIELD, WI 54449. Ask for the Sea-Bond sample. There is a limit of one sample per household.

Oil of Olay Bath Bar: A free sample Oil of Olay Bath Bar is available by writing to: OIL OF OLAY BATH BAR, P.O. BOX 5767, CLINTON, IA 52736. Include .50 for postage and handling.

Peanuts: John Allen Farms, which ships South Georgia Roasted Peanuts and Vidalia Onion products offers a free 3-oz. sample of peanuts, a recipe and an order form for Vidalia Onions. For a free sample of roasted peanuts, send $1.00 for postage and handling to JOHN ALLEN FARMS, P.O. BOX 974, VIDALIA, GA 30474.

Sweet'N-Low: The Makers of the low-calorie sugar substitute Sweet'N-Low, offer free samples of their product. To get the free sample, send .50 for postage and handling to SWEET'N-LOW SAMPLE OFFER, 2 CUMBERLAND STREET, BROOKLYN, NY 11205. Be sure to request Sweet'N-Low samples.

Hair Spray: The makers of Alberto VO5 offer a free trial-size sample of Crystal Clear 14 Hour Hold Hair Spray. This offer is good while the supplies last only. Write to VO5 FREE HAIR SPRAY OFFER, P.O. BOX 7777-K11, MT. PROSPECT, IL 60056-7777.

Crochet Pattern: Crocheting Forever offers a free fashion doll wedding gown pattern. The pattern comes with complete detailed instructions and illustrations. For a free pattern, send a long SASE to CROCHETING FOREVER, 11511 PUCKER ST., NILES, MI 49120-9036.

Wheat Germ: Get a free package of wheat germ and a brochure, "Growing Younger: Eating and Exercising Smart after 50", By writing to KRETSCHMER WHEAT GERM, P.O. BOX 530, DEPARTMENT N., BARRINGTON, IL 60011.

Tea: Get two free samples of Lipton "Soothing Moments" Teas— Cinnamon Apple herbal tea and Orange and Spice-flavored tea by writing to LIPTON SOOTHING

MOMENTS SAMPLE OFFER, P.O. BOX 1206, GRAND RAPIDS, MN 55745-1206.

Mascara: Get a free sample of "Lush-Lash" a flame-glow mascara. Send $.75 to cover postage and handling to DEL LABORATORIES, LUSH-LASH DEPART-MENT, 565 BROAD HOLLOW ROAD, FARMINGDALE, N.Y. 11735. Ask for the Lush-Lash sample and specify the color you prefer— black or brown/black.

Body Lotion and Bath Gel: While supplies last, sample packets of Bath Shoppe Shower & Bath Gel and Bath Shoppe Body Lotion by Yardley are available free upon request. To get the sample, send a #10 SASE to YARDLEY BATH SHOPPE, 170 EAST 61ST STREET, 5TH FLOOR, NEW YORK, NY 10021.

Shampoo: The makers of Neutrogena Shampoo offer a free sample size of their product. To get the sample of Neutrogena, send $1.00 to cover postage and han-dling to NEUTROGENA SHAMPOO OFFER, P.O. BOX 45062, LOS ANGELES, CA 90045.

Sunscreen: Protect yourself from the sun with "Soothing Berry" a sunscreen from Blistex. Get a free sample of this sunscreen, by writing to BLISTEX SAMPLE OFFER. 1800 SWIFT DRIVE, OAK BROOK, IL 60512.

Freebies From Uncle Sam (U.S. Government?)

Air Travel Guide: Find out which airline has the best on-time rate, which airline loses the least amount of luggage, and other information which can help you choose the best airline in the monthly publication, "The Air Travel Consumer Report". Write to the OFFICE OF CONSUMER AFFAIRS, U.S. DEPARTMENT OF TRANSPORTATION,400 7TH STREET S.W., ROOM 10405, WASHINGTON, DC 20590.

CD-ROM Catalog: "Information Dissemination: Federal CD-ROM Titles" (GAO/IMTEC 93-34FS) is a catalog listing over 100 CD-ROM publications which are available to the public. The first copy of the CD-ROM catalog is free; there-after, copies cost $2. To get the CD-ROM, write to U.S. GENERAL ACCOUNTING OFFICE, P.O. BOX 6015; GAITHERSBURG, MD 20877.

CD-ROM "National Sellers List": This free CD-ROM lists people who are licensed in the U.S. to sell properties which have been seized by the U.S. Marshal Service. The CD-ROM is available free upon request by writing to :
 THE U.S. MARSHAL SERVICE, NATIONAL SELLERS LIST,
600 ARMY NAVY DR., ARLINGTON, VA 22202-4210.

Endangered Species Information: You can get a series of one-page publications about various endangered species from the U.S. Fish and Wildlife Service. Also available is a copy of the Endangered Species Act and a list of endangered species. To get this information, write to U.S. FISH AND WILDLIFE SERVICE PUBLICATIONS UNIT, MAIL STOP 130 WEBB, U.S. DEPARTMENT OF THE INTERIOR, WASHINGTON, DC 20240.

Economic Development Sources: The U.S. Small Business Administration provides a free publication, "Working Together: A Guide to Federal and State Resources for Rural Economic Development", which provides information on sources of loans, counseling, and other assistance. The publication is available upon request from the OFFICE OF RURAL AFFAIRS AND ECONOMIC DEVELOPMENT, U.S. SMALL BUSINESS ADMINISTRATION, 409 3RD STREET S.W., WASHINGTON, DC 20416.

Earthquake Safety Information: Information about earthquakes and earthquake safety measures is available upon request from the NATIONAL EARTHQUAKE SAFETY INFORMATION CENTER, U.S. GEOLOGICAL SURVEY, MAIL STOP 967, BOX 25046, FEDERAL CENTER, DENVER, CO 80255.

Nutrition Information: Free reading lists and other information on proper nutrition resources are available from the Food and Nutrition Information Center. Write to the Center at the U.S. DEPARTMENT OF AGRICULTURE, NATIONAL AGRICULTURE LIBRARY, ROOM 304, 10301 BALTIMORE BLVD., BELTSVILLE, MD 20705.

Congratulations From The White House: The White House mails congratulatory cards to parents during the first month after the birth of a child. The White House congratulations is available free by sending the child's name, date of birth and parents' names to the WHITE HOUSE GREETINGS OFFICE, 1600 PENNSYLVANIA AVE. N.W., WASHINGTON, DC 20500.

Government Jobs: Information about government jobs worldwide, including qualifications and contacts is available from CAREER AMERICA CONNECTION. Call (912) 757-3000.

Sources of Money For College: College and trade-school students can find out about financial-aid programs, eligibility requirements, and how to fill out applications by calling the FEDERAL STUDENT AID INFORMATION CENTER at (800) 433-3243.

American Flag: The U.S. Department of Veterans Affairs provides American Flags to families of deceased veterans. Write to the U.S. DEPARTMENT OF VETERANS AFFAIRS, 941 CAPITOL STREET N.E., WASHINGTON, DC 20241.

Business Booklets: The Federal Trade Commission provides free booklets dealing with mail-order marketing, credit, and other business-related subjects. The booklets are available free upon request by writing to the FEDERAL TRADE

COMMISSION, PUBLIC REFERENCE BRANCH, ROOM 130, 6TH STREET AND PENNSYLVANIA AVENUE N.W., WASHINGTON, DC 20580.

HUD Homes Hotline: A free pamphlet providing information on buying properties owned by the Department of Housing and Urban Development is available by calling the HUD HOMES HOTLINE at(800) 767-4483.

CFTC Annual Report: The Commodities Futures Trading Commission (CFTC) will send you a free copy of its annual report. Send your request for the free report to the COMMODITIES FUTURES TRADING COMMISSION, OFFICE OF PUBLIC AFFAIRS, 2033 K. ST., N.W., 8TH FLOOR, WASHINGTON, DC 20581.

"Education Programs Catalog": This catalog features information about educational programs which are sponsored by the Department of Energy (DOE). The catalog also provides a list of educational programs sponsored by the National Laboratories which are either run by or affiliated with the DOE. To get a free copy of the catalog, write OFFICE OF ENERGY RESEARCH, OFFICE OF SCIENCE AND EDUCATION PROGRAMS, U.S. DEPARTMENT OF ENERGY, 1000 INDEPENDENCE AVE. S.W., ROOM 5B-168, WASHINGTON, DC 20585.

Surplus Government Property Booklet: The Department of Defense auctions a wide assortment of government surplus property, including office equipment, sporting equipment, tents, computers, furniture and other items. Information about the auctions is available in a free booklet, "How To Buy Surplus Personal Property From the United States Department of Defense". To get the booklet, write DEFENSE REUTILIZATION AND MARKETING SERVICE, NATIONAL SALES OFFICE, 2163 AIRWAYS BLVD., MEMPHIS, TN 38114.
OR PHONE (800) 222-3767.

Miscellaneous Freebies

Arthritis Information: A free booklet, "MetLife HMO and the Arthritis Foundation Presents: Basic Facts About Arthritis", provides information about arthritis and several exercises to help improve joint flexibility. The booklet is available by writing to ARTHRITIS METLIFE HMO, 57 GREEN FARMS RD., WESTPORT, CT 06880. Include a SASE with 52 cents postage.

Auto Care Booklet: The Firestone Company offers a free booklet, "Car-Care Tips" which features easy-to-understand instructions for routine auto care and maintenance. The booklet also features a chart for keeping a record of car maintenance. To get the booklet, call (800) 9- FIRESTONE.

Craft Instruction Kit: "Teach Your Child Origami!" features "how-to" instructions as well as paper for making several origami creations. To get a kit, send a long SASE to FASCINATING FOLDS, P.O. BOX 2820-235, TORRANCE, CA 90509-2820.

Sewing Kit: Get a free mini-sewing kit which features thread, needles, needle threader, measuring tape, button, and a safety pin. To get the kit, send $1.00 to cover postage and handling to ASSIDUITY INDUSTRIES, P.O. BOX 1147, WILLITS, CA 95490.

Sleep Problems Brochure: Get a free brochure, "40 Tips for 40 Winks", and take an interactive quiz to help you determine whether or not you're getting enough sleep or have a sleep problem by calling (800) SHUTEYE [748-8393.

Tomato Seeds: Get a free packet of Stakeless Tomato Seeds for your garden by sending $.25 for postage and handling to Stakeless TOMATO SEED OFFER, GURNEY SEED COMPANY, 3101 PAGE STREET, YANKTON, SD 57079.

Free Tree: The National Arbor Day Foundation will send you a free tree to plant as part of the "Trees for America" program. Plant a free tree and help the ecology. Write to the Foundation at ARBOR AVE., NEBRASKA CITY, NE 68410. Request a free tree to plant.

Slide-Rule Device: The Franklin Mutual Fund Family offers a free slide-rule-type device that translates an assumed rate of return on tax-free securities into the equivalent taxable yield. You can get a slide-rule device by calling Franklin at (800) 342-5326.

Lead-Based Paint Brochure: "Dealing With Lead-Based Paint: A Practical Guide for Consumers", provides a step-by-step approach for managing lead paint . The brochure has been prepared by the National Paint & Coatings Association and is available free by sending a SASE to LEAD BROCHURE, PAINT AND COATINGS INDUSTRY INFORMATION CENTER, 1500 RHODE ISLAND AVE., N.W., WASHINGTON, DC 20005.

Termite Termination: The U.S. Department of Agriculture (U.S.D.A.) offers a free 36-page booklet, "Subterranean Termites" — Bulletin 64, which offers information on pest control.To get the booklet, write to the USDA FOREST SERVICE, BOX 96090, WASHINGTON, DC 20090.

Foot Care Guide: This guide provides information on prevention and treatment for dry skin, corns and calluses and other common foot maladies. Get a free copy of the guide by writing to NATIONAL INSTITUTE ON AGING, INFORMATION CENTER, BOX 8057, GAITHERSBURG, MARYLAND 20898.

Mental Health Publications Directory: A list of National Institute of Mental Health (NIMH) publications with information about mental illnesses and their treatment is available free upon request from the INFORMATION RESOURCES AND INQUIRIES BRANCH, NIMH, ROOM 15C-05, 5600 FISHERS LANE, ROCKVILLE, MD 20857. Surgeon General's Report: Get a free copy of the 1993

"Surgeon General's Report to the American Public on HIV Infection and AIDS", by calling (800) 342- AIDS [2437].

Air Pollution Information: For information about the Environmental Protection Agency's publications on air pollution issues, call the NATIONAL AIR TOXICS INFORMATION CLEARINGHOUSE, (919) 541-0850.

Lightning Safety Guidelines: Get a free booklet, "Lightning Facts and Fallacies." The booklet provides several safety precautions. Write to COLORADO CHAR- TERED PROPERTY AND CASUALTY UNDERWRITERS, 4380 S. SYRACUSE STREET, SUITE 200, DENVER, CO 80237. Include a business-sized SASE.

Recycling Kit: The makers of Reynolds Wrap offer a free recycling bag for col- lecting used aluminum. Also included in the recycling kit is a refrigerator magnet, a brochure featuring children's activities and puzzles about recycling, and a coupon for Reynolds Wrap. To request a free kit, call (800) 344- WRAP [9727].

Seafood Hotline: Get information on buying, storing and handling seafood. Also learn about seafood labeling and nutrition in free publications available from the FDA. Write to the SEAFOOD HOTLINE, FOOD AND DRUG ADMINISTRATION, 200 C STREET S.W., HFS-555, WASHINGTON, DC 20204.

Moving Booklet: If you are planning a long-distance move, this 27-page booklet, "Guide To A Good Move", from Allied Van Lines provides some valuable informa- tion. Learn how long-distance moving operates, how to file a claim if your goods are damaged or delivered late, and how to prepare children and pets for such a move. Get a free copy of this booklet by writing to ALLIED VAN LINES, P.O. BOX 4403, CHICAGO, IL 60680.

Fabric Care Guide: The makers of RIT Dye offer a free guide, "The RIT Dye Fabric Treatment Guide to Fabric Care." To get a copy, write to RIT DYE, DEPARTMENT 267, BOX 307, COVENTRY, CT 06238.

Home Security Guide: Get a free guide on home security, "Keeping Your Family Safe", available from Security Link Inc. To get a free copy, call (800) 322-9797.

Drug Prevention Booklet: "Growing up Drug Free: A Parent's Guide To Prevention" is available free upon request. Call (800) 624-0100.

College Survival Guide: If you're going off to college, you'll appreciate this free booklet which provides information how to study better, stay safe on campus, eat right, and other related topics. Send a SASE to MUHLENBERG COLLEGE, ATTN: COLLEGE TIPS, 2400 CHEW STREET, ALLENTOWN, PA 18104-5586.

Allergy Management Kit: The makers of Tavist-D and Tavist-1 tablets and the American Lung Association offer an allergy-management kit available free upon request. The kit contains information on preventing upper respiratory illnesses and managing symptoms of such ailments.

There are also guidelines for outdoor activities, a resource directory, and coupons. The kit is available by calling (800) 828-4873.

Child Safety Booklet: "Accident Prevention: A Family Guide To Child Safety" providing information on how to prevent all sorts of accidents frequently involving children is available free upon request. Write to BAYLOR COLLEGE OF MEDICINE, "ACCIDENT PREVENTION", ONE BAYLOR PLAZA, ROOM 176B, HOUSTON, TX 77030. Include a business-sized SASE.

Breast Self Exam Waterproof Shower Card: The Zeta Tau Alpha/Susan G. Komen Breast Cancer Foundation offers an illustrated card which can be used in the shower. The card features step-by-step instructions on how to perform a breast self-examination. To get a free shower card, send a SASE to ZETA TAU ALPHA, 3450 FOUNDERS ROAD, INDIANAPOLIS, IN 46268.

"Non-Alcoholic Drink Ideas from the Rainbow Room": This free booklet from Sutter Home Winery features recipes for alcohol-free party drinks. Call (800) 662-5240 and request a free booklet.

Mutual Fund Cassette Tape: Paul Merriman & Associates offer a free 70-minute cassette tape, "Questions You Must Ask Before You Buy Any Mutual Fund". Send for the cassette by writing to : PAUL MERRIMAN & ASSOCIATES, MERRIMAN MUTUAL FUNDS, 1200 WESTLAKE AVENUE N., SUITE 700, SEATTLE, WA 98109.

E-Z Food Labels Survival Kit: This free kit provides tips for making food-label information easier to understand. It also includes a wallet-sized card to carry to the grocery store. To get the kit, write to E-Z FOOD LABELS SURVIVAL KIT, THE NUTRASWEET COMPANY, P.O. BOX 830, DEERFIELD, IL 60015.

Home & Auto Tips

50 Useful Products Or Booklets You Can Receive Free

There's one certainty about making things run smoothly around your home — you never know what will go wrong, so you can never have enough information available. To that end, we though we'd start this section by offering you a variety of free information sources — and, for good measure, a few free products — that you might want to take advantage of. The giveaways are usually for promotional reasons, and you should remember to allow four to six weeks for delivery. Also include any postage fee or self-addressed, stamped envelope requested. Be sure to ask for the product you want by name. Finally, some offers may have been discontinued by the time you read this. Nevertheless, here's a list of offers, along with the addresses to write:

1. "Cool Tips for a Hot Season" — Consumer Information Center Dept. 616Z, Pueblo, CO 81009; include a stamped, self-addressed legal-size envelope.

2. Chemistry Project Ideas Booklet — American Chemical Society, Education Dept., 1155 16th St. NW, Washington, DC 20036.

3. Microwave Instructions and Recipes — Consumer Services, Box 599, Cincinnati, OH 45202.

4. "You and Your Blood Pressure" — The Will Rogers Institute, 785 Mamaroneck Ave., White Plains, NY 10605; include a stamped, self-addressed legal-size envelope.

5. "Coping with Unemployment" — National Mental Health Association, Dept. BL-2, 1021 Prince St., Alexandria, VA 22314.

6. "Tips for Energy Savers" — Consumer Information Center, Dept. 572Y, Pueblo, CO 81109; include a stamped, self-addressed legal-size envelope.

7. "Gambling Catalogue" — John Patrick Productions, Box 289, Short Hills, NJ 07078.

8. "A Guide to Massage Therapy in America" — American Massage Therapy Association, 820 Davis St., Suite 100, Evanston, IL 60201.

9. "A Salad Tour of the U.S.A.," send 29 cents postage to H.J. Heinz, Box 57, Pittsburgh, PA 15230.

10. Free Sample of Sweet 'n Low — A sugar substitute from Sweet 'n Low, 2 Cumberland St., Brooklyn, NY 11205.

11. Dog Training booklets, free for a self-addressed, stamped envelope, from Gaines Obedience Lists, Box 1007, Kankakee, IL 60901.

12. "How to Panel a Room" — A 68-step guide from Masonite Corp., Box 311, Towanda, PA 18848.

13. Free Recipe Books — Ann Pillsbury Kitchens, Pillsbury Co., Minneapolis, MN 55402.

14. First Aid Wall Chart — From Family Health, 420 Lexington Ave., New York, NY 10017.

15. Baby Care and Nutritional Booklets — Free from Gerber Products, 445 State St., Fremont, MI 49412.

16. Beginner's Sewing Guides (10 different ones) — Free from Belding-Lilly, Consumer Information, Box 88, Shelby, NC 28150.

17. Stainless Steel Teaspoon Sample — $1 postage, Oneida Sample Center, Box 9777, New Brighton, MN 55197.

18. Spunkey's Tree-Care Booklet — Send a long self-addressed, stamped envelope to American Forestry Institute, Box 2000, Washington, DC 20013.

19. Colorado Spruce Tree Seeds — Free from Waukesha Seed Co., Box 1820, Waukesha, WI 53187; send envelope with 55 cents postage.

20. Free Cents-Off Coupons (for many items) — From Carol Wright, 1000 Donnelley Drive, Elm City, NC 27822.

21. "Create Special Parties" — Send 55 cents postage to Reynolds Wrap Entertaining Ease, Box 6704, Richmond, VA 23230.

22. Three Do-It-Yourself Wood Deck Plans — 35 cents from Western Wood Products, 1500 Yeon Building, Portland, OR 97204.

23. Magnet Sample — From Magnet Sales, 11250 Playa Court, Culver City, CA 90230; ask for Catalog H.

24. "Moving With Children" — From Consumers Services Dept., United Van Lines, United Drive, Fenton, MO 63026.

25. Hand Washables Bonus Pak and Samples — Call 1-800-443-0602, Ext. 111.

26. Silver Polish Sample — From W.J. Hagerty, Ltd., Box 1496, 3801 W. Linden Ave., South Bend, IN 46624.

27. "How to Respect and Display Our Flag — Booklet from the U.S. Marine Corps, Dept. of Navy, Washington, DC 20380.

28. American Baby Magazine — Three issues for $1 postage, from American Baby Magazine, 352 Evelyn Street, Paramus, NJ 07652.

29. Free Tomato Seeds — Stakeless Tomato Offer, Gurney Seeds, 3101 Page Street, Yankton, SD 57079; include 32 cents postage.

30. MyoFlex Analgesic Creme — Free sample tube from Warren-Teed Labs, Box 2450, Columbus, OH 43215.

31. Free Health-Care Samples — Consumer Healthcare List, Pfizer Pharmaceuticals, Box 3852, Grand Central Station, New York, NY 10163.

32. Sewing Booklets — Free from Coats & Clark Inc., Box 1010, Toccoa, GA 30577; include a stamped, self-addressed envelope.

33. "Balancing Money and Menus" — Free recipes from Quaker Oats, Box 5008, Young America, MN 55397.

34. Blistex Cream for chapped lips — 55 cents from Blistex Sample, 1800 Swift Drive, Oak Brook, IL 60512.

35. "How to Get Rid of Household Pests" — Pest Control Association, 8100 Oak Street, Dunn Loring, VA 22027; include envelope with 57-cent stamp.

36. Shareware Computer Program Disk — Send $1 for postage to FREE-WARE, Box 3726, Crofton, MD 22027.

37. Diet and Exercise Booklet — Send 55cents to Mazola Corn Oil, Box 307, Coventry, CT 06238.

38. "Mortgage Money Guide" — 16-page booklet, Mortgages, Federal Trade Commission, Washington, DC 20580.

39. Oat Bran Tablets — Free sample from Swanson Health Products, Box 2803, Fargo, ND 58108.

40. Denture Adhesive Sample — Free trial size of Sea Bond from Combe, Inc., 1101 Westchester Ave., White Plains, NY 10604.

41. Free Swab Dispenser — Q-Tips Dispenser Offer, Box 1009, Jefferson City, MO 65102; include 32 cents for postage.

42. Christmas Card Samples and Sales Kits — $1 postage, Creative Card Co., 4401 W. Cermak Road, Chicago, IL 60623.

43. "Natural Health" — Sample newsletter from National Health Outreach, 6821 E. Thomas, Scottsdale, AZ 85251.

44. Mystery Gift — Free from Frazier's, 4 Cedar, Fair Haven, VT 05743.

45. "Defensive Driving Tips" — Booklet from National Safety Council, 444 N. Michigan Avenue, Chicago, IL 60611; include legal-sized, stamped, self-addressed envelope.

46. Free Sample Toy — From Lauri, Inc., Phillips-Avon, ME 04966; include 55 cents postage.

48. Wedding Stationery Samples — From Rexcraft, Rexburg, ID 83441.

49. "Health and Beauty Tips" — Booklet from Castle and Cooke, Box 7758, San Francisco, CA 94119.

50. Free Sample of Balmex (for skin irritation) — From BALMEX Sample, 1326 Frankford Ave., Philadelphia, PA 19125.

Get Cable TV Service Absolutely Free

In spite of the best efforts of Congress, monthly charges for cable TV just keep on rising. However, there are several ways you can reduce those charges — or get your service absolutely free.

If you have the money, you can bypass the cable service entirely by getting your own satellite dish and pulling signals for all channels , including some pay TV services-- right out of the air. However, satellite dishes are expensive — as much as

$4,000 to $5,000 . More and more broadcasters are scrambling their signals. Thus, it's probably not worth your effort just to try to save $40 or $50 a month.

A cheaper alternative is to buy your own converter box — which will run from $100 to $250, depending on the quality — and hook it into the cable service lines yourself. Of course, there's a major debate about the legality of such activities — and you also have to live in a house or apartment that's already wired for cable.

The best approach — and the one that costs you only a bit of time — is to strike a deal directly with your local cable company to get free service. This can be accomplished through a trade-out deal in which you either work as a commissioned salesperson for the company, taking free cable service as part of your payment, or provide referrals to the company and get a discount on your monthly bill for each new client the cable firm signs up. You can also offer to serve as an endorser of the cable service in ads in exchange for free service.

These trade-outs are a lot easier to sell than you might think. Most cable companies generate most of their sales through phone calls, mailings or ads on broadcast television channels — none of which are as powerful as personal sales calls, referrals or recommendations. Cable companies also need as much help as possible in battling their current image as profit-hungry monopolies — and getting personal endorsements is one way to do this.

Give it a try; it could save you $40 or $50 a month — or even more.

Why You Should Never Buy Colored Toilet Paper

Colored toilet paper can dress up your bathroom — but it can also be harmful to your health. The dyes in the colored paper often irritate the anal area and lead to painful hemorrhoids. In addition, colored papers are bad for the environment since most waste water treatment facilities can't fully remove all the dyes.

Shoulf You Lease Your Car?

In spite of all the ads in your newspaper's weekend Classified Section extolling the benefits of leasing rather than buying, the answer is most likely "no." Even though less cash is needed up front, the overall cost of leasing a car for three years is usually 15 percent to 20 percent higher than buying a vehicle and maintaining it for the same period yourself. Most ads also cite the tax benefits of leasing, but there really are none — all business auto expenses are already deductible. In spite of these drawbacks, there are three times when leasing makes sense:

1. When your business needs a number of vehicles, but doesn't have the money for down payments.

2. When you need to improve your balance sheet by reducing long-term liabilities (which is where car loans would fall)

3. When a poor driving record has forced you into the costly assigned-risk insurance pool and the leasing company can offer cheaper coverage.

If you do lease, don't buy a full-maintenance contract; they're over-priced. Also beware of excessive surcharges for driving too many miles each year.

Save Thousands Of Dollars On Like - New Cars

If you want a new car but can't muster up the money, consider buying a "demo," or salesman's sample. At any given time, large dealerships have five or six cars — usually their most popular models — that salespeople drive and use to give customers test rides. Because the dealers want to put their best foot forward on demonstration drives, these cars are fully and regularly serviced to ensure top performance. They're also retired from demo service after 1,500 to 2,000 miles and placed back on the sales lot. However, because of the mileage, they can't be sold as new, so the dealer will often knock as much as $4,000 off the sticker price (depending on the model). Demos are often advertised, but if they're not, simply ask if the dealer has one in the model you're looking for when you start shopping. You still get the full factory warranty, just as if you were buying a new car. One drawback — selection is extremely limited, so you can't pick and choose among many different cars to get the exact color or options you want.

Use Your Home To Finance Your Car

Since consumer interest is no longer deductible, many people have turned to financing auto purchases with a home-equity line of credit, interest on which is still deductible. If you own a home and already have an equity credit line, this is definitely a worthwhile financing strategy for car purchases. Not only will the interest be deductible (meaning Uncle Sam will reimburse you for up to 36 percent of your interest cost), but you'll also get a big break on the actual rates. Equity credit-line rates are currently 3 to 6 percentage points below those charged on a typical new car loan — and 6 to 9 points below used car loan rates.

However, the advantages aren't sufficient to warrant getting a new equity credit line just to finance a car purchase. Many lenders demand an application fee, some require a title search and nearly all will want an appraisal of your house, all of which will cost you money. You may also have to pay points (an up-front loan fee). As a result, it could take 10 years or more of interest and tax savings on car pur-chases to recover your initial cost. Another drawback — if you default on a car loan, all you lose is the car, but if you default on a home—equity loan, the lender could start foreclosure proceedings on your house.

For more information on using equity lines of credit, send a stamped, self-addressed envelope to "Home Equity," CUNA Inc., Public Relations Dept., Box 431, Madison, WI 53701.

Get A Good Deal On A Car Without All The Haggling

If you want to save time, money and your sanity when looking for a new car, then hire a car-buying service to find the car of your dreams and get you the best price for it. For a fee of around $135 to $395 — depending on the type of auto you desire — a car-buying service will find the make, model and style of car you want in the color you want with the options you want. Then they'll shop around at a minimum of five local dealerships and make offers. You get a package with all the submitted bids, then make your decision. Some companies even offer to deliver the car to your door so you never have to set foot in a dealership! For information on car-buying companies, call Car bargains at 1-800-475-7283 or Consumers Automotive at 1-703-613-5161.

Protect Yourself Against Roadside Trouble

Nothing can spoil your day faster than getting stranded on a busy freeway or deserted country road because of car troubles. These simple equipment checks and service tips can help keep you rolling, regardless of the road conditions:

* Check the water level regularly. Overheating is the biggest cause of roadside troubles.

* Check the tires at least once a month. Improperly inflated tires are more likely to blow out or lose their seal with the rim. Rotate the tires at least once every 5,000 miles.

* Check all hoses regularly. The rubber should be smooth and pliable, not hard or cracked.

* Test all belts to make sure they aren't worn, cracked or loose. A worn or loose belt can slip, reducing fan and alternator efficiency, which can lead to overheating or a weak battery. A cracked belt is ready to break. To check belt tightness, press down on it with your thumb at a point about midway between pulleys or sprockets. The belt should go down about half an inch — no more, no less.

* Check for leaks. Place a piece of wide white paper (you can probably get a roll-end free from your neighborhood butcher) under the engine and drive train of your car when you park for the night. Slide it out the next morning, and you'll know if there were leaks — and where they came from.

* Clean the battery terminals. Corrosion can prevent the starter from getting enough current to turn over the engine. Use steel wool, a wire brush or a knife blade to scrap the battery posts and cable clamps until you see a silver shine. Avoid getting the corrosive material on your skin as it is acid based and can sting or burn.

* Check shock absorbers. Push down on the fender as far as you can and then let go. If the car bounces more than once, the shocks are getting weak. Replace shocks every 35,000 to 40,000 miles — or sooner if they start to leak.

* Check wiper blades. They should bend back and forth and the rubber should be soft to the touch. Replace hard or cracked blades. If the blade is soft, but the edge Is glazed or hard, run some sandpaper over the edge to expose a more pliant surface.

* Check your spare tire once a month. A blowout's doubly frustrating if your spare is also flat.

* Check to make sure your jack is clean and working at least once a year and that your lug wrench is still in the trunk. A properly inflated spare does you no good if you can't lift the car or loosen the tire. Special safety check: Any time your car is up on a service station rack, check the exhaust system. A bad exhaust can leak carbon monoxide into the passenger compartment, causing the drive to get drowsy — or even pass out — leading to a crash.

Two Instant Tip-Offs To A Dishonest Auto Repair Shop

A dishonest repair shop has a million scams to rip you off — but not if you know these two simple tip-offs, which can warn you to take your business elsewhere:

1. When you bring your car in for a tune up, ask for a list of standard services that includes. If they have no established definition of a tune up and can't provide a list of services they will preform, it usually means the sky's the limit and you're likely to get charged for items that are far outside the realm of a normal tune up. A good rule of thumb is to review your owner's manual and decide what you want or need to have done on your car before you take it in for servicing.

2. If the repair shop wants to charge you to run a diagnostic on a newer car — look out! If your car is less than five years old or has less than 50,000 miles on the odometer, it's against EPA rules to charge for diagnostic testing involving emission repairs — and shops that attempt to do so probably aren't on the up and up. Go elsewhere for your auto service.

How To Get Free Car Repairs After The Warranty Expires

Keeping up with auto repair costs can keep you in the poor house. To beat the post-warranty blues, don't buy an expensive dealer service contract when you buy a car — instead, contact your insurance company and buy a contract from them for a fraction of the cost. Then your repair costs will be free after the factory warranty expires.

Be aware, too, that most major auto manufacturers offer free repairs on defective parts even after the warranty expires. These special "hidden warranty" policies are widely publicized, but automakers have found them essential in fending off potential lawsuits. If such a warranty involves a safety hazard, you should get notification of the available repairs in the mail. Major safety problems, involving a large general recall, are also usually publicized in the media.

Smaller, non-safety related problems likely won't be publicized, but you can still get free parts (and sometimes labor as well) if you simply ask the dealer to outline any other factory defects that may have surfaced on your model. Remember, though, the dealer won't tell you about these hidden defects, so be sure to ask about them.

Get A Car Phone Or Cellular Phone For Free

Earlier, we talked about using trade-out deals to get free cable television service — and the same thing can work when it comes to getting a free cellular telephone. Many cellular phone sales companies will give you a free phone in exchange for referrals or as a commission on any sales you generate for them. However, the easiest way to get a cellular phone — for your car or for personal use — is to strike a deal with the telephone company that provides cellular service in your area. If you can guarantee that you'll maintain a certain level of calling — generating perhaps $200 a month in billings — many cellular phone provides will actually give you a phone, just to lock in your business (which they wouldn't be getting if you didn't have a phone). You may have to put down a deposit as security on the phone until you demonstrate your calling volume, but it's still worth the effort since it could eventually save you as much as $500 on the cost of a phone.

Get A Better Car Deal At Government Auctions

Buying a car at government auctions can be a good deal, especially for people able to do their own repairs. Some of these vehicles have been abandoned, others are never-claimed towaways and others were impounded for evidence in connection with crimes. However, you need to take some steps to protect yourself. Here are six rules for buying a car at an auction:

1. Check the cars the day before the auction. Match the auction number on the windshield with the official list. Then check current prices for the same model and make in newspaper ads or the Blue Book.

2. You probably won't be able to turn on the motor, but note tire wear, open the doors and windows, write down the mileage and generally inspect the interior. Then check under the hood. Look at the block, wiring, hoses and fluid levels.

3. Get an official bidding number from the auctioneers. And bring cash. You must pay full price, plus tax — and all sales are final.

4. Don't let competing bids take you beyond your self-imposed price limit. Stick to half the Blue Book value — and one-third is even safer. This way, you'll be okay even if major repairs are needed.

5. Get a bill of sale in order to register the vehicle with your state motor vehicles department. If you're from another state, check to see what documents are required to register the car in your state.

6. Even if the car runs or you can start it with jumper cables, you won't be able to drive it away without license or insurance. You'll have to have it towed home — and within a day or two of the auction.

One additional warning: Don't fall for TV or newspaper ads or "900" hotlines offering to tell you when and where auctions are and how to buy. The fees these people charge are very high, and you don't need them. Government sales in your area are always well advertised in your local paper, and some agencies even have mailing lists to notify past customers of upcoming auctions.

Higher Deductibles Can Cut Your Insurance Costs

Whether you're insuring your car, your house or other personal property, lower deductibles can translate into big savings on insurance coverage — even if you have a claim. With cars, for example, you can cut 20 percent to 30 percent from your annual collision and comprehensive premium cost simply by raising your deductible from $250 to $500. To translate this into dollar terms, if you have one auto accident every seven years (the recent national average), you'll save over $1,000 in premiums for every $250 extra in deductibles you pay. And, if you raise your deductible to $1,000, your savings will be even greater.

A tip for filling the gap: Many people reject the potential cost savings of maintaining higher insurance deductibles because they're afraid they won't have the cash to cover them should an accident or other claim occur. However, there's a simple, no-cost solution to this dilemma, too. Just get a no-annual-fee credit card with a loan limit higher than your insurance deductible — and reserve it specifically for emergency use.

Skip The Specialty Auto Insurance Coverages

As much as 10 percent of the premium of many auto insurance policies is the result of "specialty" coverages for things such as emergency towing or the rental of a replacement car while yours is being repaired. Insurance salesmen push these costly coverages because they offer high profit margins for the company — but you don't really need them. If you have an auto club membership, you've already got towing cover-age, and the money you save on the premiums will more than offset the cost of renting a car should you need one. (Your no-fee credit card will also protect against not having cash for such a rental.)

One exception — if you have a high-priced cellular phone or a car stereo system worth more than $1,000, the premium for specialty theft coverage on these items is a good investment.

Don't Be Afraid To Ask For Insurance Discounts

Regardless of what you're insuring, be sure to ask for all possible discounts that might apply to you — otherwise, insurers sometimes won't tell you about them.

Here are some common auto insurance discounts:

1. Multi-car policy — Multiple vehicles lower processing and administrative costs for the company, which can then afford to pass some of the savings on to you. Savings can range from 10 percent to 25 percent of the normal cost on liability, collision and medical payments coverage.

2. Auto-homeowner combination — Companies offer a 5 to 15 percent discount as an incentive to get more of your business (it's cheaper than advertising).

3. Good driver — Offered at renewal to policyholders who maintain a good driving record (no tickets, no claims); usually 5 percent to 10 percent.

4. Defensive-driving course — Take a state-approved course to improve your driving skills and get 5 percent to 10 percent off most of your coverages. Discounts are mandated by law in around 30 U.S. states, though the discounts may be restricted to drivers 55 and older.

5. Mature driver — Usually starts at age 50, but may apply only to noncommuters. Reductions range from 5 percent to 15 percent on most coverages.

6. Student discounts — Many companies offer discounts on youthful—driver premiums if your teen-ager has successfully completed a driver—training program, maintains good grades in school (usually requires a B average or better) or is away at college (usually must be at least 100 miles from home). These discounts can range from 5 percent to 40 percent, meaning they represent substantial savings since the addition of a teen-age driver to your policy can often triple your normal liability and collision premiums.

7. Safety equipment — Air bags can earn you a 20 percent to 60 percent reduction in medical payments and personal injury coverage; automatic seatbelts get 10 percent to 30 percent off the same coverages. Anti-lock brakes are worth 5

percent to 10 percent off medical, liability and collision coverages.

8. Anti-theft devices — From 5 percent to 50 percent off comprehensive premiums, depending on the device.

And, here are some common discounts for homeowners insurance:

1. Smoke alarms and fire extinguishers — Because these can help head off trouble in its early stages, insurers will usually give you a discount of 5 percent to 15 percent.

2. Fire-retardant roofing or siding materials — Again, these help prevent a total loss of your property and are thus deserving of a 10 percent to 15 percent discount.

3. Multi-policy discounts — Insure your home and car, or your home and your life through the same company and get a better rate on all the policies involved.

The Most Valuable Home Improvements

Everyone wants their home to be as nice as possible, but not all home improvements are worth the cost it takes to make them. Here are 15 popular improvements, with an estimate of how much of the expense you can expect to recover when you sell (figures are based on return per $1,000 of cost):

1. Central air conditioning — $1,150.

2. Exterior landscaping, including a gazebo or other permanent improvements as well as flowers and shrubs — $1,120.

3. An interior facelift, including carpets, paint and wallpaper — $1,090.

4. Bathroom remodeling, including new toilet, tub (or shower tile), vanity, flooring and faucets — $950.

5. Fireplace — $940.

6. Addition of a two-car garage — $900.

7. Finishing the basement — $860.

8. Kitchen remodel, including new appliances — $860.

9. Exterior paint and trim — $820.

10. A new furnace — $810.

11. Addition of an outside deck — $750.

12. Attic conversion to add two rooms with closets and addition of double-hung windows — $550.

13. Room addition, including finishing, decorating and carpet — $530.

14. An in-ground swimming pool — $350.

15. Vinyl siding and/or awnings — $310.

Does Your House Need A Security System?

Alarm equipment and installation is expensive — and you may not even need a security system if you take some basic precautions. The insurance industry has just issued a free brochure that tells you how to "case" your home the same way a burglar would — and provides tips on how to make it harder for thieves to get in and out. For a copy, send a stamped, self-addressed, business-sized envelope to the Insurance Information Institute, Publication Service Center, 110 William St., New York, NY 10038.

Deduct Your Child's Allowance And Save On Taxes

If you have children, those children are going to want spending money — probably lots of it. Fortunately, there's a way you can pro-vide that spending money and get a tax deduction at the same time — simply give the child a job with your company. Children can earn up to $3,000 a year without having to pay income taxes, but you still get to deduct the payments as a legitimate business expense. In addition, if your company is not incorporated, wages paid to children are not subject to Social Security or unemployment taxes until they reach 18 years of age. Be sure to keep records of the actual work performed and make sure that the compensation rate is fairly set. While there is nothing illegal about this arrangement, the IRS may demand detailed explanations in the event you are audited. Note: Your children's earnings won't impact their dependent status on your tax return, so long as you continue to provide more than 50 percent of their total support.

Buy Direct And Save On Vacuums And Encyclopedias

At one time or another, almost everyone has answered their door to find a salesman for vacuum cleaners, encyclopedias or some other product. In most cases, the products offered by legitimate door-to-door salespeople are of good quality, which may tempt you to buy them — especially if you really need a new vacuum or are interested in getting a reference set for your child. However, we'd advise against it — simply because you can get the same products for much less by buying direct from the manufacturer or publisher. Items sold door to door always feature a mark-up —designed to cover the salesman's commission — of from 15 percent to 50 percent. Instead of buying at your door, take a piece of the sales literature that lists the name of the company that makes the product. Then check with "800 information" — i.e., dial 1-800-555-1212 — and see if the company has a toll-free number. If they do, call and ask for the sales department, requesting a price on the specific item you're interested in, as well as ordering instructions. If you can't find a toll-free number for the firm, sit down and write a letter explaining what you're interested in and asking for a price quote and an order form by return mail. Either way, you'll find you can get the same items offered door to door, but at a substantial savings.

"Dirty Little Tricks" Grocery Stores Use

Grocery stores want you to pay higher prices — but you can outsmart them once you know a few of their "dirty little tricks" — and how to avoid them. Here are some insider tips:

* Markets stock their high-priced, high-profit items at eye level, so bend down or look up for the cheaper, but comparable items.

* When produce is priced by the bunch, weigh it and find the heaviest bunch. Purchase that one and get the extra pounds free.

* Coupon or market specials often sell out quickly, and markets know this. They assume customers will buy the more expensive product if the cheaper one is out of stock. Don't fall for that. When the advertised merchandise is sold out, ask the store for a rain check. Then you can buy the item for the cheaper price when it is available again.

* Many supermarket scanners make mistakes. They often overcharge customers for one out of every ten items. So always check your receipt for the right amounts before you leave the market.

* Always buy staple items in volume when they are on sale. Watch for the sales on items such as detergents, paper products, soda, canned goods, toothpaste, etc., and buy them in bulk at the lower prices. Each time you manage to get $50 worth of goods at 25 percent off, you will in effect make a 33 percent return on the $37.50 you invest — better than most pros can do on investments in the stock market. There's only one possible catch: Make sure you'll actually use the items you buy in bulk. A bargain price is no bargain if it's on something that will later spoil or go to waste.

Help In Recognizing Credit-Card Fraud

What ever you do around the house or yard, it's likely you'll need to make use of your credit card from time to time. And, while the credit-card industry takes great pains to maintain its integrity and protect its customers, incidents of credit-card fraud and other abuses are still rampant. To help prevent yourself from becoming a victim, order a copy of a special industry brochure called "Credit-Card Safety," which explains the most common types of credit-card crime and offers tips on how to protect yourself against them. The cost is $2.50, and the booklet can be ordered by writing the National Association of Credit Card Merchants, 217 N. Seacrest Blvd., Box 400, Boynton Beach, FL 33425.

Get Satisfaction, Regardless Of What You Buy

Many people let themselves become victims of bad business practices or out-right rip-offs through carelessness, ignorance or fear of trying to fight the system. You should work extremely hard not to fall into such traps. Learn how to protect yourself in the marketplace — and how to get satisfaction if you do get a bad deal on a purchase. Here are some tips provided by consumer experts:

1. Shop wisely. Deal only with established, reputable businesses. Know what things are worth, and be suspicious of products or services that seem to be too much of a bargain. If you're dealing with a mechanic, contractor or other type of workman, your best protection is a recommendation from someone who has used the person and been satisfied. (The same applies to doctors, lawyers and other professionals.)

2. Buy with a credit card. If you're dealing with a store for the first time — or if you're buying by mail — your best protection is to use a credit card. That way, if you have a problem with the product or service, you can legally refuse to pay the bill when the merchant won't give you satisfaction. The credit-card company will then credit your account for the amount in question, and check on the matter with the merchant. If your complaint proves valid, the credit will stand. Note: To fully protect yourself in these cases, you must explain your problem in writing to the credit-card issuer. Simply calling won't do the job.

3. Use the right return method. Faulty small appliances and electronics equipment, defective clothing items, etc., should be returned to the store from which they were purchased — preferably to the person who made the sale or the supervisor of the appropriate department. Problems with large items or in-home services should be reported first by phone and then by mail, with supportive evidence such as photographs if possible.

4. Don't get angry. Regardless of how frustrated or upset you are — and how justified those feelings may be — don't let your anger show. Wait until you can discuss the problem calmly and rationally before you return to the store or sit down to make a call or write a letter. Ranting, raving, yelling or idle threats won't help your cause — and may damage your credibility.

5. Complain to the right person. As we've already noted, the best place to start is with the same person who sold you the product or service. Tell the person your name and ask his or hers. Then state your problem in general terms and ask for a resolution. If that person doesn't have the authority to resolve your problem, ask who does. If the person claims not to know, move on to his or her supervisor or ask to be referred to customer service. If you are dealing with a large company,

this latter step may be a waste of time. In many big companies, the customer service division is merely a bureaucracy of mid level managers whose job it is to defuse complaints rather than help the consumer. If you encounter an uncooperative person at this level, don't waste your time. Instead, get the name and/or phone number of the supervisor and immediately go to that person. And don't stop there — if necessary go all the way to the company president or chief executive officer.

6. Be specific about your problem. Explain the trouble with the product or service in precise terms. Speak slowly and clearly, whether in person or on the phone, and try to set up a congenial resolution to the problem.

7. Support your claims with good records. When you make your com plaint, be sure to take along your receipt and creditcard slip, a copy of the ad you responded to if appropriate, the warranty and serial number of the defective product and any other information (such as records of service calls) about the product or problem. As you progress through the complaint process, maintain a file of all information — including a record of dates and times of store visits, telephone calls and letters sent and received. Include the names and titles of all people you've spoken to at the company, as well as notes regarding the conversations. Companies perceive complainers who are organized as credible and determined to win, and are thus more likely to resolve their problems.

8. Suggest solutions. Don't just complain aimlessly. Know what you want before you make your first contact, whether it's repair of the product, a full replacement, a store credit or a repeat of work done. You may also want to ask for a discount on future purchases or services as compensation for the problems you've encountered. However, be realistic — don't ask for something to which you're not really entitled.

9. Get someone on your side. If you have no luck complaining on your own, don't give up — get reinforcements. Sometimes merely telling a merchant you plan to take your complaint to a consumer agency or regulatory body will produce satisfaction. Other times, you may have to actually seek help from one or more of these varied sources:

* The Better Business Bureau (BBB) can not only help you resolve complaints but also lets you check up on stores before doing business with them.

* The Consumer Affairs Office in many states will help you deal with retail and other consumer problems.

* The Department of Motor Vehicles (DMV) will hear complaints against car dealers and repair shops, and may revoke business licenses in some states.

* The Public Utilities Commission (PUC) can help with problems involving the phone company (including "900" number services), the gas company, the electric company and, in some areas, cable TV providers. Many cities and counties also have utility boards or commissions to hear complaints.

* The State Insurance Commission in most states licenses insurance companies and can help with problems in that area.

* Newspapers and TV stations in many cities have consumer reporters who will investigate your charges and do stories on rip-off artists. You'll find that, even though these advocates carry no legal weight, their ability to threaten public exposure of grievances can quickly lead to settlements.

* Your state Attorney General's office is the ultimate arbiter of consumer disputes. They can file both civil and criminal cases against merchants who abuse your rights under state consumer laws.

Keep Your Mailbox From Becoming Cluttered

As convenient and economical as shopping by mail can be, there comes a time when your mailbox becomes so packed with catalogs and other direct-mail offerings that you can't find your regular mail. If you've reached that point, there's a simple way to stop a big chunk of the advertising mailers you receive. Simply write the Direct Marketing Association, P.O. Box 9008, Farmingdale, NY 11735, and request that your name be removed from all lists (four times a year, DMA member companies check the requests and purge names from their mailing lists). For this to work, however, you must be sure to list your name exactly as it appears on catalog mailing labels — and, if it's listed more than one way, be sure to include all variations. There's no charge for this service.

If there are one or two catalogs you'd still like to receive, you'll have to contact each company individually and ask them to keep you on their list — but to stop renting or selling your name to other mailers. This can be done by calling the "800" number on the catalog, or by sending a written request to the company, enclosing the actual mailing label from the last catalog you received.

MONEY POWER

CHAPTER 9

Travel & Leisure Tips

How You Can Upgrade And Fly First Class --Free

Ever flown first class? They say that once you, do you never go back to coach. And what's better than flying first class? Flying first class free!

Actually, getting a free first class upgrade is fairly simple — and there are several ways you can do it. The most common approach starts with joining the "frequent flier" programs the airlines offer. Then, once you've made a few trips, you can get a free upgrade from coach to first class using your frequent flier miles. This option is available on most domestic flights, except for those that have a business class. Upgrades on international flights require more miles, but you can also get those once you've built up a substantial balance.

Another upgrade secret: Look in the newspaper or on TV for promotional upgrades offered by the airlines throughout the year. Airlines often offer such promotions during slow periods — subject, of course, to seat availability.

Surprisingly, there's one other way to get a free upgrade to first class — just ask? Most airline gate agents are extremely helpful, and will do everything possible to make you more comfortable. Thus, if you are especially tired or not feeling well, explain this nicely to the agent and ask if you might possibly move up to first class if there are seats available. You'll be amazed how often a helpful check-in agent or flight attendant will grant your request.

Free Information For Potential Travelers

Sometimes planning your trip can be almost as much fun as taking it — but only if you have enough information to work worth. Here are some booklets and travel guides you can get for the price of a postage stamp — or less:

* Canadian Tourist Information — From Canadian Consulate General, 1251 Avenue of the Americas, New York, NY 10020.

* Free Mexico Travel Kit — From Sanborns, P.O. Box 1210, McAllen, TX 78501.

* Ireland Travel Packer — Irish Tourist Board, 681 Market St., San Francisco, CA 94105.

* Free Books on Australia — Australian Information Bureau, 636 5th Ave., New York, NY 10020.

* Italian Travel Guides — Italian Government, Tourism Department, 630 5th Avenue, New York, NY 10111.

* Information on France — French Embassy, 972 Fifth Avenue, New York, NY 10021.

* Bermuda Travel Information — From Bermuda Department of Tourism, 630 5th Avenue, New York, NY 10021.

* "Kampgrounds of America" — A booklet listing 800 campsites around the United States; send a first-class stamp to KOA Handbook, Box 30558, Billings, MT 59114.

* Information on Tickets to TV Shows — From ABC, Guest Relations, 7 West 66th St., New York NY 10023, or ABC, 4151 Prospect Ave., Holly-wood, CA 90027.

* American Fishing Guide — From Sheldon's, Inc., Antigo, WI 54409; send 32 cents postage.

* "Traveling With Your Pet" — A free booklet from Alpo Pet Center, Box 4000, Allentown, PA 18001.

Get "Bumped" From A Flight On Purpose
And Get A Free Ticket

Air travel costs are always rising. How can you get a free flight? When flying, find popular flights that are most likely to be "over-booked." When this happens, airlines routinely ask if any passengers are willing to give up their seat — or be "bumped" — from the flight. Offer to do so. Of course, you will be able to take another flight with the ticket you are holding. In addition, however, the airline will give you a free fight voucher for your next trip. Sometimes they will also pay for a free hotel room and meals should there not be another flight out until the next day. And, if they are really desperate, they may even offer you a cash payment in addition to the ticket. So, if you have the time to spare and plan it right, you could have another night out of town for free, a couple of free meals, some extra cash to spend — and a free airline ticket for a future trip! What a deal!

Seven Words That Almost Always Get
A Free Hotel Room Upgrade

"I'd like the room I had before." These seven magic words almost always guarantee a free room upgrade in most quality hotels. You see, most major (and many smaller) hotel chains keep nicer rooms reserved for their frequent or returning patrons.

Doubletree, Marriott, Hilton and Sheraton also offer membership in "clubs" — like the frequent flier clubs of the airlines — for guests who stay more than twice a year at their hotels. Club membership is open to anyone, is generally free and can be obtained any time before your stay. Once you arrive, you simply inform the hotel that you are a preferred guest, or one who has stayed there before, and a free room upgrade is usually offered without question.

Two Travel Insurance Offers You Should Always Decline

One of the ways travel-related companies boost their profits is through the sale of overpriced insurance. Here are two such insurance offers you should always refuse:

1. Travel insurance sold at airports. Your chances of dying in a commercial airline accident are remote. However, if you still feel the need for travel insurance, but it directly from an insurance company — the coverage will be much less expensive. (Note: If you buy an airline ticket with most major credit cards, you automatically get from $25,000 to $100,000 in free travel life insurance.)

2. Optional collision-damage coverage on rental cars. Premiums for insurance on rental cars can add as much as $20 a day to the price of the rental. However, if you carry liability, collision and comprehensive coverage on your own car, you're most likely already covered — meaning you don't need rental-car insurance. To find out for sure, check your auto insurance policy, which will usually explain your rental coverage in a clause headed either "Coverage for the Use of Other Cars" or "Rental Car Deductible Expense Coverage." You may want to make a copy of this page of your policy and carry it with you when you travel, just so you can prove coverage if need be.

Even if your own auto policy doesn't cover you when you rent, you can still avoid paying for rental insurance by charging the car rental on a credit card that provides this service automatically for its customers. American Express, Diners Club, MasterCard and Visa all offer this benefit — in varying amounts from $3,000 up to $50,000 — to preferred cardholders. Check your card's statement of benefits and services to see if you are covered — and, if you are, use that card to pay for the rental.

Caution: If you do charge a rental on your credit card and then have an accident, most rental companies will immediately put a hold on your credit card account for the amount of the deductible — even if you refuse to sign the charge slip. If that happens, immediately notify the credit card company of the situation, explain that your insurer will be making a direct settlement with the rental company and advise them that you will be disputing the charge. In most cases, the credit-card issuer will remove the hold, though you may have to talk to a supervisor to get approval.

An Exception To The Rental Insurance Rule

Regardless of how good your personal auto insurance coverage is, it probably won't cover you when you are driving a car in a foreign country. As a result, you should always take the insurance coverage on overseas car rentals. This insurance will protect you against any peculiarities in local laws, perhaps even preventing your arrest following an accident — something your domestic policy can't do.

Besides, you probably need the extra insurance overseas — simply because your lack of familiarity with local traffic laws, driving habits and road conditions will increase your chances of having an accident.

Answers To Other Travel Insurance Questions

Insurance can also come into play in other travel situations — some-times involving coverage you don't even know you have. Here are a few examples:

* Your homeowner's policy will usually cover lost luggage, stolen purses or wallets and property taken in rental car or hotel room breakins. It may also cover unusual accidents — such as damage by vandals or motor vehicles — and property lost or damaged while moving.

* American Automobile Association (AAA) members have automatic hospital and death benefits if hurt in a car accident.

* Family health insurance policies — even those involving health maintenance organizations (HMOs) — nearly always include provisions for coverage while you are traveling. Check your policy or with your HMO representative or insurance agent.

* If you're traveling on business, it's likely your company's insurance policies provide extra coverage for you, including excess life insurance, medical coverage, liability in the event of an accident and, perhaps, even coverage against theft. Check with your benefits office if you want to know for sure.

An Insider's Way To Save On Car-Rental Charges

If you arrive in a city late in the day and are staying at a hotel near the airport, don't head straight for the car rental counter. Instead, take the free hotel shuttle or a cab to the hotel, spend the night and rent your car the next day (you can take the shuttle back to the airport). This will save you a day's rental charge.

Cashing In On Airfare Wars

Naturally, most air travelers seek the lowest possible fare — and assume their travel agents will come up with it. However, fares change rapidly — sometimes on a daily basis. In fact, a lower fare may be offered after your ticket is booked and before it's issued (a period which can be up to two weeks for vacationers).

Make sure your travel agent uses a computerized program that auto-matically hunts for lower fares up to the time the ticket is booked. Such search software generally discovers a lower rate for one out of four tickets. One software company claims the average savings is 28 percent of the ticket cost, anywhere from $68 to $130. These programs are increasingly available, both in big agencies like Thomas Cook and many small bureaus.

Yes, Virginia, There Are Ways To Travel For Less

Got a travel itch you think you can't afford to scratch? Well, think again. With a little planning and ingenuity, you can travel almost anywhere for nothing — or next to it. You just need to take advantage of the opportunities that for too long have been known only to a lucky few. Here are five freebie tickets to exotic adventure.

1. Air couriers — Since customs laws can require that someone accompany cargo, some firms will pay you to chaperone one of their shipments. Don't worry, you won't have to lug crates — only carry forms with cargo information, hand it over to a contact at your destination, then take off for your own vacation. Using this little—known method, you can usually bring in your trip for 50 percent to 70 percent off a normal fare. However, you probably won't be able to check baggage since most shipping companies use your baggage allowance as part of the shipment. For more information, order: "Air Courier Bargains — How to Travel World-Wide for Next to Nothing," by Kelly Monaghan ($14.95), by calling 1-800-356-9315.

2. Tour escort or planner — If you can round up enough family or friends for a vacation on the same plane, you can fly free depending on the airline. Some require a group of 10, others 15. This can also work for ski trips and cruises. To arrange this, you should make a deal with a good travel agent and get a percentage of the agency commissions (10 to 15 % of airfare, hotels and tours that you arrange).

Bonus: Once you're in the travel business, all your trip expenses are deductible.

3. RV delivery — How about delivering a brand-new recreational vehicle to its new owner somewhere in America or Canada — and getting a vacation en route. Naturally, you'll sleep for free right in the RV. And, as long as you reach your destination in a week or so, the route is up to you. With a little planning, you can even get back home again, picking up more money with a return vehicle. These jobs are ideal for college students on summer break or retired couples sharing the driving. In fact, some people regard this as a "retirement career." To qualify you need only be between 18 and 88 with a driver's license. No special training is required. RV's aren't trucks; they drive just like cars. And some companies prefer retirees because of their maturity. How much will it pay? Believe it or not, some people make up to $50,000 a year. Two companies that hire drivers are Transfer Drivers, Inc., 10920 East McKinley Hwy., Osceola, IN 46561; and TOMCO, P.O. Box 384, Forest City, IA 50436. For other dealers, check your local Yellow Pages under "Motor Homes" or "Recreational Vehicles."

4. Travel industry jobs — Airlines may be going through tough times, but there are opportunities in other travel-related businesses — car rental, hotels, cruise ships and many others. And, most of them carry fringe benefits of travel bargains. Cruise ships, by the way, are always looking for employees with experience in everything from food service to entertainment. Another way to enjoy free or deeply discounted travel is to start your own travel agency. This isn't as difficult as it may sound. Start-up help is available from the Independent Travel Agencies of America Assn. (ITAA) in Rochester, NY, 1-800-947-4822.

5. Small-Item Importer — This can be like an extended hobby, not nearly as complicated as you might think. You'll simply buy stuff overseas at outdoor bazaars and bring it back in empty suitcases. The U.S. charges no duty on artwork or handicrafts — and, once you're home, you can sell the items on consignment to local gift shops or sell them right out of your house. The profit will at least help pay for your trip — and your travel costs will be tax-deductible. For help, consult The Learning Annex's "Guide to Starting Your Own Import-Export Business" (Carol Publishing, $8.95).

Low -Cost Travel Options For Families

As most parents know, taking the kids on the road to a resort or theme park can bust any vacation budget. But the alternative isn't just staying at home and staring at the back yard. In fact, some of the most rewarding family trips can also be the least expensive. Here are some valuable suggestions:

1. Budget hotels — Don't hit the road without a list of motel or hotel chains that offer special rates to families.

2. Hostels — These are now open to families and offer hotel-style lodging at a fraction of the cost.

3. Fairs and festivals — With a little research, you can come up with a long list of regional or city celebrations that provide loads of family fun with no ticket price. They range from biggies like the New Orleans Mardi Gras to little-known annual events like the Strawberry Festival in Troy, Ohio, or the Garlic Festival in Gilroy, California.

4. Nature hikes — These educational outings are offered by most national, state and local parks.

5. Museum field trips.

6. City walking tours — Most cities offer them, either providing guides or brochures for self-guided discovery walks.

7. Washington, DC. — Not only America's capital — and perhaps its most beautiful and enjoyable city — but a bargain destination for families. All those wonderful monuments and museums are admission-free.

8. Factory tours — Check with chambers of commerce for factories that have guided tours, especially any that offer free samples of their products. Winery tours can be included in this category.

Special Savings For Kids

Family vacations can be fantastic — and fantastically expensive. All those extra tickets and snacks and fares and Happy Meals have forced many to rethink or cancel carefree summer plans. But, if you're married with children, you should know that more and more holiday destinations are offering kiddie discounts. Here's a short list:

1. Most major hotels don't charge for kids who share your room. Marriott Suites and Embassy Suites both offer adjoining rooms at a discount for kids.

2. Free teen-age programs are offered by other hotels and resorts. For instance, teens vacationing with parents at many Hyatt holiday destinations can take part in "Rock Hyatt," a program offering day and

evening entertainment for the 13-to-17 set. Amusements include videos, arcade games, rock music, sightseeing, sports and social activities.

3. Amtrak cuts coach fares in half for passengers between the ages of 2 and 15 — that is, if they bring an adult along. Passengers under 2 ride free.

4. Some airlines offer fare breaks for college students. Check with your travel agent — or American Express, which has a "Student Privileges Program" for student cardholders who pay for their tickets with the American Express card. Call Amex at 1-800-582-5823.

5. To drastically cut costs of family travel accommodations, consider hosteling. For about $25 a night you and your brood can bed down in a special "family" room

at any American Youth Hostel. AYH accommodations vary from mansions to lighthouses. To qualify, you need a one-year family membership for $35 — or get an introductory guest card for $3 per night, good for three nights' stay at any hostel. Members also receive discounts on Alamo or National rental cars. Call AYH at 1-202-783-6161 and ask for the Travel Center. Warning: Hostels usually don't accept kids younger than 5.

Savings Tip For Train Travelers

Most U.S. railway fares these days have a heavy front-end load, so be sure to book round-trip tickets. For example, a one-way Los Angeles—to-Las Vegas Amtrak ticket costs $65 (rates subject to change), but a round-trip ticket is only $68. Also be sure to ask for excursion fares, which are designed for short-stay, round-trip travelers. A regular New York-to-Philadelphia-and-back ticket on the Metroliner recently cost $92, while a round-trip excursion fare was just $47..

Deduct Atleast 50 Percent Of Your Vacation Costs

In spite of tighter IRS rules on travel and entertainment expenses, it's still possible to combine business and pleasure travel and get a deduction for 50 percent or more of your expenses. All expenses that would normally be incurred in the course of your business activity are fully deductible, even if you also spend some time on pleasurable activities. However, you may have to make some rate adjustments if your spouse goes along. For example, the spouse's airfare and meals won't be deductible, nor will any extra charge for a double room as opposed to a single. However, a spouse's presence won't affect car rental charges, cab fares or other expenses that you'd incur even if you were alone.

You can also fully deduct certain luxury items, such as hotel suites and a limo to and from the airport and the hotel if they are necessary for the business you're conducting (say, you need the suite for a business meeting or the limo because you are on a tight business schedule).

As mentioned earlier, many travel-related expenses can also be de-ducted if you get yourself involved in a travel-related business, even on a part-time basis.

Heading For The Gambling Meccas

Las Vegas is one of the most popular adult vacation destinations in America — and, with the opening of a number of new "theme" hotel/casinos, some of which even include amusement parks, it is fast becoming an equally popular family destination. Part of the reason is the value you can get for your food and hotel dollars. You can easily feed a family of four three "all-you-can-eat" meals a day for less than $20 each — and hotel rooms can be had for as little as $20 a night, even if you have four people in your party. Junkets and special airfare packages to Las Vegas (and Atlantic City and Reno) are also available from most major U.S. and Canadian cities, so travel expenses can be cut as well. The catch, of course, is that you're expected to gamble while you're there — and a couple of bad sessions at the tables can wipe out all your savings on your other expenses.

Regardless of how well you play a casino game, the house always has an edge — otherwise, it wouldn't be in business. However, with sensible wagering and money-management strategies, you can cut that house advantage to around 2 percent — or even less. Here's how:

* When you head for Las Vegas, Reno or Atlantic City, take along a gambling stake equal to about 40 times your usual minimum bet for each day of your stay. You can't play wisely or comfortably with anything less. Divide your stake into two parts, but not less than $100 per gambling session, which is the bare minimum for survival at a $5 table. (If you go mid-week, most casinos have $3 or even $ 2 tables, meaning you can live with a smaller stake.)

* When you're losing, don't borrow from the next session's stake. If you go through the entire $100, walk away from the table — and the casino. You can gamble another time. If you're losing, or barely holding your own, set a time limit for the session — say, 30 minutes — and quit if nothing happens in the period.

* If your budget is limited, work harder to preserve your stake. When you lose half, stop playing.

* If you're winning, secure your original stake as soon as you double your money. Take the chips off the table and put them in your pocket — and don't remove them until you're ready to cash out. You'll then be playing with the casino's money. Continue removing money each time you hit another plateau — say $50 in winnings — so that you always have only $100 to $150 on the table (assuming you started with $100). If your luck turns, quit when you've lost 50 percent of the money on the table.

* If you lose your gambling money, spend the rest of your trip by the pool or sightseeing, but don't go back to the tables. You can also improve your odds by checking out some of the following items, which provide tips on various gambling endeavors.

Finding Slot Machines Programmed To Make Money

The best places to gamble are Las Vegas and Reno, which offer 92 to 98 percent paybacks on their slot machines (Atlantic City has some unusual state gaming laws that mandate lower payouts). However, the best machines are found off the main "strip" in each city — with some offering 100 percent paybacks, or even more! And, the longer you play these generous machines, the better odds you have to win.

To find these "money machines," look for a row with lots of activity — a deserted area in a busy casino means players have left for an area where the payback is hotter. Casinos also sometimes boost the payout ratio on machines at the ends of long rows, or near the entrances to the casino. They want these machines to pay off loudly to attract pass-ers-by into the gaming area and toward the more remote machines, which usually don't pay as well.

Actually, all slot machines go through cycles — paying part of the time and going cold at others. During a pay cycle, the machine can pump out far more than you put in — and stay hot for a hundred pulls or more. Unfortunately, cold cycles can last just as long — and empty your wallet. Here are some tips on finding machines already in or about to enter a pay cycle:

* Watch before you play. If you see a $1 machine gulp $100 or more (even with a few small payouts) and the player walks away empty, give it a try. It may be time for its pay cycle. (For a 25-cent machine, look for a rapid loss of $20 to $30.)

* If you walk up to machine "blind," feel the coins after your first payoff. Warm coins have been sitting inside a while, indicating a pay cycle may be due. If coins are cool, try another machine.

* Ask a change clerk to recommend a hot slot. Casinos don't mind, and you are likely to get a good tip. If so, tip the clerk back — 10 percent of your winnings off that machine.

* Try machines near gaming tables. They sometimes pay better since they're used to lure wives watching their husbands play black jack or craps. Machines in less conspicuous spots have less advertising potential and, thus, pay fewer jackpots.

* Look for three-reel machines with a cherry in the middle. This can be a sign that a pay cycle is coming.

* Single-line dollar slots have the best odds. You get more jackpots with multiple-line slots, but the payoffs are smaller. Play the maximum number of coins on each wager.

* "Progressive" slots with jackpots growing to $1 million usually only pay off when the jackpot is within a programmed range. Unfortunately, it's not easy to discover just what that range is.

* New machines are programmed to pay generously for the first couple of days in order to draw more business later. If you see one being uncrated and set up, grab it.

Be A Consistent Blackjack Winner

More than any other casino game, blackjack (21) is a game of skill as well as chance. According to Doug D'Elia, a professional player from Las Vegas, knowing the right way to play can reduce the house advantage to as little as 1.2%, depending on the circumstances. Here are his guidelines:

* When the dealer has a 2, 3 or 4 up, hit if you have 12 or less, and stand with 13 or more.

* When the dealer has a 5 or 6 up, hit if you have 11 or less, and stand with 12 or more.

* When the dealer has a 7, 8, 9, 10 (face cards) or ace up, hit if you have 16 or less, and stand with 17 or more.

Splitting pairs to make two hands — and doubling your bet in the process — can also reduce the house advantage. Here are some basic rules:

* Never split 4's, 5's, 6's or 10's.

* Always split aces, even though most casinos allow you take only one additional card on each ace.

* Split 2's and 3's only when the dealer is showing a 2, 3, 4, 5, 6 or 7.

* Split 7's only when the dealer's up card is 4, 5, 6 or 7.

* Always split 8's unless the dealer has a 9, 10 or ace up.

* Always split 9's unless the dealer has a 10 or an ace up.

D'Elia notes, however, that playing well isn't enough to guarantee a win at the blackjack table. Even more important is good money management. Wins and losses tend to come in bunches, so you need to maximize your winnings when the deck is hot and minimize your losses when it's cold. A good way to do this is to use what is known as a "winning progression," increasing your bet steadily as long as you keep winning. You'll never be a winner betting the same amount each time (the house odds will eventually wear you down) or betting $10 one hand and $100 the next, based on hunches or whatever. And, a "losing progression" — where you double your bet each time you lose — is a sure road to ruin (you'll either run out of money or hit the table limit). Here are some suggested winning progressions for four popular starting bets:

$2 bettor: $2, $4, $4, $6, $10, $10, $15, $25, $40, $40, $60, $100.

$5 bettor: $5, $10, $10, $15, $25, $40, $40, $60, $100, $150, $150.

$10 bettor: $10, $20, $20, $30, $40, $60, $60, $100, $150, $200.

$25 bettor: $25, $50, $50, $75, $100, $150, $150, $250, $400.

Note that, in each case, you bet the same amount on the third hand in a progression. This returns your original bet, plus a one bet profit, and means you are playing on the house's money throughout the rest of a given progression. Remembering this can often keep you from getting nervous when you — a normal $2 bettor — suddenly hit a hot streak and wind up with a $100 wager on the table.

When you lose a hand, at whatever point you happen to be in a pro-gression, go back to your starting bet and keep betting that amount until you begin winning again. (Note: Ignore pushes, or ties, continuing with the same bet on the next hand.) This makes it very difficult for you to give back your winnings. For exam-ple, if a $10 bettor wins six hands in a row before losing, his profit on that run will be $120 (excluding any extra winnings due to splits, doubles or blackjacks — which, by the way, should not alter your progression). That means he will have to lose 12 times to give back what he won in six hands.

When to Quit: A good rule of thumb is to get up any time you lose 50 percent of the chips you have on the table — until you double your original stake. At that point, you should quit any time you lose an amount equal to 50 percent of your starting stake, regardless of how high your winnings rise. For example, if you sit down with $100 and run your total to $160, you should quit if you give back $80. However, if you run your total to $250, you should quit if you fall back to $200. That way, you guarantee you'll quit a winner.

Scoring Big With Football Bets

Football is the most popular sport among American betters — from those who plunk a dollar down in an office pool to those who wager thousands at the Nevada sports books. And, because of the massive publicity surrounding both the sport and the betting lines, it's also one of the most difficult in which to gain an edge.

The odds makers, both legal and illegal, monitor events constantly and regularly adjust the lines to reflect changes in personnel, weather conditions, etc. As a result, you may do better playing some of the specialty bets — such as the over/under (whether the total points scored will be over or under a certain level) — rather than trying to pick the winner versus the spread, simply because these bets aren't adjusted as quickly as the main line. If it's announced, for example, that a key player has been hurt in practice, the overall line will shift instantly. However, you may still have time to place a bet on the "unders" before the betting level is lowered to reflect the player's loss.

Winning At The Sweepstakes Games

Being picked as a sweepstakes winner is everybody's dream come true. And knowing a simple secret can increase your odds of winning. If the winning sweep-stakes ticket is chosen from a drum or barrel, fold your entry on the diagonal or into an accordion shape. This will give it more surface area so the judge will have a better grip. If it's a mail in sweepstakes, use an oversized envelope to give the judge's hand a bit more to grab on to.

Little-Known Sweepstakes With Excellent Odds

It's almost impossible to win one of the heavily advertised major sweepstakes. Most have minimum odds of 20 million to 1 or more, and you wind up competing with 30 million or 40 million other entrants for the prizes. However, that doesn't mean playing sweepstakes is a waste of time — you simple need to focus on smaller, lesser-known promotions with better odds. But, how do you find these sweepstakes?

Most dedicated entrants rely on one of several specialty newsletters or magazines, which report on both the major and the more obscure sweeps and contests being offered around the country. Here are some possibilities, with addresses to write for sample copies and subscription information:

* "Winning" Magazine, will send you a second place sweepstakes prize and a sample issue of the magazine for $1.95. Send your check to "Winning," P.O. Box 55550, Boulder, CO 80322-5550.

* The Contest Newsletter covers all sorts of contests and sweepstakes, with a special focus on smaller or specialized promotions. For a sample copy, write to P.O. Box 2676, Boulder, CO 80322.

* The American Contest Association Bulletin is a trade publication that lists current and scheduled contests and sweeps promotions being planned by members or affiliates. For a sample, write ACA, P.O. Box 356, Hamilton, OH 45012.

Tips For Bettering Your Sweepstakes Odds --
And Avoiding Scams

Here are five tips for improving your sweepstakes odds and spotting rip-off attempts by bogus sweeps promoters:

1. Print your entry clearly in dark ink. Avoid handwriting, calligraphy and peculiar shades of ink. Addresses written with felt-tip pens can smear in the rain.

2. If the entry is a post card, fill out the mailing address in black ink — which post office machines can read — then fill out your entry in red ink — which post office machines can't read. This will insure your post card gets delivered, not sent back to you by the post office.

3. Don't accept COD prizes. If you're being asked to pay on delivery for some "prize," it's a scam. Refuse it.

4. Beware of phony sweepstakes with entry fees. It's against the law for a sponsor to demand a fee to enter a sweeps contest. If you get one, notify your postal inspector.

5. Follow all sweepstakes instructions and rules. For instance, you may be disqualified if you don't copy the address exactly as shown.

Free Information For Hobby Enthusiasts

Hobbies play an important role in the lives of many people, filling uncounted hours of leisure time with pleasure. If you have a hobby, you already know the joys — but, if you're still looking for one that's just right for you, you may be interested in some additional information. Here are some booklets and brochures, most of them free, that could spark your interest in a new endeavor:

* "How to Collect Postage Stamps" — A free booklet from the Littleton Stamp Co., Littleton, NH 03561.

* "Stamp Collecting for Fun" — A free booklet from the U.S. Postal Service Advertising Director, 475 L'Enfant Plaza West S.W., Washington DC 20260.

* Introduction to Model Railroading — From Model Railroader Maga-zine, 1027 N. 7th St., Milwaukee, WI 53233; include 32 cents postage.

* "Author in Search of a Publisher" — A free 40-page guide for writers from Vantage Press, 516 W. 34th St., New York, NY 10001.

* "Sky and Telescope" Magazine — A free copy of this publication for astronomy buffs, from Sky Publishing, 49 Bay St. Road, Cambridge, MA 02138.

* "Chess Life and Review" — Sample copy of magazine from U.S.Chess Federation, 186 Rt. 9W, New Windsor, NY 12550.

* "The Art of Needlecraft" — A large folder of instructions from TNNA Fun Projects, 230 Fifth Avenue, New York, NY 10001; enclose 32 cents postage.

* "Official Softball Rules" — Send 32cents postage to Hillerich & Bradsby Promotions, Box 18177, Louisville, KY 40218.

* "Horseshoe Pitching Rules" — Free from Horseshoe Pitcher's Digest, 1307 Solfisburg Ave., Aurora, IL 60505.

* "Table Tennis Guide" — From U.S. Table Tennis Association, Box 815, Orange, CT 06477; include 32 cents postage.

Fine Dining At Half The Price

Eating out is also one of the most popular leisure time activities in America — but it can also be a costly one. Fortunately, it's not that hard to get discounts at many major restaurants. In fact, a lot of them advertise two-for-one specials in the local newspapers or tourist guides (you don't have to be a tourist to pick these up at any major hotel in the area), and many others participate in discount programs in conjunction with major credit-card issuers such as American Express and Visa.

However, for consistent value all across America (and in Canada too), its diffi-cult to beat the program of ENTERTAINMENT Inc., P.O. Box 1014, Trumbull, CT 06611. ENTERTAINMENT publishes value books — each containing hundreds of two-for-one and discount coupons — for more than 100 cities or areas around the country. Each book has a section on fine dining, featuring 30 to 40 of the city's best restaurants, as well as sections on casual dining, fast food outlets, movies, theaters, sporting events, tourist attractions, car rentals and hotel and resort savings in nearby areas.

In larger cities, such as Baltimore, Boston, Chicago, Detroit, Long Island, Los Angeles, north New Jersey, New York, Philadelphia, Seattle and Washington, there are even books for different areas of the city. The books are generally sold for $30 to $35 as part of fund-raising drives by local charitable and civic organizations. However, you can purchase up to four different books (only one per city) directly from the publisher for only $22, plus $3 shipping and handling. Just call 1-800-374-4464 and use your Visa or MasterCard to order.

Reasonable Reading

Reading is another popular leisure-time activity that has been hit by inflation. However, there are a number of methods you can use to reduce your book-buying costs:

* You can save 10% to 25% on new books — even best sellers — by shopping the discount stores rather than the retail shops. Among the best-known and most readily available are Crown, SuperCrown and Book-star. Check your local Yellow Pages for the location nearest you.

* Both discount and full-price stores generally have bargain racks, with books marked down 50 percent to 75 percent — or even more. Crown and SuperCrown also have special racks labeled "Books Near a Buck" and "Books Near $3" — prices that represent even larger savings. Admittedly, some of the books on these racks are real dogs, but lots of them aren't. In fact, if you wait a few months after the release date, you may even find works by some of the most popular authors on the bargain racks — simply because the store ordered too many copies.

* Book clubs and mail-order publishers generally offer rates 25 percent to 33 percent below retail prices on the newest releases. Be aware, however, that you usually have to pay shipping and handling charges, which could more than offset your savings on the price of the book.

* Many of the country's largest publishing houses not only supply re-tailers and book clubs, but also have their own catalogs, which usually offer discounted prices. The catalogs, which generally come out twice a year, also feature stock-reduction sales on books that were overprinted, offering savings of 60 percent or more.

* Wait for the paperback edition to come out.

* For really big savings, check the used book stores. More and more of these operations are popping up these days, and they usually feature a wide selection of fairly recent editions. Hardbacks normally go for about 25 % of the original retail price, with paperbacks selling for around a third of their original cost.

* Garage and yard sales can also be fertile ground for book shoppers, offering paperbacks for as little as a dime and hardbacks for a quarter.

NOTES

_____

_____

_____

_____

_____

_____

_____

_____

_____

_____

_____

_____

_____

_____

_____

_____

MONEY POWER

Appendix

Resources for Job Outlook Information

You can contact any of the following to obtain State and local job outlook and opportunities information (see chapter 7 section, titled "Where To Find High-Paying Jobs With Great Benefits":

— State Employment Security Agencies

Alabama— Labor Market Information, Department of Industrial Relations, 649 Monroe Street, Room 422, Montgomery, AL 36131; (205) 242-8855.

Alaska— Research & Analysis, Alaska Department of Labor, P.O. Box 25501, Juneau, AK 99802-5501; Phone: (907) 465-4500.

Arizona— Department of Economic Security, P.O. Box 6123, Site Code 733A, Phoenix, AZ 85005; Phone: (602) 542-3871.

Arkansas— Labor Market Information, Employment Security Division, P.O. Box 2981, Little Rock, AR 77203-2981; Phone: (501) 682-3198.

California— Labor Market Information Division, Employment Development Department, P.O. Box 942880, MIC 57, Sacramento, CA 94280-0001; Phone: (916) 427-4675.

Colorado— Labor Market Information, 393 South Harlan, 2nd Floor, Lakewood, CO 80226-3509; Phone: (916) 323-6544.

Connecticut— Research & Information, Employment Security Division, 200 Folly Brook Boulevard, Wethersfield, CT 06109; Phone: (203) 566-2120.

Delaware— Office of Occupational and Labor Market Information, Department of Labor, P.O. Box 9029, Newark, DE 19702-9029; Phone: (302) 368-6962.

District of Columbia— Division of Labor Market Information, Department of Employment Services, 500 C. Street NW, Room 201,

Washington, DC 20001; Phone: (202) 639-1642.
Florida— Bureau of Labor Market Information, Department of Labor
and Employment Security, 2112 Capitol Circle SE, Room 200,
Tallahassee, FL 32399-2151; Phone: (904) 488-1048.

Georgia— Labor Information System, Department of Labor, 148
International Blvd. NE, Atlanta, GA 30303; Phone: (404) 656-3177.

Hawaii— Research & Statistics Office, Department of Labor and
Industrial Relations, P.O. Box 3680, Honolulu, HI 96813; Phone:
(808) 548-7639.

Idaho— Research & Analysis, Department of Employment, 317 Main
St., Boise, ID 83735-0670; Phone: (208) 334-6169.

Illinois— Economic Information & Analysis, Department of
Employment Security, 401 South State Street, Room 215, Chicago,
IL 60605; Phone: (312) 793-2316.

Indiana— Labor Market Information, Indiana Workforce
Development, 10 North Senate Ave., Indianapolis, IN 46204; Phone;
(317) 232-7460.

Iowa— Audit & Analysis Department, Department of Employment
Services, 1000 East Grand Ave., Des Moines, IA 50319-0209; Phone:
(515) 281-8181.

Kansas— Labor Market Information Services, Department of Human
Resources, 401 SW. Topeka Blvd., Topeka, KS 66603-3182; Phone:
(913) 296-5058.

Kentucky— Research & Statistics Department, Department For
Employment Services, 275 East Main St., Frankfort, KY 40601;
Phone; (502) 564-7976.

Louisiana— Research & Statistics Section, Louisiana State Dept.
of Labor, P.O. Box 94094, Baton Rouge, LA 70804-4094; Phone:
(504) 342-3141.

Maine— Division of Economic Analysis & Research, Department of
Labor, Bureau of Employment Security, 20 Union St., Augusta, ME
04330; Phone: (207) 289-2271.

Maryland— Office of Labor Market Analysis and Information,
Economic and Employment Development, 1100 North Eutaw St., Room
601, Baltimore, MD 21201; Phone: (410) 333-5000.
Massachusetts— Department of Employment and Training, 19
Staniford St., 2nd Floor, Boston, MA 02114; Phone: (617) 727-6868.

Michigan— Financial & Management Services, Employment Security
Comm., 7310 Woodward Ave., Detroit, MI 48202. (313) 876-5904.

Minnesota— Research & Statistics Office, Department of Jobs and Training, 390 North Robert St., St. Paul, MN 55101; Phone: (612) 296-6546.

Mississippi— Labor Market Information Division, Employment Security Commission, P.O. Box 1699, Jackson, MS 39215-1699; Phone: (601) 961-7424.

Missouri— Research & Analysis, Division of Employment Security, P.O. Box 59, Jefferson City, MO 65109; Phone: (314) 751-3591.

Montana— Research & Analysis, Department of Labor and Industry, P.O. Box 1728, Helena, MT 59624-1728; Phone: (406) 444-2430.

Nebraska— Labor Market Information, Department of Labor, P.O. Box 94600, Lincoln, NE 68509-4600; Phone: (402) 471-9964.

Nevada— Employment Security Research, Employment Security Division, 500 East Third St., Carson City, NV 89713; Phone: (702) 687-4577.

New Hampshire— Economic Analysis and Reports, Department of Employment Security, 32 South Main St., Concord, NH 03301; Phone: (603) 228-4123.

New Jersey— Policy & Planning, Department of Labor, Labor and Industry Bldg., P.O. Box CN056, Trenton, NJ 08625-0056; Phone: (609) 292-2643.

New Mexico— Economic Research and Analysis Bureau, Employment Security Division, P.O. Box 1928, Albuquerque, NM 87103; Phone; (505) 841-8645.

New York— Division of Research and Statistics, New York State Dept. of Labor, State Campus, Bldg. 12, Room 400, Albany, NY 12240-0020; Phone: (518) 457-6181.

North Carolina— Labor Market Information Division, Employment Security Commission, P.O. Box 25903, Raleigh, NC 27611-5903; Phone: (919) 733-2936.

North Dakota— Research & Statistics, Job Service of North Dakota, P.O. Box 1537, Bismarck, ND 58502-1537; Phone: (701) 224-2868.

Ohio— Labor Market Information Division, Bureau of Employment Services, P.O. Box 1618, Columbus, OH 43215; Phone: (614) 752-9494.

Oklahoma— Research & Planning Div., Employment Security Div., 2401 North Lincoln #310, Oklahoma City, OK 73105. (405) 557-7116.

Oregon— Research & Statistics, Employment Division, Dept. of Human Resources, 875 Union Street NE., Room 207, Salem, OR 97311-9986; Phone: (503) 378-3220.

Pennsylvania— Research & Statistics Division, Department of Labor and Industry, 1213 Labor and Industry Building, Harrisburg, PA 17121; Phone: (717) 787-6466.

Rhode Island— Labor Market Information and Management Services, Department of Employment, 107 Friendship Street, Providence, RI 02903; Phone: (401) 277-3704.

South Carolina— Labor Market Information Division, Employment Security Commission, P.O. Box 995, Columbia, SC 29202-0995; Phone: (803) 737-2660.

South Dakota— Labor Market Information Division, Department of Labor, P.O. Box 4730, Aberdeen, SD 57402-4730; Phone: (605) 622-2314.

Tennessee— Research & Statistics Division, Department of Employment Security, 500 James Robertson Pkwy., 11th Floor, Nashville, TN 37245-1000; Phone: (615) 741-2284.

Texas— Economic Research and Analysis, Texas Employment Commission, 1117 Trinity Street, Room 208-T, Austin, TX 78788; Phone: (512) 463-2616.

Utah— Labor Market Information, Department of Employment Security, P.O. Box 11249, Salt Lake City, UT 84147-1249; Phone: (801) 536-7425.

Vermont— Policy and Public Information, Department of Employment and Training, P.O. Box 488, Montpelier, VT 05602; Phone: (802) 229-0311.

Virginia— Economic Information Service, Employment Commission, P.O. Box 1358, Richmond, VA 23211; Phone: (804) 786-7496.

Washington— Labor Market and Economic Analysis, Employment Security Department, 605 Woodview Drive, SSE, Lacey, WA 98503; Phone: (206) 438-4800.

West Virginia— Labor and Economic Research Section, West Virginia Bureau of Economic Security, 112 California Ave., Charleston, WV 25305-0112; Phone: (304) 348-2660.

Wisconsin— Bureau of Workforce Policy And Information, Department of Industry, Labor and Human Relations, P.O. Box 7944, Madison, WI 53707-7944; Phone: (608) 266-5843.

Wyoming— Research & Planning, Employment Security Commission, P.O. Box 2760, Casper, WY 82602-2760; Phone: (307) 265-6715.

— Bureau of Labor Statistics Regional Offices
Boston— 10th Floor, 1 Congress Street, Boston, MA 02114; Phone: (617) 565-2327.

Chicago— 9th Floor, Federal Office Building, 230 South Dearborn Street, Chicago, IL 60604; Phone:(312) 353-1880.

Dallas— Room 221, Federal Building, 525 Griffin Street, Dallas, TX 75202; Phone: (214) 767-6970.

Kansas City— 15th Floor, 911 Walnut Street, Kansas City, MO 64106: Phone: (816) 426-2481.

New York— Room 808, 201 Varick Stret, New York, NY 10014; Phone: (212) 337-2400.

Philadelphia— 3535 Market Street, P.O. Box 13309, Philadelphia, PA 19101; Phone: (215) 596-1154.
San Francisco— 71 Stevenson Street, P.O. Box 193766, San Francisco, CA 94119; Phone: (415) 744-6600.

— RTC Sales Center Offices

National Sales Center, 1133 21st Street NW, Washington, DC 20036; Phone: (202) 416-4200.

Western Region:

Central Western Consolidated Office, 2910 North 44th Street, Phoenix, AZ 85018; Phone: (602) 224-1100.

Coastal Consolidated Office, 1901 Newport Boulevard, Costa Mesa, CA 92627; Phone: (714) 631-8380.

Intermountain Consolidated Office, 1515 Arapahoe Street, Denver, CO 80202; Phone: (303) 556-6500.

Southwestern Region

Metroplex Consolidated Office, 300 North Ervay, Dallas, TX 75201; Phone: (214) 683-0036.

Gulf Coast Consolidated Office, 100O Memorial Drive, Houston, TX 78217; Phone: (713) 683-3476.

Southern Consolidated Office, 1777 NE Loop 410, San Antonio, TX 78217; Phone: (512) 820-8164.

Northern Consolidated Office, 4606 South Garnet, Tulsa, OK 74146; Phone: (918) 627-9000.

Central Region

Mid-central Consolidated Office, Board of Trade Building II, 4900 Main Street, Kansas City, MO 64112; Phone: (816) 531-2212.

Lake Central Consolidated Office, 2100 East Golf Road, Rolling Meadows, IL 60008; Phone: (708) 806-7750.

North Central Consolidated Office, 3400 Yankee Drive, Eagan, MN 55122; Phone: (612) 683-0036.

Eastern Region:

Bayou Consolidated Office, 10725 Perkins Road, Baton Rouge, LA 70810; Phone: (504) 769-8860.

Northeast Consolidated Office, East 6th Street, Red Hill, PA 18076; Phone: (215) 679-9515.

Southeast Consolidated Office, 220 East Madison Street, Tampa, FL 33602; Phone: (813) 870-5000.

Mid-Atlantic Consolidated Office, Building 400, Suite 900, Colony Square, Atlanta, GA 30361; Phone: (404) 881-4840.

YOU MAY CUT OUT THESE REPORTS AND PUT THEM IN A SEPARATE BINDER
FOR FUTURE REFERENCE

How To Get Free Cable TV

Imagine getting all cable TV channels including HBO, Showtime, the Movie Channel, and many others absolutely free! What's more, no illegal equipment is required. The strategies for getting free cable TV are easy and proven to be successful. All that's required is that you live in an area where cable is offered and that you be willing to make a special "working" arrangement with a local cable company. The special arrangement you make can save you $30 and more a month that you would ordinarily pay for cable TV.

Independent Contractor

One insider strategy for getting free cable TV involves working as an independent contractor for a local cable company. You will need to make an arrangement with a local cable company wherein you agree to contact potential subscribers in exchange for "free cable" service in your home. Obviously, this type of an arrangement will require some work on your part, but it shouldn't be too difficult or too taxing. Most local cable companies should jump at such an arrangement because of the opportunity to sign up many new subscribers from your contacts.

Obviously, you'll want to live up to your part of the arrangement and have your contacts with potential subscribers be as successful as possible. You can do that by having the cable company run a special promotion for new subscribers. You could suggest that the company offer "free installation" for a limited time only, or a "buy one month's cable service—get one free" deal. You also can have several hundred door hangers printed up with a brief description of the cable company's service along with its local office address and phone number. You can then canvass the area which the cable company serves, leaving the doorhangers on the front doors of potential customers who will in turn call the cable company if they are interested in subscribing.

Getting free cable service will more than make up for the minimal amount of time and effort you'll need to put in contacting potential subscribers. In fact, this type of an arrangement is beneficial to both parties involved. You get free cable TV and the cable company gets a contact source for bringing in new subscribers.

Trouble Shooter

Another strategy for getting free cable TV involves being a "trouble shooter" for a centralized cable company. This strategy can be used if you live in an area where a cable company serves seven or eight communities without having an office in each community. You can visit the company's main, centrally-located office and offer an arrangement wherein you will be the cable company's trouble shooter in your area in exchange for free cable. As a trouble shooter you would be responsible for making sure there are no problems with the service in your area. Your "duties" as a trouble shooter would include switching through all the channels offered, making sure there are no problems with reception, audio or other areas of service. If you noticed such problems, or if the cable goes out, you would contact the central office and file a report. The company would then send a qualified repairman to restore service to the area.

Both of the above strategies for getting free cable TV require some salesmanship on your part. You'll need to convince cable company officials that you can provide a valuable service in exchange for free cable. In short, you'll need to sell yourself. If you can do that, you should soon be enjoying all the cable channels absolutely free.

Drive A New Luxury Car Free

You don't have to be rich in order to drive a brand-new luxury car every year. In fact, there is a proven business strategy that, if used properly, will enable you to own and drive a new car at no cost whatsoever! The strategy works by taking advantage of legitimate, IRS-approved tax shelters. Hundreds of people are already using this strategy to drive their very own Corvettes, Jaguars, Mercedes, Cadillacs, and other luxury cars. The strategy will work for any kind of car, whether priced at $20,000 or $50,000, or higher.

In order for this plan to work, you will need initiative and a basic understanding of business financing and current tax laws. Actually, with a little research and study, the strategy is easy to use. It involves forming a small car-leasing corporation, making an agreement with a new car dealer, contacting several top professionals in your area, and then "selling" the plan to potential stockholders. If you are successful in each of these steps, you could be driving a new luxury car at no cost in just a matter of months.

Step 1: Incorporating

The first step in this strategy requires that you organize a small car-leasing corporation. Generally, the purpose of incorporating your car-leasing operation is to keep it separate from other businesses and to minimize federal income-tax liability. The leasing arrangement also makes the company's assets (new cars) available for corporate use.

The actual process of incorporating is fairly simple, and it can be done at little cost to you. In fact, in most states incorporation costs around $50 and can be as easy as completing a simple one- or two-page form. While the requirements vary great-ly from state to state, you may be able to contact your state government's division of corporations and request the necessary forms to incorporate. You also may want to consult with an attorney or an accountant to help guide you through the legal steps involved in incorporating.

In order to incorporate, you'll need to get approval from your state government. That's because corporations can exist only through the permission of individual state government. The first, and typically most important, step in getting state approval involves filing articles of incorporation with the secretary of your state. In most states, articles of incorporation must provide the following:

— The proposed name of the corporation. For example, the "XYZ Leasing Company".

— The address of the corporation. This should include the location of the corpo-ration's main office.

— The purpose of the corporation. Simply put, you'll need to explain why the cor-poration is being formed.

— The names and addresses of three or more incorporators.

— The number and type of shares of capital stock to be issued.

— The amount of capital required at the time of incorporation.

Depending upon the state, there also may be other requirements either before or after you file articles of incorporation. For example, many states require that you also file a statement naming the elected officers. You also may need to request permission to issue stock.

If you plan to incorporate by yourself, without consulting an attorney, you will need to learn everything you can about the incorporation laws and requirements of your state. Whatever the requirements, once they have been met, and the state grants corporate status, you are ready for the next step in the plan.

Step 2: Purchasing Cars For Your Company

Once your car-leasing business is incorporated, you'll need to locate a source for several cars. Visit a car dealer who offers the type of vehicle you want and make the following proposal: you will agree to purchase 10 new cars per year for the next five years. In return for making such a sizable purchase, the car dealer will supply you with a new car for yourself each year. Most car dealers will readily agree to such a proposal because they rarely have the opportunity to sell so many cars to one customer. You'll be offering to make a large volume purchase (50 new cars over a five-year period) in exchange for a discount (5 new cars for yourself over that same 5-year period). It's a good deal for both parties involved, and providing discounts for quantity purchases is a common business practice.

Step 3: Contacting Potential Stockholders

The next step is to locate prospective stockholders. The key here is to find several top professional people in your area who are in a high tax bracket. These should be people who, because of their tax status, are likely to be interested in a legitimate tax shelter. You can locate these professionals by consulting the Yellow Pages. Write down the names and addresses of attorneys, executives, doctors, dentists, and so on. Your final list should include 250 to 300 names of the top professionals in your area.

Another way to locate professionals who may be interested in your leasing plan is to use the services of a reputable mailing list broker. You can contact a local broker and obtain a list of top professionals for a small fee of $50 to $75 per 1000 names.

Once you've compiled a list of the top professionals in your area, you can begin contacting them in writing. It's important that your initial contact be in writing rather than through a phone call because of the image you can project. You are more likely to impress prospects and get responses by sending them a brief, businesslike introductory letter, composed on high-quality letterhead stationery, than by making a possibly intrusive phone call.

Your letter may be similar to the following example:

Dear Mr./Ms. Smith,

As a representative of XYZ Leasing Company, Inc., I would like to request an opportunity to speak with you and explain a special leasing plan. The plan would enable you to drive and own a brand new car every year at no cost.

The plan works by taking advantage of IRS-approved tax shelters. It is designed especially for top professionals such as yourself, who are in a 50% tax bracket. The plan will enable you to drive a new automobile for an entire year. At the end of that year, you will then take delivery on another new automobile. This
arrangement may be extended for as long as you like.

I would be happy to meet with you in person and explain this leasing plan in complete detail. Please call me at (000) 000-0000 to arrange a meeting. I look forward to meeting you.

Sincerely,
ABC

Remember, your letter should be on the highest quality stationery featuring your leasing corporation letterhead. The letters also should all be individually addressed and include an expensive business card. While presenting such a successful and professional image won't guarantee response to your proposal, it is likely to make a positive impression and increase your chances for success.

Step 4: Selling Your Plan

Once you begin receiving calls of interest in response to your letter, you can begin arranging appointments. You should be prepared to explain the plan completely and to answer any questions each prospect may have. Your meetings should be brief, cordial, and low key. An aggressive, hard-sell approach is likely to put off most prospects. The main thing is to provide your prospects with enough information to enable them to understand your proposal. The best way to do that is to be clear, concise and straightforward.

You should stress to each prospect that the plan works by taking advantage of legitimate tax shelters, the 50% tax bracket, and by maintaining a high resale value for each automobile. The leasing arrangement makes the corporation's assets (automobiles) available for corporate use. Each stockholders' monthly payment to the corporation (rental income) is tax deductible. Other possible tax deductions include interest paid on the loan(s) financing the acquisition of the automobiles, depreciation, insurance, and administrative costs. Be sure that each prospect understands that the success of the plan depends on each automobile retaining its resale value at 2/3 or more of original cost.

You also should provide each prospect with copies of the corporation's financial statement. The statement should provide a detailed breakdown of the leasing plan's financial arrangements. It should include the following:

— The amount of the loan being financed to acquire the assets (10 cars). For example, 10 cars at $25,000 each = $250,000.

— Each stockholder's (10) equity in the corporation. For example, 10 stockholders' equity of $5,000 each = $50,000.

— Balance to be financed. Using the above two examples, the balance to be financed would be $200,000 ($250,000 - $50,000 = $250,000).

— Payment on $200,000 for one year.

— Monthly Loan Payment (including interest).

The financial statement also should include each stockholder's monthly tax deductible payments (rental income) to the corporation, each stockholder's total tax deduction (figuring in the 50% tax bracket of each stockholder); and the resale value of each car at the end of one year.

If the cars retain a resale value of around 2/3 of their original cost and the tax deductions are taken advantage of, the net cost to each stockholder will be zero. The result is that each stockholder will be able to own and drive a brand new car every year as long as the leasing arrangement is in effect. And you will have a new car of your own every year at no cost as part of your original arrangement with the car dealer.

Keys To Success

The success of this strategy is contingent upon several factors. First of all, you'll need to be well prepared and willing to invest the time and effort required to organize your car-leasing corporation. That means learning all you can about the incorporation laws and requirements of your state and filing all the necessary forms correctly.

Locating successful professionals and "selling" your plan is another key to your ultimate success with this venture. Keep in mind that successful professionals are not likely to take you seriously unless you present yourself and your proposal in a professional and businesslike manner.

Finally, the overall success of this strategy depends on each car retaining a high resale value at the end of one year. You should encourage each prospect to study the plan and have their tax advisors or accountants go over the financial statement. Once your prospects understand that the plan is legitimate and that it can work for them you should be on your way to a successful venture. Success for you will be owning and driving a brand new luxury car absolutely free!

Get Anyone To Do What You Want

How often have you fantasized about being able to get other people—men or women—to do exactly what you want them to do? You may even know people who appear to possess such a power. Such people are typically highly successful in both their personal and professional lives. From your vantage point it may seem that these people wield magical or super-natural powers of mind control that are shrouded in secrecy.

The truth is, these special powers that some people possess are neither magical nor super-natural. Nor are they secret. They have actually mastered certain mind-control techniques similar to those used by modern clinical hypnotists. The techniques themselves are not new. In fact, the ancient Hindu Veda, written well over 3000 years ago, recounts the use of certain "hypnotic-like" techniques and procedures. And Hindu fakirs and Indian yogi have been using mind control techniques for thousands of years.

Many of today's most successful and influential people have studied, refined, and mastered this ancient mind control "secret" and have used it to help them accomplish their goals. Their mastery comes not through force or intimidation. Nor do they use the techniques to make people do things that would cause harm to anyone. Instead, through subtle suggestion and indirect commands, they can get people to do things that are of benefit to all parties involved.

The good news is that anyone can learn and use the techniques upon which this ancient method of mind control is based. In fact, anyone willing to make the effort required will find that the techniques are actually easy to learn and master. Indeed, if you have a basic understanding of human behavior, you've already mastered one of the most important elements required for getting other people to do what you want. What you need to learn is how to make other people feel relaxed and completely at ease around you. Once you have developed that skill, people will be open to your suggestions and subtle commands. The techniques required for developing this skill are described below and can be mastered by a dedicated "student" in less than an hour.

Establish Harmony

No one is likely to be open to your suggestions and indirect commands if you are disagreeable. In order to make other people feel at ease and comfortable, it is essential that you establish a friendly and open rapport with them. And the best way to do that is by finding areas of agreement. You should make every effort to avoid being critical or argumentative. Instead, try being as accommodating as possible. By building on the areas of agreement you find, you will establish an easy rapport or harmony and other people will be drawn to you.

Be A Mirror

If you emulate a person's posture, body language, and attitude, he/she is much more likely to feel relaxed around you. To master this technique you must be subtle. The other person must not be consciously aware of what you are doing but instead sense a feeling of unconditional acceptance on your part. The important thing is to make the other person feel that he/she is with a "kindred spirit". By adopting the other person's posture, body language and attitude, you can create such a feeling.

Create And Build Upon A Feeling Of Trust

One of the key elements in being able to get anyone to do what you want them to do is trust. If a person doesn't trust you, for whatever reason, your power of suggestion is likely to fall upon deaf ears. The first two techniques described above can help you create trust, but you also will need to convey sincerity. If other people feel that you are simply being polite or patronizing they are likely to question your motives. Instead of being a kindred spirit, you will be disingenuous. Instead of harmony you'll have mistrust. Your sincerity in your appreciation and acceptance of other people must be genuine in order to gain their trust and break down any resistance they might have to your suggestions and indirect commands.

Eliminate All Distractions

The key to using these subtle mind control techniques successfully is in making other people completely open to the power of your suggestions and commands. In order for the techniques to work, you must eliminate all distractions. When dealing "one-on-one" with another person, he/she must see and hear only you. In other words, you must gain the other person's undivided attention. By speaking in a clear, slow manner and by making direct eye contact you can actually direct another person's entire focus upon you. Once you have gained the other person's undivided attention, he/she is in effect, "under your power". Your suggestions and commands, even if unspoken, are likely to be met with little or no resistance.

The Power To Be Successful

Most of today's highly successful professionals— lawyers, business executives, politicians— have gained their measure of success in part by using the techniques described in this report. Many of these people are considered "mesmerizing" by those amazed at their powers of persuasion. The secret of their power is anability to control other people through subtle suggestions and indirect commands, rather than by being domineering or forceful. These people have learned to use ancient techniques based on an understanding of basic human behavior. These techniques work not by direct and blatant attempts to control other people, but rather by the power of subtle suggestion and indirect commands. If you are willing to take the time to master the techniques described in this report you too can "wield" this power and get anyone to do exactly what you want them to do.

How To Make $75,000 A Year From Your Hobby

Wouldn't it be great if you could quit your "9-to-5" job, be your own boss, and make much more money? Many people have done just that by turning their hobbies into highly successful home-based businesses. In fact, men and women across the country are converting their love of crafts, artwork, photography, reading, sports, cars, fishing, animals, and other special interests into money-making part- and full-time businesses. If you have an interesting hobby, such as photography, artwork, crafting, etc., you too can be among the home-based entrepreneurs earning $75,000 or more a year.

There are several advantages to turning your special interest or hobby into a full-time home-based business. Consider the following: You'll be getting paid to do what you most enjoy; you'll be your own boss; your work hours will be flexible; you can take advantage of IRS-approved tax deductions. However, before you hand your boss a letter of resignation, there are several other things you should consider.

First of all, does your hobby or special interest offer anything of value to other people— something they would pay to receive? To answer that question, it might be helpful to look at what types of hobbies and interests other people have turned into money-making businesses. Here are some of the most successful hobby-turned-business opportunities:

— Creating arts and crafts. Your hobby could generate a good income if you produce anything. Hand-crafted items that are skillfully produced, are in constant demand.

— Selling antiques or collectibles. Many people have turned a love of antiques and/or collectibles into highly profitable full-time businesses.

— Appraising collections. If you are an experienced and knowledgeable collector, you may be able to offer your knowledge and services as an appraiser of art, stamps, coins, etc.

— Teaching special skills. You can give lessons and teach paying customers your special skills. For example, people who enjoy and are skilled at dance and exercise can offer classes to teach others those skills.

— Breeding, training, and grooming dogs. Animal lovers can earn a good income by providing such services to pet owners.

While the above hobbies and special interests offer some of the best full-time business opportunities, virtually any hobby has money-making potential. The question is, are there enough paying customers in your market area to support your hobby as a full-time business? To answer that question you'll need to analyze the market and calculate the costs involved in operating your own business. Once you have thoroughly investigated the possibilities and developed a plan of action, you can move forward. However, it's best to hold onto your "day job" and start out on a part-time basis. That will give you time and an opportunity to find out whether or not your hobby can be converted into a profitable home-based business.

Step-By-Step Plan For Success

There are several ways you can go about generating financially rewarding results from your hobby. The approach you take depends on your hobby or interest and the products or services you offer. Here are several easy-to-follow steps that could help you turn your hobby into a high-profit home-based business;

— Sell your products to friends, neighbors and colleagues.

Regardless of the type of product you produce— stuffed animals, dolls, ceramics, artwork, quilts, knitted/crocheted items, wreaths/dried flower arrangements, baskets, and so on—you'll need to test the waters to find out if there is a market for your work. Rather than forcing your products on the people you know, you can hold a garage sale and invite them to attend. Have samples of your work on display at this sale to see if they generate any sales.

— Offer your products and services to a larger market.

Once you find out whether or not you can make a profit with your products, you can begin to expand your base of customers. The best way to do that is through advertising. While word-of-mouth advertising will bring in many new customers, you'll need to reach as many potential buyers as possible. You can run a classified ad in area newspapers and/or have several hundred flyers printed at relatively little cost. You also can take advantage of free advertising space on public bulletin boards. The important thing is to let as many potential customers as possible know what you are offering.

— Sell at craft fairs, flea markets and swap meets.

Craft fairs are often held at shopping centers and in malls. Several times a year, craftspeople can rent space and sell their products from booths which are located in high-traffic areas. These events are typically well-advertised and attract large crowds interested in hand-crafted items. Craft fairs provide an excellent opportunity to sell your products at substantial profits.

Flea markets and swap meets tend to offer a variety of items that attract collectors, dealers, tourists, and bargain-hunters who are looking for well-made, handmade items. Just about any product can be sold at flea markets and swap meets. Hobbyists have sold everything from homemade cookies and other baked goods to wood art at these events. Flea markets and swap meets can be held both indoors and outdoors and are excellent opportunities to sell your merchandise. You can usually rent space at these events for less than $20 a day and your profits can more than make up for expense. In fact, many flea market vendors earn over $75,000 selling their merchandise only six to eight months of the year. If your hobby produces anything that can be sold at flea markets and swap meets, you are well-advised to take advantage of these money-making opportunities.

A good source of information about flea markets and swap meets is the American Vendors Association (AVA). The AVA publishes information guides for vendors and exhibitors. Its annual Special Events Directory features a listing of over

16,000 special events taking place throughout the U.S. and Canada each year. For information, write to American Vendors Association, P.O. Box 702 Dept. FP, Palmyra, NJ O8065. Or call, (800) AVA-9909.

— Sell On Consignment

Many hobbyists generate income by selling their work on consignment. Selling by consignment involves making arrangements with store owners to leave your work on display in their stores. You get paid only after the stores sell your products. You set the price you want to make for your work. Store owners then mark up your work anywhere from 75% to 100% to insure that they also make a profit. Consignment selling is fairly common among smaller stores which have low profit margins. It's a good way to get your work displayed before a broad range of potential customers.

— Prepare and distribute a monthly newsletter

If you have a hobby that is shared by thousands of other people, you also have an opportunity to generate a good income. People who share your interests are likely to pay for timely news and information which caters to those interests. With a minimal initial investment you can prepare and distribute a monthly newsletter to subscribers across the country. In time, such a newsletter could generate substantial profits.

Pricing your work

The amount you get paid for your work depends on several factors. First of all, you'll need to develop a budget. Figure in the cost of your supplies and materials. Be sure to figure in the cost of electricity if you use power tools and shipping charges if you order your supplies by mail. As a rule, you should charge at least four times your cost. You also may want to do some market research and find out the average price of products similar to yours. The important thing is to set a price that ensures you of a nice profit for your work while not being out of the range of most potential customers.

Another factor to consider in pricing your work is the time and labor involved. You'll need to have a good idea of how many items you can prepare in a day, and how much time and labor is involved. Some hobbyists set their prices based on how much they want to get paid per hour.

Tax Deductions

As a hobbyist, your tax deductions are basically limited to whatever income the activity generates. If you operate your hobby as a business, you can deduct your business expenses, even if they are greater than your business income. You can take advantage of business-related tax deductions only if the IRS is convinced that you are operating your business with the intention of making a profit. It is important to remember that if your hobby activity is not carried on for profit, your deductions will be limited and business losses will not be allowed to offset other income.

Generally, The IRS presumes that an activity is being carried on for profit rather than as a hobby if it produces a profit in three out of five consecutive years (two out of the past seven years for breeding, showing, training, or racing horses). If you are just starting your hobby as a business and you can not yet show three years of profit, you can file IRS Form 5213 and postpone any IRS determination for five years. In that event, the IRS is not likely to question whether or not your activity is being engaged in for profit. Nor will it challenge any deductions you might claim relating to that activity until the five years are up.

If you decide not to postpone a determination on your business status, you'll need to prove that you are indeed trying to profit from your activity. Here are several insider tips that can help you provide such proof:

— Register your business name with your local county clerk. This involves filing a "doing business as" statement.

— Document your business plan, listing your business goals and strategies.

— Set up a business bank account.

— Use professional business cards and stationery.

— Get a listing for your company in the Yellow Pages.

— Advertise in local newspapers, and through direct mail ads to potential customers.

— Keep accurate books and records.

By operating your hobby as a business you could save hundreds, even thousands of dollars in taxes every year. Generous tax deductions are available if you can show the IRS that you are trying to profit from a legitimate business venture.

You can get free publications on all aspects of the tax code by calling the IRS at (800) 829-3667. Available publications of interest to home-based business operators include the following:

__ "Tax Guide For Small Business"... Publication # 334

— "Self-Employment Tax"... # 533

— "Business Expenses"... # 535

— "Taxpayers Starting A Business"... # 583

— "Business Use Of Your Home"... # 587

Your hobby can be your key to personal fulfillment and financial success. By following the steps outlined in this report, many former hobbyists have turned their special interests and talents into profitable businesses. You can too.

The income you generate from your hobby can range anywhere from $10,000 to $75,000 or more a year, depending on the time and effort you are willing to put into the venture. If you apply yourself and take advantage of your special talents you could soon quit your job, be your own boss, and earn a good living doing something you enjoy.

Become A Real Estate Millionaire

Many of today's wealthiest real estate investors started out with little or no money or credit. Using insider techniques, these people were able to purchase homes, apartments, shopping centers, office buildings, and other properties with little or no money down. They then rented or re-sold these properties for huge profits. Many of these entrepreneurs became real estate millionaires in just a few years by buying for next-to-nothing and then renting and/or selling their properties.

The insider techniques used to turn real estate investments into high-profit money-making ventures will work for anyone, even if there's little or no capital available to invest. The secrets to success involve knowing how to find valuable property that you can buy when you have a relatively limited amount of money to invest, how to choose the right type of property to invest in, and how to finance such transactions.

This report provides information on some of the most successful insider techniques for turning real estate into money-making investments. The techniques include buying "options" on properties when you have limited funds for investment, buying foreclosed or distressed property, and taking advantage of government financing. Used properly, these techniques could help you acquire virtually any type of property which you can then rent or re-sell for huge profits. If done wisely, you could become a real estate millionaire in just a few years.

Options To Buy

This technique is easy to use and is an invaluable tool when you have little money to invest. It allows you to "tie up" profitable real estate opportunities using only a small deposit. In the meantime, you can develop, renovate or repair the property and then re-sell it at a substantial profit. The only money you invest is the small deposit required to purchase the option. It is entirely possible that you can turn an initial option fee of a few hundred dollars into a profit of $50,000 to $100,000 and more.

Generally, an option is the right or reservation to buy something at a predetermined price within a set time period. To acquire that right (option) you have to pay a small fee. Once you've paid an option fee (also known as an option consideration) the seller is obligated to sell the property only to you during the option period. You then locate a buyer who is willing to pay more than the option price you negotiated, thus ensuring you a profit. As soon as you locate such a buyer, you exercise your option, buy the property, then resell immediately.

Let's say you know someone who has a ten-acre piece of land for sale at $5,000 an acre ($50,000). You're confident that, if properly developed, the property is worth twice that much. In order to buy the property you will have to come up with $5,000 to $10,000 for a down payment. You'll also need to find the necessary financing, pay closing costs, make monthly payments, and so on.

Considering the amount of money you'll need to buy outright, you decide instead to purchase an option on the property for a few hundred dollars. You pay the option fee, agreeing to pay $50,000 for the property before the predetermined option period of one year runs out. You now have 12 months to find a buyer who is willing to pay your price of $75,000 to $100,000 for the property. If you've done your homework, you should be able to find a buyer who is interested in developing the land into a mobile home park, housing development, apartment building site, etc. As soon as you find such a buyer, you arrange for the necessary financing, exercise your option, buy the property, and then re-sell immediately for a profit of $25,000 to $50,000.

When looking for bargain real estate to invest in using the above technique, you might first consider concentrating on properties which have problems that are easy and inexpensive to fix. Problems such as leaky roofs, scuffed or peeling paint, or some other repair needed, often lead owners to sell at substantial discounts from their property's real value. However, before you attempt to persuade an owner to sell you an option to buy such property, you should be certain that you can resolve the problem(s) inexpensively. You also should determine how much rental income or resale value you can collect once the property is in good shape.

Another way to find valuable property which you may be able to purchase using the option technique is to look for a building that sits on a lot which has several acres of land that could be developed. You might be able to rent the building as well as sell part of the land for substantial profits.

The above is just one example of how options can be used as a technique to generate huge profits. There are several other ways this technique can be used, all of which would require little investment on your part. The key to success with this technique is in being certain of the property's profit potential. You should know whether or not you can find a buyer and resell the property for a worthwhile profit before you exercise an option to buy. Or if you plan to rent, you should be certain you can find tenants who are willing to pay the amount of rent to ensure you of a solid rental income.

Investing In Foreclosed Property

Many fortunes have been made in real estate by purchasing foreclosed or distressed property. Such property can often be purchased at discount prices and used as investment opportunities to resell and to generate rental income. As investment opportunities, foreclosed properties often can be purchased at far below market value and resold for handsome profits. Purchased as rental properties, foreclosures not only generate rental income, but they can provide substantial tax benefits as well.

Distressed properties are available nationwide and can be obtained through foreclosure auctions or through the Resolution Trust Corporation (RTC). However, potential buyers should be aware that such property is typically sold in "as is" condition. That means you should investigate and inspect each property thoroughly before bidding. Some foreclosed property is in such poor condition that you would need to invest thousands of dollars in repair and renovation. While you can find many exceptional bargains in foreclosures, you'll need to be careful of what you buy.

Obviously, in order to be successful with this insider technique, you'll have to know where to find foreclosed properties. There are actually several good sources of foreclosure information. Here are nine sources most commonly used by successful real estate investors:

1) Resolution Trust Corporation

The savings and loan scandals of the 1980s led to the creation of this government agency. The RTC was established to dispose of the assets of failed S & L's. Those assets, totaling more than $180 billion, include thousands of residential and commercial properties. Specifically, the properties include single- and multi-family houses, townhouses, condominiums, mobile homes, and office and apartment buildings.

To liquidate S & L assets, the RTC has established Sales Centers at national, regional and local levels (See the Appendix in "Money Power" for a listing of these Sales Centers). All property is sold in "as is" condition. Smart investors will examine these properties thoroughly before making a bid.

To order a list of foreclosed properties in your area, call the RTC at (800) 782-3006. The list is priced at $5.00.

2) Bank REOs

Even though they don't advertise it, many solvent banks also have foreclosed properties. These foreclosures are known as Real Estate Owned (REO) and are disposed of at each bank's discretion. The best way to obtain information about REOs is to contact each bank in your area. You can write to the bank's foreclosure or REO department and make an appointment for a personal meeting. You should explain to the person in charge of that department what type of property you're interested in and ask him/her to contact you if such a listing occurs. You also may be able to get some banks to put you on their mailing lists. In some areas REOs also may appear occasionally in real estate classified ads. In any event, when looking for REOs, persistence is the key. You may eventually find several foreclosure bargains that you can resell for sizable profits.

3) Thrifts In Conservatorship

Another way to find banks that are likely to have foreclosed property for sale is to contact the RTC at (202) 842-2970 to obtain information about thrifts in conservatorship. These are banks which have been taken over by the RTC, but are not yet in receivership. A conservator has been placed in each of these banks to oversee their operations and to sell their REOs. Most thrifts in conservatorship are eager to sell their foreclosures and, as such, provide a good source for some potential bargains.

4) Department Of Housing And Urban Development (HUD)

HUD foreclosures may include single-family homes, condominiums, townhomes or 2-4 unit properties located in communities nationwide. These properties are put up for sale when borrowers default on mortgages which have been insured by the Federal Housing Administration (FHA). In many cases, sales prices for HUD foreclosures will be less than market value. Some investors have even purchased HUD properties for as little as $100 down. Like the foreclosures sold by the FTC, HUD foreclosed properties also are sold in "as-is" condition. It is the buyer's responsibility to take care of repairs and maintenance and to make sure the property is up to local codes. Potential buyers should be sure of the condition of the property before submitting any bids.

You can contact your local HUD office to get a list of HUD foreclosed properties.

5) Veterans Administration

Many real estate investors take advantage of the favorable terms offered by the VA on property that it has repossessed. The VA "repos" are properties which have been foreclosed on after the armed forces personnel who bought them failed to make their payments. You can get a listing of VA foreclosures in your area by contacting your state Veterans Administration Office. Local real estate brokers also may have information about VA foreclosures.

6) Internal Revenue Service

As a means of collecting on unpaid federal taxes, the IRS can seize and "sell off" a delinquent taxpayer's property. Virtually any type of property, including real estate, can be found at IRS levied property sales. Such sales are conducted either as public auctions or by sealed bid. You can contact your IRS district field office to get your name on a mailing list to receive information about upcoming sales in your area. Be sure to specify that you are interested in real estate.

7) Tax Sales

When property taxes go unpaid, local tax collectors can seize delinquent taxpayers' property. The property then can be sold at public auction to recover the unpaid taxes. Public notice of impending delinquent property tax sales are published in local newspapers. You also can get a list of tax sale properties as well as sale dates and locations by contacting your county assessor's office.

8) Federal National Mortgage Association (Fannie Mae)

Fannie Mae also maintains a listing of foreclosed properties it offers for sale. To order the list, call (800) 553-4636

9) Foreclosure Research of America

This company publishes material on how to buy foreclosed properties at bargain prices, fix them up and resell them at a profit. You can send for a free brochure "The Pre-Foreclosure Hot List" by writing to Foreclosure Research of America, P.O. Box 10236, Rockville, MD 20849.

Government Financing

The federal government sponsors a number of little-known programs that can help people buy and repair real estate. Favorable loan programs with low down payments or no down payments required, low interest rates, and assumable mortgages are available to qualified buyers. Many of these loan programs can make it possible for you to start from scratch and invest in homes and apartment buildings to fix up for rental income or to resell. There also are loan programs designed for people who have credit problems and who may not qualify for conventional loans. If you are investing in an apartment house, a government program may even help you find tenants and subsidize your rents.

The Federal Housing Administration (FHA), which is an agency of HUD, offers dozens of low-cost loan programs for buying or renovating houses, mobile homes, apartment buildings, and other properties. FHA financing typically requires a 3%-5% down payment rather than the usual 10% to 20%. The Veterans Administration (VA) and the Farmers Home Administration (FmHA) also sponsor low cost loan programs to help individuals to buy and own real estate or to rehabilitate run-down property.

Your real estate agent or local lender may be able to give you information about these loan programs. You also can find information, including qualifications and who to contact, in government publications such as "The Catalog of Federal Domestic Assistance" which is available in many local libraries.

If you qualify, government assistance can enable you to buy property with little or no capital to invest. You can fix up this property for rental income or to resell at substantial profits.

By using the insider techniques described in this report, it is possible for virtually anyone to make money investing in real estate. How much money you can make depends on how much time and effort you put into understanding, locating and managing investment real estate. While you won't become a real estate millionaire overnight, you can, using the techniques described in this report, take great strides in obtaining financial security for you and your family. Borrow $50,000 In Just 72 Hours

How To Borrow Large Sums of Money

Raising large amounts of money in a hurry may not be as difficult as you might think. Regardless of your present financial situation— little or no credit, or even bad credit— there are ways that you can borrow the money you need in as little as 72 hours. What's more, you can borrow this money as unsecured loans. That means no collateral, no co-signers, and no credit check. You can have "cash in hand" on your signature alone. And you can use the cash to pay off pressing debts, make new purchases, save, or invest. In some cases, you can even take up to 40 years to pay the money back!

The creative financing techniques described in this report have been used successfully by hundreds of people to borrow $50,000 and more. Depending on your financial need and credit status you can use these techniques to get "quick cash" through credit card loans and bank overdraft protection. If you have credit problems, there are government loan programs designed to help you get the money you need. With careful planning and preparation, these techniques could enable you to raise enough cash to take care of all your financial needs.

Credit Card Loans

Credit card issuers offer "open-end" or "revolving" credit which can provide card holders with a predetermined line of borrowing power. As a card holder you can use this borrowing power either to make purchases or to obtain a cash advance. In either case, you can pay back the money as quickly or as slowly as you want. You'll receive a bill each month which specifies the balance due, the interest being charged, and the minimum payment. In order to stay current, you'll need to remit at least the minimum payment each month.

Ordinarily the best way to use a credit card is to pay off the balance due each month. You not only avoid paying interest but you also avoid the risk of running up unmanageable credit-card debt. As a rule, limiting the number and dollar amount of your cash advances is also advisable. There are, however, exceptions to every rule. If you've carefully thought out how you plan to pay back the money, credit card loans can be an excellent source of $500 to $50,000 and more in quick cash.

Most everyone has credit cards. Millions of Americans carry as many as 20 to 30 cards. The credit limits on those cards range anywhere from $500 for first-time card-holders to $5000 or more for people with established creditworthiness. Such cards can be used as sources for unsecured loans to raise the cash you need. For example, suppose you have 10 credit cards with pre-approved credit limits averaging $5,000 each. That means you have up to $50,000 in unsecured credit you can tap whenever you need quick cash. By taking advantage of such pre-approved cash advances, you can have the cash you need in 72 hours or less.

So, how can you get 10 or more credit cards? The answer to that question may be in your mailbox. Credit card issuers are constantly looking to sign up new customers. The competition for business is fierce with many lenders offering low rates and other enticements. They flood the mail with applications for credit cards with pre-approved cash advances. In fact, insider estimates are that almost 60% of new credit card accounts are obtained through direct mail. Instead of discarding those applications as junk mail, look them over carefully. Apply for the cards which offer the lowest interest rates and no or low fees for cash advances. If your credit is in good shape, you should have no trouble obtaining several such cards. If you are married, you and your spouse may be able to apply separately for cards with pre-approved cash advances. If you own a small business, you also can apply for cards in the name of the business.

Once you obtain several cards with pre-approved cash advances, you can begin borrowing the money you need. You can borrow any amount up to your credit limit with no questions asked. No collateral, credit checks, or co-signers are required. The loans were approved as soon as you received the credit cards.

While you can pay back your credit card loans slowly by making minimum monthly payments, it's best to pay off the loans as quickly as possible. By doing that you can keep the interest from piling up, reducing the overall cost of the loans. Also, paying off your loans in timely fashion will strengthen your creditworthiness. In that event, many lenders will automatically increase your credit line, providing you with even more potential borrowing power.

Overdraft Protection

Another relatively easy-to-use technique to raise "quick cash" involves using overdraft protection as a line of readily accessible credit. For many people, overdraft protection is just that— protection. It provides for the transfer of money into their checking accounts whenever their account balances are overdrawn. Other people have discovered, through wise planning and careful preparation, that overdraft protection also can provide a quick source of cash for investments, purchases or other purposes.

In order to get the most borrowing power out of overdraft protection, you'll need to set up accounts at several banks. Here's an example of how this creative financing technique might work: Open checking accounts in at least five banks in your area. Apply for overdraft protection with a $5,000 credit line at each bank. Some banks may turn you down, especially if they know you already have similar accounts in other banks. For that reason, it's important that you be able to convince each bank that you are not overextended. Don't be discouraged if a bank does turn down your application for overdraft protection, or gives you a credit line lower than you requested. Stay with the bank for several months and then reapply. If you maintain your credit in good standing, and can show the bank that you are not overextended, your application will most likely be accepted.

If each bank approves your application for overdraft protection, you will then automatically have a credit line of $25,000. Since each account has a credit line of $5,000, you can write five checks for $25,000 or just one check on one account for $500. All that will be required is your signature and the money will be yours in whatever amount you choose, up to $25,000 in 24 hours or less. Obviously, your borrowing power with overdraft protection depends on the number of accounts you open and the amount of your credit lines at each bank. Overdraft protection credit lines can range anywhere from $500 to $20,000 and more depending on your account and the policy of the bank.

Using overdraft protection as a line of credit can provide you with a steady source of "quick cash", but it also can get you into trouble. Many people are guilty of overdraft abuse. These people are constantly tapping this line of credit to make monthly bill payments. The problem with that is that overdraft protection is expensive. Most banks charge a very high interest rate of 15% to 20% for overdraft credit. Borrowing on a regular basis can lead to deeper and deeper debt. In order to avoid such an eventuality, you should use your overdraft credit line only when necessary and only when you are certain you can repay the loan in a timely manner.

Government Loans

The first thing you should know about government loans is that they are not a source of quick cash. While you can borrow money at good terms through government programs, it will take more time to get the cash in hand than by using the other techniques described in this report. However government-sponsored loans are often available at lower interest rates than conventional loans, and at terms that could give you up to 40 years to pay the money back. What's more, there are government sponsored loan programs designed to help people who have credit problems and who otherwise would not qualify for conventional bank loans.

If you own a small business, have credit problems, and/or you need to raise cash in order to take advantage of an investment opportunity, say in real estate, you'll most likely qualify for a government-sponsored low-cost loan program. There are hundreds of such programs available covering a wide range of financial needs. Here are a few examples:

— Business and Industrial Loans

Guaranteed and insured loans are available for individuals through the Farmers Home Administration (FmHA). Applicants must be in rural areas. The amount of loans given through this program ranges from $30,000 to several million dollars. Contact your county or state FmHA for application and requirement information.

— Rental And Cooperative Housing Loans

This loan program, sponsored by the U.S. Department of Housing and Urban Development, offers guaranteed and insured loans. Eligible applicants include individual investors in new or rehabilitated market-rate rental or cooperative housing developed for moderate-income families and the elderly. Terms may include up to 40 years to pay back the loan.

— Manufactured (Mobile) Home Loan Insurance- Financing Purchase of Manufactured Homes As Principal Residence of Borrowers

This is another HUD-sponsored program which provides guaranteed and insured loans to cover the purchase of mobile homes. Any buyer who will use the mobile home as a principal residence is eligible to apply. The maximum loan is $48,600.

For information, contact Director, Title-I Insurance Division-HUD, Washington, DC 20401.

— Mortgage Insurance- Manufactured Home Parks

Individual investors and/or developers are eligible to apply for guaranteed and insured loans offered through this program. The loans are available for mobile home park development, new or rehabilitated, with five or more spaces. Contact Policies and Procedures Division, Office of Insured Multifamily Housing Development-HUD, Washington, DC 20410.

— Loans For Small Businesses

The Small Business Administration (SBA) provides direct loans to small businesses which are either owned by low-income individuals or located in areas with a high rate of unemployment. To qualify, business must be independently owned and operated and not dominant in its field. Loans up to $150,000 are available. For information, contact your nearest SBA field office.

The five loan programs described above are just a sample of the wide range of government-sponsored programs available. For a comprehensive listing of government assistance, you can consult such sources as the "Catalog of Federal Domestic Assistance" (U.S. Government Printing Office); and the "Government Assistance Almanac" 1994-95 (J. Robert Dumouchel, Omnigraphics, Inc.). Both publications can be found in most public libraries.

By taking advantage of government-sponsored loan programs for which you qualify, you can raise the money you need, even if you are currently experiencing credit problems. In some cases, you may be able to borrow $50,000 or more through such a program and take up to 40 years to pay it back.

Comparing One Loan To Another

Regardless of the type of credit you're interested in, the federal Truth-in-Lending Act requires that all lenders provide you with certain information. You can use this information to compare one loan to another in making your decision. If you take the time to make such a comparison, you could save yourself a lot of money and get the best loan deal possible. Here is some of the most important information lenders must provide:

— The name of the company offering the loan or credit line

— The amount of the loan or credit line in dollars

— The finance charge, both in dollars and as an annual percentage rate (APR)

— The repayment schedule, including monthly payment dates and minimum payments required

— Annual fees (if any)

— The length of grace period (if any) before payment is required

— Payment penalties (if any) and how those payments are calculated

— Late payment fees (if any) and how they are calculated

Before you borrow money from any lender, make sure you are provided the above information. Study the information and compare potential loans carefully. It is important that you not only get the best deal possible, but that you also understand and accept the terms.

The Bottom Line

Regardless of your financial need and current credit status, there are creative financing techniques that if used properly can enable you to borrow money on favorable terms. The techniques described in this report will work for anyone, but should be used prudently. If you want to borrow money, you should be certain you can make a timely repayment. If you can, the financing techniques in this report can help you raise the money you need in just a matter of days. How To Receive 124 Products Free

You can write to the following addresses and request a variety of items free of charge. Be sure to include money for postage and handling and SASEs when required.

How To Receive 124 Products Free

Free Things For Kids

Animal Iron-Ons: To get 10, 5" x 6" animal iron-ons, send 75 cents for postage and handling to DOG'S WORLD, 498 NEW ROCHELLE ROAD, BRONXVILLE, NY 10708.

Skateboard Bumper Sticker: Get a free skateboard bumper sticker and the rules of skateboarding safety by writing to ROLLER SPORTS, 1855 CASSAT AVE., JACKSONVILLE, FL 32210.

Coloring Book & Poster: Discover ways to have fun with your pet with this free coloring book and poster. Lots of safety tips too. Write to PETS ARE WONDERFUL COUNCIL, 500 NORTH MICHIGAN AVE, SUITE 200, CHICAGO, IL 00611.

Iron-On Decals: The makers of Heinz ketchup are offering a free 8" x 7" "Give Me A Squeeze iron-on decal. The decal is available upon request by writing to HEINZ KETCHUP, BOX 28, PITTSBURGH, PA 15230.

Olympic Swimming Decal: Get a red, white and blue U.S. swimming team olympic decal by writing to UNITED STATES SWIMMING, INC., PROMOTIONS DEPARTMENT, 1750 EAST BOULDER STREET, COLORADO SPRINGS, CO 80909.

Bumper Sticker: The Juvenile Shoe Co. offers a free bumper sticker of its "Lazy Bones" logo. To get the free bumper sticker, write to JUVENILE SHOE CO., 331 CARNATION DRIVE, AURORA, MO, 65605-0331.

Math Activities Brochure: Learn how to figure out basic math and have fun doing it with the information provided in this free booklet. For a free copy, send a SASE to NATIONAL COUNCIL OF MATH TEACHERS, 1906 ASSOCIATION DRIVE,RESTON, VA 22091. Ask for the "Family Math Activities" brochure.

Oral Health Coloring Book: You can get a free 26-page coloring book, titled "The ABC's Of Good Oral Health". Write to, AMERICAN DENTAL ASSOCIATION, 211 E. CHICAGO AVE., CHICAGO, IL 60611. Include 25 cents for postage.

Bike Safety Coloring Book: Have fun while learning about bike safety. Get a free coloring book by writing to SANDOZ-TRIAMINIC, ROUTE 10 EAST, E. HANOVER, NJ 07936. Ask for the Bike Safety Coloring Book.

Large Coloring Book: Kids will love to color in "Tuffy Talks About Medicine". This coloring book is available free, by writing to AETNA SPECIAL SERVICES LIBRARIAN, 151 FARMINGTON AVE., HARTFORD, CT 06156.

Play It Safe Coloring Book: This coloring book was developed by the U.S. Department of Justice for elementary school children. Besides having fun coloring, children also can learn about personal safety and burglary prevention strategies. To get a free coloring book, write to AETNA LIFE & CASUALTY, PUBLIC RELATIONS DEPARTMENT, DA21, 151 FARMINGTON AVENUE, HARTFORD, CT 06156.

Honey Bee Coloring Book: Get a free copy of this coloring book, which tells the story of honey production, by writing to DADANT & SONS, INC., HAMILTON, IL 62341.

Bookmark/Ruler: This plastic 6-inch ruler also serves as a bookmark. It's yours free by writing to UNION LABEL DEPARTMENT, ILGWU, 1710 BROADWAY, NEW YORK, NY 10019. Include a business-size SASE.

Recipes

"Pasta": Get a free booklet featuring 15 pasta recipes by sending a long SASE to MUELLER'S ENDLESS PASTABILITIES, P.O. BOX 307, COVENTRY, CT O6238.

"Fingerman's Fingerfood Favorites": ZIPLOC offers this recipe booklet filled with ideas for party finger foods. To get a free copy, write to FINGERMAN'S FINGER-FOOD FAVORITES, ZIPLOC STORAGE BAGS, BOX 78980, NEW AUGUSTA, IN 46278.

Light Brown Sugar Recipes: To get a free booklet of recipes using light brown sugar, write to DOMINO BROWNULATED RECIPES, P.O. BOX 17037, HAUP-PAUGE, NY 11788.

"75 Years Of Good Eating": This free booklet features 23 recipes using Mazola corn oil. To get a copy of the booklet, send 50 cents for postage to MAZOLA ANNIVERSARY COOKBOOK, BOX 307, COVENTRY, CT 06238.

"It's A Breeze To Freeze": This guide to freezing food also provides tips and recipes. For a free copy, write to "IT'S A BREEZE TO FREEZE", ZIPLOC FREEZ-ER BAGS, P.O. 78980, NEW AUGUSTA, IN 46278.

Wyler's Bouillon Recipes: For 18 recipes using Wyler's Bouillon, write to TASTE THE FLAVOR RECIPES, P.O. BOX 8927, CLINTON, IA 52736.

"California Baby-Cut Carrots": This brochure from the California Fresh Carrot Advisory Board provides several recipes featuring baby carrots. For a free copy, write to CALIFORNIA BABY-CUT CARROTS, 15 WILLOW STREET, SALINAS, CA 93901.

Pizza Recipes: Get a collection of unusual and delicious pizza recipes from WIS-CONSIN MILK MKT. BOARD, SPECIAL EDITION PIZZA RECIPES, 8418 EXCELSIOR DRIVE, MADISON, WI 53717.

Vegetable Recipes: All vegetable recipes are featured in this free booklet. Write to, VEG-ALL RECIPES, THE LARSEN COMPANY, P.O. BOX 19026, GREEN BAY, WI 54307-9026.

Tomato Recipes: These recipe cards feature 10 dishes made with spicy tomato sauce. To get the recipes, write to FREE PACE RECIPE CARDS, BOX 169, EL PASO, TX 79977.

"Salad Tour of the U.S.A.": A variety of salad recipes are featured in this free recipe book. To get the free recipe book, send 29 cents for postage and handling to H.J. HEINZ CO., P.O. BOX 57, PITTSBURGH, PA 15230.

Blueberry Recipes: You can get several recipes using blueberries, free, by writing to BLUEBERRY COUNCIL, P.O. BOX 38, TUCKAHOE, NJ 08250. Include 29 cents for postage and handling.

Turkey Recipes: Dozens of creative turkey recipes are featured in this free recipe collection from the NATIONAL TURKEY FEDERATION, CONSUMER DEPART-MENT, 11319, SUNSET HILLS ROAD, RESTON, VA 22090.

Chicken Recipes: If you like chicken, this free booklet featuring several award winning recipes from a national chicken cooking contest is for you. To get the booklet, send $1.00 for postage and handling to RECIPE BOOKS, ZACKY FARMS, 2000 N. TAYLOR AVENUE, SOUTH EL MONTE, CA 91733.

"Prego's Easy Italian Cooking": Twenty easy-to-prepare Italian recipes are fea-tured in this cook book which is available free by writing to PREGO'S EASY ITAL-IAN COOKING, BOX 964, BENSALEM, PA 19020.

"29 Recipes Using Apple Juice": This recipe booklet is available free from SPEAS COMPANY, 2400 NICHOLSON AVENUE, KANSAS CITY, MO 64120.

Booklets

"Bonds: What They Are, How They Work, What To Look For": This booklet pro-vides information about government-issued bonds, municipal bonds and bonds issued by corporations. For a free copy, write to NEUBERGER AND BERMAN MANAGEMENT INC., 605 THIRD AVE., SECOND FlOOR, NEW YORK, NY 10158.

Educational Booklets: An assortment of free educational booklets are available from the AMERICAN TRUCKING ASSOCIATION, OFFICE OF PUBLIC AFFAIRS, 2200 MILL ROAD, ALEXANDRIA, VA 22314. Write to the association and ask for a copy of its list of available booklets.

"Reading and Your Adolescent": Provides information on how parents can help their teens learn to enjoy reading. Also includes a suggested reading list. For a free copy, send a business-size SASE to CENTER FOR THE STUDY OF REAING, DISSEMINATION DIRECTOR, 51 GERTY DRIVE, CHAMPAIGN, IL 61820.

"Don't Make Waves": Boating safety tips and water regulations are provided in the free booklet. For a copy of the booklet, write to STATE FARM PUBLIC RELA-TIONS, ONE STATE FARM PLAZA, DEPARTMENT R, BLOOMINGTON, IL 61701.

"Schemes, Scams and Flim Flams: A Consumer's Guide To Phone Fraud": Get a copy of this booklet free by writing to the NATIONAL FRAUD INFORMATION CENTER, ATTN: NATIONAL CONSUMER'S LEAGUE, 815 15th STREET NW, WASHINGTON, DC 20005.

Skin Cancer Prevention Booklet: Skin Cancer Foundation offers a free booklet featuring information on skin cancer and tips on how to protect yourself from exposure to the sun. To get a free copy of this booklet, write to the SKIN CANCER FOUNDATION, BOX 561, NEW YORK, NY 10156.

"What You Need To Know About Breast Cancer": This booklet features information on detection, treatment, current research, breast self-examinations and more. To get a free copy, write to the NATIONAL CANCER INSTITUTE, OFFICE OF CANCER COMMUNICATIONS CODE PO17, 31 CENTER DRIVE, MSC 2580, BETHESDA, MD 20892.

"Jobs Of The Future For Women": Published by the Business & Professional Women's Foundation, this free booklet describes the job outlook for women through the year 2000. To get the booklet, send a self-addressed mailing label to WOMEN'S BUREAU, DEPT. "P", DEPT. OF LABOR, 200 CONSTITUTION AVE. N.W., WASHINGTON, DC 20210.

"MANAGING MENOPAUSE": For a free copy, write to the NATIONAL INSTITUTE ON AGING, INFORMATION CENTER, BOX 8057, GAITHERSBURG, MD 20898.

Mortgage Money Guide: This 16-page booklet provides information on 15 different types of mortgage plans. You'll also learn the advantages and disadvantages of each plan. For a free copy of this booklet, write to MORTGAGES, FEDERAL TRADE COMMISSION, WASHINGTON, DC 20580.

"Recovering From A Stroke": This free booklet is available upon request from The AMERICAN HEART ASSOCIATION, STROKE CONNECTION, 7272 GREENVILLE AVE., DALLAS, TX 75231.

"How To Collect Stamps": Here's a free booklet for would-be stamp collectors. To get a copy, write to LITTLETON-MYSTIC STAMP COMPANY, 96 MAIN STREET, CAMDEN, Nj 13316.

"Nine Ways To Lower Your Auto Insurance Costs": Get a copy of this booklet free by writing to INSURANCE INFORMATION INSTITUTE, 110 WILLIAM STREET, NEW YORK, NY 10038.

"The Savings Bond Question & Answer Book": This booklet offers answers to over 50 of the most frequently asked questions about bonds. For a free copy, write to DEPARTMENT OF THE TREASURY, US SAVINGS BONDS DIVISION, WASHINGTON, DC 20226.

"What You Should Know Before Declaring Bankruptcy": Find out the warning signs of debt, alternatives to bankruptcy and more in this free booklet. Write to, CONSUMER CREDIT EDUCATION FOUNDATION MATERIALS, DEPARTMENT DB, 919 18TH STREET NW, THIRD FLOOR, WASHINGTON, DC 20006. Include a business-size SASE.

"Tips For Choosing Safe Toys": Features information about safety features to look for when purchasing toys and other toy-safety guidelines. Write to: PREVENT BLINDNESS AMERICA, 500 E. REMINGTON RD., SCHAUMBURG, IL 60173.

"Travel and Fashion Guide": This booklet is available free upon request from the CONSUMER AFFAIRS DEPARTMENT, ILGWU-GARMENT WORKER'S UNION, 1710 BROADWAY, NEW YORK, NY 10019.

"Coping With Pet Odors": This booklet provides information on how to remove pet odors from carpeting and upholstery. For a free copy of the booklet, write to "COPING WITH PET ODORS", CHURCH & DWIGHT COMPANY, P.O. BOX 7648, PRINCETON, NJ 08543. Include a business-sized SASE.

"Credit Cards: An Owner's Manual": For a free copy of this booklet, write to VISA FULFILLMENT, BOX 100, ST. CLOUD, MINNESOTA.

Health

Nutrition and Exercise Booklet: Get a free copy of "Shaping Up For The Long Run" by writing to NUTRITION FOR THE WAY WE LIVE, P.O. BOX 307, COVENTRY, CT 06238.

Health Chart: This chart, "Guide To Eating For A Healthy Heart", is available free upon request from MERCK SHARP & DOHME, HEALTH INFORMATION DEPARTMENT, P.O. BOX 1486, WEST POINT, PA 19454. Include a business size SASE.

"Strokes: A Guide For The Family": This free booklet provides information about strokes including causes and treatments. The booklet also offers advice on how families can help loved ones recover. For a copy of the booklet, write to the AMERICAN HEART ASSOCIATION, BOX SG, GREENVILLE AVENUE, DALLAS, TX 75231.

Fitness Guide: Get a free booklet featuring information and safety tips on jogging and running. You can get a free copy of "Simple Tips For A Safe Workout" by writing to AMERICAN RUNNING AND FITNESS ASSOCIATION, 9310 OLD GEORGETOWN ROAD, BETHESDA, MD 20814.

Personal Medical Data Card: This pocket-size card provides space to list all of your medications (prescription and non-prescription). Carry it in your wallet or purse and you'll have your medical information with you at all times. To get a free card, send a business-sized SASE to PFIZER, P.O. BOX 1608, WEST CALD-WELL, NJ 07007.

Calorie Counter and Carbohydrate Guide: Get both free, by writing to HOLLY-WOOD DIET BREAD, 1747 VAN BUREN STREET, HOLLYWOOD, FL 33020.

First Aid Chart: Get a free wall chart featuring first aid information by writing to CONSUMER SERVICES, JOHNSON & JOHNSON, 501 GEORGE ST., NEW BRUNSWICK, N.J. 08903.

Cancer & Diet Booklet: Published by the National Cancer Institute, this 50-page booklet features healthful menus and other information. For a free copy of the booklet, write to FOOD CHOICES, NATIONAL CANCER INSTITUTE, BETHES-DA, MD 20205.

Exercise Guide For The Over 40 Crowd: This booklet provides safe, effective exercises for men and women over age 40. To get a copy of the guide, write to STAYING FIT OVER 40, ADVIL FORUM ON HEALTH EDUCATION, 1500 BROADWAY, 25TH FLOOR, NEW YORK, NY 10036.

Health Care Information: The following organizations can provide you with free information and referrals concerning specific health concerns.

Dental Care: Get free booklets and folders on proper dental care by writing to the AMERICAN DENTAL ASSOCIATION, 211 E. CHICAGO AVE., CHICAGO, IL 60611.

ALCOHOLICS ANONYMOUS, 15 EAST 26TH STREET, ROOM 1817, NEW YORK, NY 10010; PHONE: (212) 683-3900.

AMERICAN CANCER SOCIETY, INC.— NATIONAL HEADQUARTERS, 1599 CLIFTON ROAD NE, ATLANTA, GA 30329; PHONE: (404) 320-3333.

AMERICAN COUNCIL OF THE BLIND, 1156 15TH STREET N.W., SUITE 720, WASHINGTON, DC 20005; PHONE: (800) 424-8666.

AMERICAN DIABETES ASSOCIATION, INC., 149 MADISON AVENUE, NEW YORK, NY 10010; Phone: (212) 725-4925.

AMERICAN HEART ASSOCIATION, 7272 GREENVILLE AVENUE, DALLAS, TX 75231; PHONE: (214) 373-6300.

AMERICAN LUNG ASSOCIATION, 1740 BROADWAY, NEW YORK, NY 10019; PHONE: (212) 315-8700.

THE ARTHRITIS FOUNDATION, 2045 PEACHTREE ROAD, N.E., ATLANTA, GA 30326; PHONE: (404) 351-0454.

ASSOCIATION FOR ALZHEIMER'S AND RELATED DISEASES, 919 N. MICHIGAN AVENUE, SUITE 1000, CHICAGO, IL 60611; PHONE: (800) 272-3900.

ASTHMA AND ALLERGY FOUNDATION OF AMERICA, 1125 15TH STREET N.W., SUITE 502, WASHINGTON, DC 20005; PHONE: (202) 466-7643.

CANCER INFORMATION CLEARINGHOUSE, NATIONAL CANCER INSTITUTE, BUILDING 31, ROOM 10A30, BETHESDA, MD 30014; PHONE: (800) 4-CANCER (in Hawaii, (808) 524-1234).

CDC NATIONAL AIDS HOTLINE, 215 PARK AVENUE SOUTH, SUITE 714, NEW YORK, NY 10003; PHONE: (800) 227-8922.

LUPUS FOUNDATION OF AMERICA, 4 RESEARCH PLACE, SUITE 180, ROCKVILLE, MD 20850; PHONE: (800) 558-0121.

NATIONAL CLEARINGHOUSE FOR ALCOHOL AND DRUG INFORMATION, 11426-28 ROCKVILLE PIKE, SUITE 200, ROCKVILLE, MD 20852; PHONE: (800) 729-6686.

THE NATIONAL COUNCIL ON AGING, 409 THIRD STREET S.W., SUITE 302A, WASHINGTON, DC 20024; PHONE: (202) 479-1200.

NATIONAL DIABETES INFORMATION CLEARINGHOUSE, NATIONAL INSTITUTES OF HEALTH, 9000 ROCKVILLE PIKE, BOX NDIC, BETHESDA, MD 20892; PHONE: (301) 468-2162.

NATIONAL INSTITUTE OF MENTAL HEALTH, PUBLIC INQUIRIES SECTION, ROOM 15C-05, 5600 FISHERS LANE, ROCKVILLE, MD 20857; PHONE: (301) 443-4513.

NATIONAL STROKE ASSOCIATION, 8480 EAST ORCHARD ROAD, SUITE 1000, ENGLEWOOD, CO 80111; PHONE: (800) STROKES.

PLANNED PARENTHOOD FEDERATION OF AMERICA, INC., 810 SEVENTH AVE., NEW YORK, NY 10017; PHONE: (212) 541-7800.

SELF-HELP FOR HARD OF HEARING PEOPLE, 7800 WISCONSIN AVENUE, BETHESDA,MD 20814; PHONE: (301) 657-2248.

Product Samples

Hair Treatment Product: Sample the restorative powers of the Swiss herbs in St. Ives Formula Hair Treatment. Get a free sample by writing to ST. IVES HAIR REPAIR OFFER, P.O. BOX 8363, CLINTON, OH 52736.

Hand Cleaner: Get a free sample of "Fast Orange Hand Cleaner" by writing to FAST ORANGE SAMPLE OFFER, LOCTITE CORPORATION, PUBLIC RELATIONS DEPARTMENT, 4450 CRANWOOD PKWY., CLEVELAND, OH 44128-4084.

Wedding Invitations and Stationery: Free samples of wedding invitations and stationery are available upon request from DAWN STATIONERY, 300 MAIN STREET, LUMBERTON, NJ 08048.

Pet Treats: Get a 3 oz. sample of Beggin' Strips bacon flavor dog treats from Purina. Request the free sample by writing to BEGGIN' STRIPS SAMPLE OFFER, P.O. BOX 15510, MASCOUTAH, IL 62224.

Cologne: The makers of "Truly Lace" cologne will send you a free sample of their new fragrance. To get the free sample, send $1.00 for postage and handling to TRULY LACE SAMPLE, P.O. BOX 5567, NEWTOWN, CT 06470-5567.

Bath Bar: Oil of Olay offers a free sample bath bar. Send 50 cents for postage and handling to OIL OF OLAY SAMPLE OFFER, P.O. BOX 5767, CLINTON, IA 52736.

Bath Products: Get the "Shower 2000" trial offer which features one ounce each of Bath-SHOWER GEL, deodorant and moisturizer by writing SHOWER "2000" OFFER, BONNE BELL, 18519 DETROIT AVENUE, LAKEWOOD, OH 44107. Include $1.00 for postage.

Silver Polish: Get a free sample of Hagerty's Silver Polish by writing to W.J. HAGERTY LTD., BOX 1496, 3801 W. LINDEN AVENUE, SOUTH BEND, IN 46624.

Skin Ointment: You can get a free sample of Balmex, for treating skin irritations and diaper rash, by sending 25 cents for postage to BALMEX SAMPLE OFFER, 1326 FRANKFORD AVENUE, PHILADELPHIA, PA 19125.

Tampax Tampons: The makers of Tampax Tampons offer a free sample and a helpful booklet. Write to TAMPAX TAMPONS, SAMPLE OFFER, P.O. BOX 4138, MONTICELLO, MN 55565-4138.

Denture Adhesive Powder: Denture wearers can get a free sample of Klutch Denture Adhesive Powder by writing to KLUTCH FREE SAMPLE OFFER, I. PUTNAM, INC., P.O. BOX 444, BIG FLATS, NY 14814.

Flower Seeds: A free packet of annual flower seeds is available from ALBERTA NURSERIES, P.O. BOX 20, BOWDEN, ALBERTA CANADA TOM-OKO. Include 29 cents for postage and handling.

Skin Care Treatment: Get a free sample of Bonne Bell's "Ten-O-Six" Skin Care Treatment. The sample includes one ounce each Deep-Clean Antiseptic, astringent and medicated facial wash. To get the sample, send $1.00 for postage to TEN-O-SIX SAMPLE OFFER, BONNE BELL, 18519 DETROIT AVE., LAKEWOOD, OH 44107

Seed Packets: You can get a free sample package of vegetable or flower seeds by sending a long SASE to ACE HARDWARE, P.O. BOX 630, GWINN, MI 49841. Be sure to specify what type of seeds you want— vegetable or flower. You can get both by including 29 cents with your request.

Oat Bran Tablets: Swanson Health Products offers a free sample (100 tablets) of Swanson Oat Bran Tablets. To get a free 30-day supply, send $1.00 for postage and handling to SWANSON HEALTH PRODUCTS, P.O. BOX 2803, FARGO, ND 58108.

Shampoo: To get a free sample size container of Neutrogena Shampoo, send $1.00 for postage to NEUTROGENA SHAMPOO OFFER, DEPARTMENT 1765, P.O. BOX 45062, LOS ANGELES, CA 90045.

Miscellaneous Freebies

Free Poster: Get a free 25" x 32", four-color poster by writing to: U.S. NATIONAL ARBORETUM, PUBLICATIONS DEPT., 3501 NEW YORK AVENUE NE, WASHINGTON, DC 20002.

U.S. Flag: This flag is 4" x 6" and comes on a staff with safety ball. The flag is available free from PARKER, DEPARTMENT JA, 5746 PLUNKETT STREET, SUITE 4, HOLLYWOOD, FL 33023-2346. Include 50 cents for shipping and a long SASE (2 stamps).

Decal Stickers: Free decal stickers and some peanut recipes are available free upon request from the TEXAS PEANUT PRODUCERS BOARD. Write to P.O. BOX 398, GORMAN, TX 76454.

Pierced Earrings: Get a pair of earrings free. Your choice: 14k gold or simulated diamond studs. Both come with hypoallergenic posts. To get a free pair of earrings, write to KARAT CLUB OF AMERICA, 405 TARRINGTOWN ROAD, SUITE 215, WHITE PLAINS, NY 10610. Include $1.50 postage and handling per pair ordered.Also be sure to include your choice of earrings.

Flower Seeds: Get a free packet of annual flower seeds by sending 25 cents to ALBERTA NURSERIES, P.O. BOX 20, BOWDEN, ALBERTA CANADA TOM-OKO.

Wall Chart: This free wall chart depicts "The Story of Cotton". The story begins with planting and continues through spinning and weaving. Write to the NATION-AL COTTON COUNCIL OF AMERICA, P.O. BOX 12285, MEMPHIS, TN 38112.

No Smoking Sign: This sign is shaped like a stop sign and is available free upon request from the American Lung Association, Send a postcard to the AMERICAN LUNG ASSOCIATION, GPO BOX 596, NEW YORK, NY 10001. Request #0121 Lungs at Work sign.

Tomato Seeds: Get a free packet of tomato seeds for your garden and a seed cat-alog by sending 29 cents postage to GURNEY SEED COMPANY, 3101 PAGE STREET, YANKTON, SD 57079.

Bumper Stickers: Quarter horse lovers can send for free bumper stickers and ref-erence guide books all about the Quarter Horse breed. To get these free quarter horse items, write to AMERICAN QUARTER HORSE ASSOCIATION, AMARIL-LO, TX 79168.

Project Planning Pack: Here's a free offer of interest to anyone planning to re-dec-orate. Get a free project planning pack which includes a color guide, floor plan designer, a booklet of do-it-yourself flooring, and more. The project pack is avail-able free from ARMSTRONG TILE, DEPARTMENT 55GCR, P.O. BOX 3001, LANCASTER, PA 17604.

Horseshoe Pitching Rules: No need to argue about ringers or leaners anymore. Get the official rules for horseshoe pitching by writing to the NATIONAL HORSE-SHOE PITCHER'S ASSOCIATION, RT. 2, BOX 178, LAMONTE, MO 65337.

Refunding Brochure: "Refunding For Fun & Profit" is available free upon request from TROPICANA PRODUCTS, CONSUMER CENTER, P.O. BOX 338, BRADENTON, FL 34206.

Currency Exchange Guide: Get a free pocket-size currency exchange guide. The guide provides currency conversion charts for over 20 European, Asian and Latin American countries and Australia. Other currency information is also provided. Send a SASE to FOREIGN CURRENCY GUIDE, RUESCH INTERNATIONAL, 1350 "I" STREET NW., 10TH FLOOR, WASHINGTON, DC 20005-3305.

Shopping By Mail Guidebook: For free consumer guidelines to shopping by mail, send a business-sized SASE to BESS MYERSON'S GUIDELINES, DIRECTMAIL MARKETING ASSOCIATION, 6 EAST 43RD STREET, NEW YORK, NY 10017.

Ballerina Bumper Stickers: This bumper sticker reads, "I'd Rather Be Dancing" and is available upon request from CAPEZIO BALLET MAKERS, ONE CAMPUS ROAD, TOTOWA, N.J. 07512. Include a business-sized SASE and 29 cents for postage.

Yard And Garden Remodeling Kit: Plan your next garden with the information and tips provided in this free kit from the GARDEN COUNCIL, 500 NORTH MICHIGAN AVENUE, SUITE 1400, CHICAGO, IL 60611.

Personal Property Inventory Forms: Use these forms to record all the valuable items in your home. Makes an excellent record for homeowner's insurance. To get the forms, write to AETNA PERSONAL PROPERTY INVENTORY, 151 FARMINGTON AVENUE, HARTFORD, CT 06156.

Table Tennis Guide: Get a complete guide and rules for table tennis by sending 29 cents for postage and handling to the U.S. TABLE TENNIS ASSOCIATION, BOX 815, ORANGE, CT 06477.

Fishing Guide: Learn the best times to fish and other helpful tips for successful fishing by sending for this free fishing guide. Write to CISCO KID TACKLE, 2630 N.W. FIRST AVENUE, BOCA RATON, FL 33432.

Basketball Fan Mail Packages: Every team in the National Basketball Association offers a package of fan-pleasers, including such things as team logo decals, photos of your favorite players, etc. To get a free NBA fan-mail package, send a business sized SASE to your favorite team, listed below.

ATLANTA HAWKS, PUBLIC RELATIONS DEPARTMENT, ONE CNN CENTER #405, ATLANTA, GA 30303.

BOSTON CELTICS, 151 MERRIMAC STREET, 5TH FLOOR, BOSTON MA 02114 (ATTN: FAN MAIL DEPARTMENT).

CHICAGO BULLS, 980 N. MICHIGAN AVENUE, ROOM #1600, CHICAGO, IL 60611-4501.

CLEVELAND CAVELIERS, 2923 STREETSBORO ROAD, RICHFIELD, OH 44286 (ATTN: FAN MAIL DEPARTMENT).

DENVER NUGGETS, PUBLIC RELATIONS DEPARTMENT, 1635 CLAY STREET, DENVER, CO 80204.

DETROIT PISTONS, 2 CHAMPIONSHIP DRIVE, AUBURN HILLS, MI 48326 (ATTN. FAN MAIL DEPARTMENT).

GOLDEN STATE WARRIORS, OAKLAND ARENA COLISEUM, OAKLAND, CA 94621-1995.

HOUSTON ROCKETS, PUBLIC RELATIONS DEPARTMENT, P.O. BOX 272349, HOUSTON, TX 77277.

INDIANA PACERS, 300 E. MARKET STREET, INDIANAPOLIS, IN 46204 (ATTN. FAN MAIL DEPARTMENT).

LOS ANGELES CLIPPERS, LA SPORTS ARENA, 3939 S. FIGUEROA, LOS ANGELES, CA 90307.

LOS ANGELES LAKERS, PUBLIC RELATIONS DEPARTMENT, BOX 10, INGLE-WOOD, CA 90306.

MILWAUKEE BUCKS, PUBLIC RELATIONS DEPARTMENT, 1001 N. FOURTH STREET, MILWAUKEE, WI 53203.

NEW JERSEY NETS, BRENDAN BYRNE ARENA, EAST RUTHERFORD, NJ 07073.

NEW YORK KNICKS, MADISON SQUARE GARDEN, FOUR PENN PLAZA, NEW YORK, NY 10001.

ORLANDO MAGIC, 1 MAGIC PLACE, ORLANDO ARENA, ORLANDO, FL 32801 (ATTN. FAN MAIL DEPARTMENT).

PHOENIX SUNS, PUBLIC RELATIONS DEPARTMENT, P.O. BOX 1369, PHOENIX, AZ 85001.

SACRAMENTO KINGS, PUBLIC RELATIONS DEPARTMENT, 1515 SPORTS DRIVE, SACRAMENTO, CA 95834.

SEATTLE SUPERSONICS, PUBLIC RELATIONS, BOX C 900911, SEATTLE, WA 98109.

UTAH JAZZ, 5 TRIAD CENTER #500, SALT LAKE CITY, UT 84180 (ATTN. FAN MAIL DEPARTMENT).

WASHINGTON BULLETS, PUBLIC RELATIONS, CAPITAL CENTRE, LAN-DOVER, MD 20785.

OTHER HEALTH AND MONEY BOOKS

The following books are offered to our preferred customers at a special price.

BOOK	PRICE	
1. Penny Stock Newsletter (12 issues)	$55.00	*POSTPAID*
2. Lower Cholesterol & Blood Pressure	$26.95	*POSTPAID*
3. Book of Home Remedies	$26.95	*POSTPAID*
4. Proven Health Tips Encyclopedia	$19.97	*POSTPAID*
5. Foods That Heal	$19.95	*POSTPAID*
6. Natural Healing Secrets	$26.95	*POSTPAID*
7. Most Valuable Book Ever Published	$16.95	*POSTPAID*
8. Eliminate Prostate Problems	$16.95	*POSTPAID*
9. Drugs-Side Effects	$16.95	*POSTPAID*
10. Govt. . Benefits For 50 or Over	$26.95	*POSTPAID*
11. Book of Credit Secrets	$26.95	*POSTPAID*
12. How To Win At Slot Machines	$30.00	*POSTPAID*
13. How To Trade Commodities	$149	*POSTPAID*
14. How To Trade Options	$149	*POSTPAID*
15. Money Power	$24.95	POSTPAID
16. Proven Wealth Creating Techniques And Formulas	$19.95	POSTPAID

Please send this entire page or write down the names of the books and mail it along with your payment

NAME OF BOOK_____ PRICE_____

NAME OF BOOK_____ PRICE_____

NAME OF BOOK_____ PRICE_____

NAME OF BOOK_____ PRICE_____

TOTAL ENCLOSED $_____

SHIP TO:

Name_____

Address_____

City_____ ST_____ Zip_____

MAIL TO: KEYSTONE PUBLISHING
POST OFFICE BOX 51488
ONTARIO, CA 91761-9827

For other fine books go to our website:
www.emarketupdate.com